D1563278

# 200

## SCRIPTURAL

## SERMON

## OUTLINES

**JABEZ BURNS** Sermon Outline Series

- 500 Sketches and Skeletons of Sermons
- 357 Sermon Outlines
- 300 Sermon Sketches on Old and New Testament Texts
- 200 Scriptural Sermon Outlines

# 200

# SCRIPTURAL

# SERMON OUTLINES

BY

## JABEZ BURNS, D.D., LL.D.

**KREGEL PUBLICATIONS**
Grand Rapids, Michigan 49501

Library of Congress Catalog Card Number 75-92502
ISBN 8254-2211-6

First American Edition . . . . . . . . . . . . . . . . . .1969
Reprinted . . . . . . . . . . . . . . . . . . . . . . . . . . . .1973

Formerly published in Great Britain in 1875 under
the title *Two Hundred Sketches and Outlines of
Sermons.*

Printed in the United States of America

## PREFACE

This volume, like the author's earlier volumes of Sermon Sketches and Outlines, is designed to be suggestive of texts, subjects, and modes of treatment. To make such a use of them will involve the necessity for reading, study and diligent preparation. It is impossible that they should supersede personal attention and labor, but rather indicate a text when needed, and a theme adapted for the occasion, and a brief view how the author in his own preaching ministry has treated them. To our lay preachers, students and young ministers, they may thus render considerable help. To others more advanced in the preaching work, they may supply topics, which may often be convenient, and save considerable time and effort. The very large demand for the previous volumes of the author, both in Great Britain and the United States, evidently prove there is a need for such help, and that the author's labors have met with appreciation. Throughout this volume prominence has been given to the great saving evangelical truths of

# PREFACE

the Gospel, and while avoiding sectarian peculiarities, he has ever felt that the Lord Jesus Christ, in His Divine Person and atoning work must always have the pre-eminence. Many of the texts selected for this volume are passages seldom used in pulpit messages and include some from nearly all the Books of the Old and New Testaments. The author has endeavored in all the Sketches to avoid wordiness and to see that every subject should have a sufficiency of ideas for its full exposition and illustration.

That these outlines and sermon sketches may be useful helps to his brethren and do good whenever they may be consulted, is the devout desire of the author.

# CONTENTS

# CONTENTS

# CONTENTS

# CONTENTS

# CONTENTS

# CONTENTS

# SCRIPTURAL SERMON OUTLINES

## I.

### THE DIVINE NATURE

" God is love."—1 John iv. 8-16.

THE grandest aphorism ever uttered—the sublimest truth ever spoken—the divinest portrait ever drawn—the most momentous principle ever exprest. It is the essence of the Gospel—the glory of Christianity—the Alpha and Omega of the Bible. It is to religion what the vital air is to our world—what the law of gravitation is to the universe. Yet, by sceptics it is denied—by some systems of religion ignored—and by others mal-treated or caricatured.

**I. Let us see what is the grand idea presented.**

" God is love "—God is benevolent, and, as the result, He is beneficent.

1. He delights in the happiness of His creatures.

2. Makes provision for it. In other words, He loves His creatures and exhibits it towards them. Right feeling and right action. As such, it is the opposite of malignity—selfishness—isolation—indifference—or apa-thy. It has no connection with hate, wrath, or maledic-tion. It is at the remotest distance from implacability and revenge. It is in direct harmony with justice,

holiness, and truth. Observe, God is love, not only
loving, but love. It is God's nature, not one of many
perfections, but the essence and perfection of all. God
is a spirit as to His essence and love, as to His moral
character, and, therefore, whatever can be said of God
as to His self-existence, eternity, unchangeableness,
infinity, almightiness, can be said of His love—His
love is self-existent, eternal, unchangeable, infinite.
More—His goodness is the stream of His love as creator,
preserver. His mercy, the stream of His love to the
miserable. His grace, the stream of His love to the
undeserving and guilty. Now have we put the great
idea before you clearly, fully? if so, let us present—

**II. The undeniable evidences of its truth.**

We see it—

1. In the *titles* He *assumes*. God is the good. He
passed by and proclaimed His name and exhibited His
glory. Exodus xxxiv. 6; so xxxiii. 18.

2. In His *glorious works*.

CREATION—in its marvellousness, vastness. Love and
goodness everywhere. Stars, worlds, systems, creatures, &c.

GOVERNMENT of the world—benevolent ruler, benignant
administrations, kindness, beneficence, no law designed
to give pain, suffering, He is good to all, and His tender
mercies are over all His works.

REDEMPTION of mankind—suspension of judgment,
exercise of clemency, annunciation of a deliverer, the
gift of His Son, "God so loved," &c. Jesus the Messiah
of love, the incarnation of love, the proclaimer of love,
the sacrifice of love; all His life, toils and sufferings,
death, &c., miracles, evidences of His love, everywhere,
to all.

3. In the *Gospel of Christ*—history of love, overtures

of love, blessings of love, salvation of love, all its glory love, its influences love, triumphs love.

4. In the *experience* of *Christians.* Their calling, love; their acceptance of love; pardon, love; justification, love; holiness, love; renewal, love; preservation, gifts, graces, &c.

5. In the *gift* of *eternal glory* to all the saints. Called to his eternal kingdom and glory—" I give," &c., "Father, I will," &c., "Then shall the King say, Come ye blessed," &c.; so the song "Unto Him that loved us," &c. Let us see,

**III. Some of the apparent difficulties which are supposed to stand in the way of this great declaration.**

1. The *existence* of *moral evil.* If God is unmixed love, why not prevent the existence of sin? A profound and difficult subject. It involves another—why create free agents? angels or men, there is no moral evil except with moral beings. Suppose by their existence God's glory should be manifested, man's dignity and blessedness enhanced, &c.

2. The *existence* of *human* suffering.

(1.) Is human suffering ever inflicted immediately by God on holy beings?

(2.) Is it not the result of unlikeness or opposition to God?

(3.) Is it not often disciplinary, and in the end a blessing? Father and child; sovereign, His subjects.

(4.) Is it ever beyond the desert of the sufferer?

(5.) Would not miraculous interferences be necessary to prevent it, as in infants and godly persons?

3. Do *not future punishments* come in collision with this *grand declaration?* We do not enter on the subject of the nature, place, nor duration of future punishment, but let us look at the subject as a whole, as a moral

principle. Now observe the relation between law and penalty—present penalties, if equitable, are right; future penalties, if so, must be right, too. Two illustrations— the case of the insane and their confinement, is it right, or should they be at liberty to the peril of themselves and the greater peril of others? The case of desperately malignant persons, of hate, wrath, violent, bloodthirsty, should they be at liberty and be unrestrained, &c.? Should punishment be inflicted and continued? If the lunacy or malignity continue, of course the restraint must continue. To deduce that God is not love from a future Hell, it would be requisite to prove—

(1.) That the undeserving became its victims.

(2.) That the punishment was disproportionate in intensity or duration. Punishment according to equity, either in this world or the next, is no evidence that God is not love. On the gates of Hell, as a place of confinement, it might be written most assuredly, "God is love." Now consider—

**IV. The use we should make of this glorious and sublime declaration.**

Observe—

1. How it *ennobles* the *religion* we possess, for the religion is as the Deity identified with it. Well may we be jubilant on this subject. Contrast the false gods of the heathen, "their rock," &c. This is the highest glory of the God of revelation, it cannot be exaggerated except we look at it aside from holiness and justice.

2. It should *produce* in *us* the *noblest trust* and *confidence*. God cannot do what is contrary to His nature. He may not interpose to prevent calamities, the result of violated laws, He may not relax what appears severe discipline, but His observant eyes and His chastening

hand will ever be guided by His essential and infinite love.

3. *True religion should inspire* with grateful joy. God is light—so is religion, God is blessed—so is religion, God is love, so we will exult and praise Him evermore.

4. The *realization* of this *principle* will transform us into the *Divine likeness*, we are changed by the spirit of this love into the same image—"he that dwelleth in God, dwelleth in love." True religion is love; as love is the very nature and essence of Deity, so it is the nature and essence of true religion.

5. As a *religion* of *love* it is to be *universal* and *everlasting*, love is to be the light of all nations, and their real power and their blessedness. Having renewed the face of the earth and prepared it for the descent of the tabernacle of God with men, it will be the song and joy and bliss of the redeemed for evermore; so let it be. Lord Jesus come quickly. Finally we see--

6. The *extreme evil* and *heinousness* of *sin* and *unbelief*.

## II

## THE MARVELLOUSNESS OF GOD'S LOVE TO HIS CHILDREN

" Behold what manner of love the Father hath bestowed upon us, that we should be called the sons of God: therefore the world knoweth us not, because it knew Him not."—1 JOHN iii. 1.

THE love of John is constantly exhibiting itself in his loving epistles. This spirit breathes throughout; he seems by his closeness to the Master's bosom to have

caught His marvellous affection.  Our text exhibits
three things.

**I. The marvellous love of the Father.**

The interrogation exhibits wonder and delight.
What manner, &c.  The manner of God's love is indeed
marvellous.

1. In its *Eternal Origin*.

2. In its *Peculiar Objects*.

Not Angels, &c., not man holy, good, lovely; but
fallen, corrupt, vile, and base, traitors, rebels, enemies,
hateful, &c.

3. In its *Costly Sacrifices*.

Love providing—

(1.) A ransom!

(2.) That ransom His own Son!

(3.) That Son to die!

(4.) To die on the cross!

Love flowing in the tears and agonies and soul offering of His beloved Son.

4. In its *processes* of *manifestation* in *Christ*.  By the
Spirit, through the Gospel ministry, agencies, providences, &c.  Now here are heights, depths, breadths,
and lengths, that surpass all knowledge.  A marvel to
angels as well as men.  See this love exhibited,

**II. In the glorious calling of the Christian.**

"That we should be called the sons, &c."  Love not
only delivering us, but calling us to be the "sons of
God."  So that we become

1. *Partakers* of *His nature* by the Spirit dwelling in us.

2. *Adopted* into *His family*.  The Prodigal.

3. *Endowed with His name*.  God's sons.

4. *Distinguished* by *privileges*.  Dwelling with God;
His table; His counsel; His care; His blessing.

5. *Heirs* to the *Divine inheritance*.  Heirs of Life, Sal-

vation, Heaven; but also of God Himself, Rom. viii. 17. "If children, then heirs." Ye shall be my children and I will be "your God." The Lord our portion.

Then see—

III. **The extraordinary ignorance of the world.**

"Therefore the world knoweth us not, &c."

1. They *don't understand spiritual things.* The carnal minded cannot have spiritual eyes and ears and senses necessary.

2. They *don't perceive spiritual operations.* Work of God is hidden. Meal, &c. Seed in the soil, &c.

3. They *don't understand spiritual principles.* Faith, self-abnegation, cross-bearing, &c.

4. They don't comprehend *spiritual experiences.* Conviction, conversion, sanctification, holy hope and joy.

5. They don't realise *spiritual graces* and holy *virtues.* Love to God, to Jesus, &c. They recognise temporal excellencies, political, &c., but not spiritual; no marvel, for they "knew Him not."

1. Did not recognise Christ.

2. Or receive Him; but hated and put Him to death. Therefore we should not be surprised nor cast down, but joyfully bear the result of men's ignorance as Christ did.


# III

## DWELLING IN LOVE

"He that dwelleth in love, dwelleth in God, and God in him."— 1 JOHN iv. 16.

JOHN was the apostle of love. His training, his nearness to Christ, on His bosom, having His spirit, ripened by a

long experience, carried into the assembly just to smile
on them, bless them, and say, "Little children love one
another." How needful we should distinctly understand
the subject, then realize it, and last of all exhibit it.
For these ends—

### I. Definitions may be essential.

The definition.

1. As to *love itself*. Obviously the same as the charity
of the xiii. of I. Corinthians. It is not to be confounded
with mere softness of human nature, a tendency to
geniality and kindness and good-nature, nor with freedom from the baser passions of hate, malignity, &c.
Love is a positive quality or attribute. It takes in
goodwill, kindness, esteem, delight, impassioned affection, sympathy, generosity. Now love, Godwards, is
reverence, confidence, admiration, delight. See 1 Cor.
xiii. Then —

2. *Love* as *our habitation*, to dwell in it, is not natural
but supernatural, not of the flesh, but of the Spirit and
of grace. It is the abode of the new man, not the old.
Into this dwelling he is brought by regeneration, here
he is enfranchised, here is the vital atmosphere of love,
here he meditates on it, here he receives supplies of love,
here is the spirit of love, the angels of love, here is the
*sanctum sanctorum :* God Himself dwells in God-loving
hearts. The elements are kindled, the spark is attracted,
the drop is in the Divine ocean, the beam in the glorious
sun. Now let us see—

### II. How we are to realize it.

1. *Abandonment* of our *natural condition*, the flesh, the
world. The flesh is selfish and sensual, and the world
hates, &c. This region must be forsaken, not of the
flesh, not of the world, not of Satan.

2. Obtain a place in the spiritual and Divine—in God's

house, by adoption; in God's nature, by regeneration; born into the kingdom of Heaven.

3. This dwelling in love must be *attested by* the Divine Spirit. Because ye are sons, the Spirit of grace and favour is given, the love of God shed abroad in the heart.

4. *It must be retained* by faith and prayer, thus communion is kept up between Heaven and earth, God and the soul, thus this love will abound yet more, &c., thus coldness, lukewarmness, and apostacy will be avoided.

Now observe, this dwelling in love and God—

III. **Must be exhibited.**

1. In the general emotions of our spirits; spirit of love, this our atmosphere ever with us.

2. In *the tone* of *our conversation;* tongue, not sword nor arrows, not the poisoning of the asp, but the sweet kindness of love. Our vocabulary is love to friends, to all, to enemies.

3. In our unselfish conduct, not greedy, not self-seeking, but looking on the things of others; "Love seeketh not her own," goes out of self, rises above it, crucifies it.

4. In our *generous beneficence*, communicating to others, imparting as we possess. Light, comfort, gifts, &c.; water to the thirsty, bread, &c., clothing, &c., and all in love.

5. In *doing all this to God's glory*, setting the Lord before us, warmed, inspired by Him, seeking to please Him, &c.

6. And this *as the habit of the soul*, not the impulse of the season, not occasionally, not under unusual pressure, but this our dwelling, our daily life, &c.

In conclusion, notice—

1. This is the *Christian's Divine* life, no other Divine life; this is the true, the real, not ideal, but the true life.

2. This is not *sectarian*, but *catholic*, love of the Father

and the whole brotherhood. This rises higher than sectarian fences and inclusive creeds or exclusive anathemas, it belongs to the whole kingdom of the saints.

3. This is the *preparation* for *Heaven*, is the little Heaven below, Heaven within, and meetness for Heaven beyond. We can thus dwell in God anywhere, in any world, in time and eternity. Do we know that we are of God, and that He dwells in us, &c. Examine, prove, seek after this.

4. To this we invite the sorrowful around us; here is a heart and home in God's infinite love and unchanging goodness.

# IV

## THE SOUL'S CRY FOR GOD

" My heart and my flesh crieth out for the living God."—Psalm lxxxiv. 2.

The law of adaptation is one prominent everywhere— light and the eye; air and the lungs; food and nutrition. So mind and knowledge, reflection, &c. So the moral nature and veneration, sublime emotions, desire for worship, a crying out for a God. Now there is most obviously often exhibited,

I. **A false and unnatural cry.**

"No God," says atheism. What folly—infatuation. This cry starves veneration and ideality and wonder, or reverence, sublimity and imagination. Then there is,

II. **A vague perverted cry.**

*All is God.* This is diseased sentimental pantheism.

A personal God ; absorbed in mountains, lakes, oceans, stars, sun's-light, ether, electricity, &c. But here there is no adaptation to the loftiest thoughts and aspirations of the soul. Then there is,

III. **The true and earnest cry of man's moral nature.**

As expressed in the text, "My heart, my affections, my flesh, my human nature, crieth &c. Now notice—

1. The *object* of this *cry* is "for God." The supreme, the infinite, the glorious deity. A Being the source of all, above all, to be adored and worshipped by all. "The one God," not any of the gods many, but the blessed God is desired.

2. *This glorious Being* "*is* the living God." Not statuary, not effigies, not personifications, not mythological fabled deities, but the living God. God existent, ever existent, unchangingly existent, eternally existent.

3. This *glorious living God* is *not visible.* Purely spiritual, the invisible God, &c. So that it is not to see Him with the eye, or hear Him with the ear; but, it is the inner man that seeks and cries out, &c. His manifestation must be in the soul, revealed to the mind, realised of the spirit.

4. The soul's cry *indicates* intense *dreariness* and *anxiety.* Man needs God. So needs God, that nothing else will do. Just as nothing will do in place of the sun, or vital air. Men, angels, works of creation won't do. "God" is wanted. All dark, all cold, all miserable without Him. So the enquiry is, "Where is God?" "Where shall I find, &c.?" "How draw near?" "How come to Him?" But in the cry of the text,

5. There is the *fullest* and *clearest satisfaction* with the *God desired.* Life in God is the one thing essential, but it must be

(1.) The living God in His boundless goodness. God

signifies " good," the good One, benevolent, beneficent,
compassionate, clement, loving, kind. This 'is the God
adapted to man's dependence and unworthiness; such
a God only meets the necessities of the soul. And it
must be

(2.) In His all sufficiency.—Knowledge, wisdom, purity, truth, omnipresence, almightiness. So said God to
Abraham.

(3.) It must be God in His gracious relationship to
us; not clothed with flame, not vengeful, not furious,
not malignant; but in friendly communion, pitying,
ready to forgive, abundant in mercy, &c. This is the
God the soul sinful, guilty, needs.

(4.) It must be God that has manifested these attributes and perfections in His Son. Now God has given
the record of His will, the portrait of His face, the incarnation of His Godhead, so as to come near to us in
Christ. He comes down, visits, shews Himself; so Jesus
is the true God, &c. " Whoso hath seen Me, said Jesus,
hath seen the Father." Hear His words, see His work,
receive His gifts. And yet as Christ is no more on
earth,

(5.) The cry must centre and terminate in the Holy
Spirit. Eighteen hundred years ago, Christ said, I go
away, &c., I ascend, &c.; but I will send the Holy
Ghost; the Spirit of Truth, and He shall abide, &c.
Now, ours is the dispensation of the Holy Ghost. The
Spirit has come. He is in the world. With the Church.
Dwelling in the souls of believers. So, if any man hath
not the Spirit of Christ, &c. And now in conclusion,
notice in this desire,

1. The love and nearness of God in the Gospel of
Jesus.

2. The necessity of faith to apprehend God thus desired.

3. The importance of earnest soul desire. Prayers. Strong cries, &c.

4. The intermediate blessedness of ordinances in relation to God, His house, worship, &c. The whole psalm is expressive of this.

# V

## GOD'S GREATNESS

"Behold, God is great, and we know Him not."—JOB. xxxvi. 26. (See also PSALM cxlv. 3).

ADMITTING the personalty of God, His greatness must follow as matter of necessary deduction. And if we hold merely some loose notions of God, as confounding His being with His works, and wandering away in the vague regions of pantheism, any belief we profess to entertain can be of little worth. One intellectual personal God, the source of all existence, and therefore, before all existence, and above all creatures and worlds, and is alike in harmony with sound philosophy and Scripture authority. And this stands out with sublime grandeur in this the most ancient of sacred writings, the book of Job. With a Bible basis let us look—

I. At the sublime declaration of the text.

"God is great"—This greatness of God will be obvious by contemplating—

1. His *eternal existence.* The God inhabiting eternity, from everlasting to everlasting; God dwelling in the far-back solitudes of eternity, before He had put forth

His creative energy, or brought one world or being into existence. Isaiah xliii. 10; lvii. 15.

2. His *absolute independence.* We see dependency through all God's works and creatures. All linked together. All having mutual relationships and cementations. Thus, all the planets of the solar system, arranged and moving in precise order and harmony. So the strata of the earth; one stratum rising above another. But God, outside and above all His works, and being in Himself, self-existent, and connected only with any of His works by the exercise of His will, and wisdom and power. The highest seraph is as dependent as the crawling worm, or insect of a day's being.

3. Then *God is great in wisdom.* This is all comprehensive, and absolutely unerring, and infinite. All His works bear manifest evidence of this. Without this His government would be dubious and imperfect.—Psalm cxlvii. 5.

4. God is *great in might.* Omnipotent. Able to do everything it is befitting Him to do. Deut. iii. 24.—Jer. ii. 13.

5. God is *great in goodness.* So often stated and reiterated. Good Himself, infinitely and unchangingly good. Good in all phases of love, pity, compassion, mercy and grace ; good to all, good always. Essentially good, for this is the very nature and glory of God. Exod. xxxiv. 6.—Psalms lxxxvi. 5; cvii. 8. But God—

6. Is *great* in *His works.* Creative of government, universal rule, and illimitable authority. Here is a wide subject for evidence and illustration, and we only add, Neh. ix. 6.—Rom. iv. 11.

7. God is greater *than all His works.* Higher than the heavens, above all seraphim and cherubim. Just as

the sun is greater than the planets that revolve around him.

Now observe

**II. The call to contemplate this greatness of God.**

"Behold" God is great.

1. It is a subject *not* to *be ignored* or *overlooked*. We can contemplate it. We have powers by which to do it, and it would be a base non-use of such power if God in His greatness should be forgotten.

2. It is a *subject* that will *reward* our *contemplations*. Will tend to our mental and moral dignity. Soul's expansion. Soul's sublime advancement. And our conformity to God by beholding His glory.

3. It is *a subject connected* with *greatest enjoyment*. The soul's rest and peace and joy are inseparably connected with a true contemplation of God's greatness. Faith, hope, veneration will all revolve around the Divine majestic greatness. A contemplation of God's greatness,

4. Will *constitute* a *leading feature* in the *services* of *eternity*. No doubt other services will engage and occupy our faculties, but this surely most of all and for evermore.

### APPLICATION

I. *This* greatness of God will *demand* the exercise of our *noblest powers*. How can we know God perfectly, how search out His wondrous works and ways? Here is a sphere for the loftiest intellect. Where the psalmist and the holy prophets Isaiah and Ezekiel and the ecstacised John in Patmos, may all wonder and adore. Sir I. Newton and Sir D. Brewster and Cuvier, were students in this divine university.

II. What profound *reverence* and *humility should char-*

*acterise* contemplations like these! How great is God! What is man? A worm, as nothing before God. How lowly, how prostrate, while he beholds God's greatness.

III. How exalted *becomes* our *Lord* and *Saviour* when contemplated as being clothed with the essential glory of the Father. One with the Father. Thought it not robbery to be equal with God. Jesus, Himself, the blessed and the true God, and the eternal life.

IV. How the *precious* aid of the *Holy Spirit* should be sought in these *contemplations*. That He may raise our souls to this lofty theme. That He may give us the power of vision for so great a sight. That He may cause us to delight in His holy exalted service. And that He may save us from self-exaltation, and give us the grace of true humility, that so God may have all the glory, while we have the transforming power and lofty emotions from such devout contemplations.

# VI

## THE DIVINE CONDESCENSION AND MANIFESTATION

" God was manifest in the flesh."—1 TIM. iii. 16.

GOD in essence is the invisible God, no man hath or can see Him, &c.; how He reveals Himself to angels we know not, but except in His works and by His voice and inspiration, no one could know God. Our first parents had both these—the Divine works, the Divine voice. Gen. ii. 16; iii. 8. Well now in after ages God thus revealed Himself, and also by expressive symbols—light and fire, bush, cloud, &c., but the last and grandest was in, and by the person of His Son, the Lord Jesus Christ. So see Heb. i. 1, &c. Now the text refers to this, "God was," &c., the reading of the text may be thus—"Who was manifest in the flesh," read verse 15. Well let us see in reference to this great subject—

I. Who was manifest—"God."

Now in a certain sense the whole Deity. In His Tri-unity, the Father, "whoso" hath seen, &c., the Holy Spirit, for Jesus had the unbroken fulness of the Spirit in Him; but, strictly, it was the Divine logos or word. See this fully stated, John i. 1, &c., and verse 18; so it is set forth Col. i. 14, 15; see also Col. ii. 9. Now these statements are sufficient as to "who" was manifest, enough for every purpose of creed or belief. We enquire—

II. What was manifest?

1. The *name* of *God*, expressly given and recorded. Rom. ix. 5.

2. The *perfections* of *God*. Knowledge, omniscience, power or almightiness, ubiquity or omnipresence, grace and mercy.

3. The *authority* of *God*. He thus spake—"All power is given to Me," &c., "I say unto you," &c., "Whoso honoureth the Son," &c.

4. The *saving influence* of *God*. "Look unto Me and be ye saved." Salvation in none other, no other name, one Saviour. Now this was exhibited in healing, purifying, pardoning in the days of His flesh, so that God was both gloriously and graciously manifested in the flesh. We ask—

III. In what was God manifest?

"The flesh," that is, in our humanity, God the Son, &c., was the Child born. By flesh is meant man's nature, body and soul, so He was the God-Man, Emmanuel,

&c., in Him dwelt all the fulness of the Godhead bodily; God was seen in the Man Christ Jesus, heard, His power felt, love embodied, so that in Christ, God is with us, near us, for us. Now this manifestation—

**IV. Is a great mystery.**

We see it and know it, but cannot—

1. *Minutely comprehend* it, nor—

2. *Fully understand* it. We have mysteries all around us, ourselves, &c., but this is the great mystery, by way of emphasis and pre-eminence—

> "The first archangel never saw
> So much of God before."

God and man united in one Lord Jesus Christ. Eternity and time, omnipotence and weakness, glory and ignominy, life and death, the infinite and the span, Jehovah and the creature. But observe—

**V. It is a great mystery of godliness.**

"A godly mystery," not a mystery of science or philosophy, but a mystery to restore godliness. The greatest of all godly mysteries, "Angels desire to look into it," &c. A godly mystery beyond dispute, no one can controvert this as a great mystery.

## APPLICATION

There can—

I. Be no objection to Christianity that it involves mystery, this is in analogy with nature and providence.

II. It is a mystery for our salvation not to excite curiosity and mere wonder.

III. A mystery which eternity may more fully develope. Let us—

IV. See our personal interest in it. It concerns us and all mankind in general, and every human being in particular.

V. By faith alone we can receive it, and realize the blessing it conveys.

## VII

## FAITH

" Now faith is the substance of things hoped for, the evidence of things not seen."—HEB. xi. 1.

FAITH or Belief is so pre-eminently important that it is of the highest consequence that we should rightly understand it. Our text is the only definition the Bible gives, and it is necessary we should clearly comprehend it. In order to do this we will endeavour to analyze the two parts the Apostle gives, and we will take the latter part of the text first.

Observe—

**I. It is the evidence of things not seen.**

That is, we acknowledge existences that we never saw. Blessed are they who have not seen and yet have believed. Now this will apply to every kind of faith.

1. Look at it *generally*.

(1.) As to persons—Homer, Alexander, Socrates, Plato.

(2.) Look at nations—Egypt, as the cradle of learning, contrast it with its present condition.

(3.) Look at the lost cities—Babylon, Nineveh, Tyre, &c., as described to us, yet unseen by us.

(4.) Look at Bible history and incidents—the flood, confusion of tongues, destruction of Sodom, deliverance of Israel, overthrow of Pharoah, destruction of Jerusalem, &c., the existence of Moses and the prophets, the advent, and work, and death of the Lord Jesus Christ, the establishment of Christianity.

Here the evidence is convincing on all these points, and we might refer to many others. Now in all these cases faith is an intellectual act, and exercises no influence on the heart or life.

But now look—

**II. At faith as the substance of things hoped for.**

We now get into the region of spiritual life and salvation. Notice things hoped for—

(1.) Must have excited our desires or emotions—as pardon, sanctification, eternal life.

(2.) Must be future, what we have not now in possession; and full salvation, eternal life, are not now enjoyed, but are desired and expected.

(3.) There must be grounds for this desire and expectation, mercy of God towards us, work of Christ for us, the Spirit's operation within us, and the promises of Holy Scripture given to us.

(4.) Faith in these and by them gives the substance, before we have the actual realization, just as a cheque is the substance of the money it represents, or the title-deed the substance of the estate it describes, or the covenant the substance of the contract made. Life now, salvation now, grace and glory, two links of the same chain.

Observe this faith—

(5.) Involves trust as well as credence, we trust God's mercy, Christ's work, the Spirit's operation, the covenant, the promises.

We trust as well as desire, and expect " as Moses," &c. Now many enter into the first, the outer court of faith, true personal believers into the second, which is the holiest of all. To give credit to a living Christ as the Saviour, and acknowledge His work and grace, may be entirely inoperative; but to desire Christ's salvation, and trust in Him as the only Saviour, will certainly secure it, and be the substance of things hoped for.

(1.) Now faith being the substance, see how it will remove terror, all dread of future wrath.

(2.) How it will bring peace into the soul.

(3.) How it will excite the emotions with grateful love, and—

(4.) Lead to willing obedience and, if needs be, to self-denial and suffering for Christ.

### APPLICATION

Observe, then, clearly what faith is, and prove yourselves, see if you have realized it, and ask for its increase more‚ assured evidence, and more earnest trust; faith more entire, more solid, more joyous, &c.—"Believing we rejoice," &c.

# VIII

## FAITH IN GOD THE CREATOR

" Through faith we understand that the worlds were framed by the word of God, so that things which are seen were not made of things which do appear."—HEB. xi. 3.

IN the text, faith is spoken of in direct relationship to the work of creation. It is reasonable that men should inquire about the origin of the universe; a variety of opinions have been formed, many we think extraordinarily absurd.

(1.) The eternity of the world, no one can comprehend the beginning of all things, except the Creator, is in harmony with all rational ideas.

(2.) The self-creation of the world, self-contradictory. A creation supposes a creator, one who did create.

Spontaneous creation is equally revolting to the human mind.

(3.) Now, no one could know about the creation without it had been revealed to him.

(4.) The Bible professes to give that revelation. To Moses, God said, or exhibited by visions, the mode of the creation.

(5.) Believers in the Bible receive this revelation as true and veritable, and the text says that it is by faith we come to know the philosophy of creation, it cannot be by sight or imagination or mere reasoning, for all sorts of errors might then be adopted, but by faith in the Holy Scriptures we understand how the worlds were framed. Now let us look at the text and consider—

I. The Creator—"God."

II. His mode of creation—by His word, and—

III. How faith realizes this.

I. The Creator—"God."

This is the first sentence in the Bible, "In the beginning God created" &c., Gen. i. 1. Now God is revealed as a Being competent to this work. No one could create but one having the qualifications for this stupendous undertaking. The revelation of the Divine Being distinctly refers—

1. To His *eternal self-existence.* He must be before all creation, He must be self-existent, or we go back to another creator. He is the "high and lofty One, inhabiting eternity," from "everlasting to everlasting." Psalm xc. 1, 2. To His—

2. *Infinite knowledge and wisdom* to design, plan, sketch, draw out; "No searching of His understanding." "His understanding is infinite." Isa. xl. 13, 14.

3. *Almighty power* to *execute* thus expressed—"Thou

the black gate of perdition. It seeks the darkness, and perpetrates spiritual self-destruction. Now the Apostle lays it down that the faith which is of God is of a two-fold character.

I. It believes in the Divine existence.

II. It trusts in the Divine fidelity.

I. It believes in the Divine existence.

"That God is," this is the first letter in the divine alphabet. The Bible never presents an argument to prove this. It does to prove the folly of atheism. It does as to the superstition of idolatry; the senseless-ness of idols, and from its representations of God's works, it leaves the divine existence as a necessary inference. Now, the belief of God's existence is—

1. The *very opposite of atheism*. The atheist says "no God." A world without a creator. A universe without a ruler. No God. Self-origination. Nature and natural laws, but no author or law-giver. The grossest credulity and disbelief meet here. Can anything be, without a source or cause. I say anything—a chiseled stone, an engraved block, the simplest machine.

2. *Belief* in God is *utterly different to pantheism*. Pantheism says, all is God and God is all things. No personal, distinct, intellectual Author exists. Hence, there is no builder, the building is the architect and the architect the building; no watch maker, the watch is the constructor and the constructor the watch. Intelligence and power are elements in the universe, and sep-arate from any outer cause. So God is not the originator, and not present with His works, but He and His works are the same. The earth is God, and the sea and heaven, and all material things, and animated ex-istences. Life is God, and death is God, and everything; and so really it comes to atheism at last. For nothing

is God personally, positive; and the negative—light and darkness, good and evil, are alike God.

3. *Belief* in God is *more than deism*. Deism admits a God, but fashions Him as reason suggests, and so we are left to conclude in a phantasmagoria, as the light or fancy of man may produce. Hence deism has no well defined God; with some He is indifferent to His works, they are left to chance, and any and every possible contingency. No supervision, no control, no direction, harmony or collision, order or confusion, beauty or foulness, all are left to chaos and darkness, or arrangement and light as it may be. A bewildered world, without governorship or control; anything more wild could not be conceived, and yet this is the necessary result of some of these conclusions. With others He is the cause of all things, good or evil. With some He will reward good and punish evil. With others He leaves actions to produce their results. Now, how different is this god to the God of the Bible—holy, just, true, good, righteous; the God of law, order, and excellency, &c. So that the deists' god is really "unknown," undefined. Besides, belief is not the right word for imagination, fancy, or even emotion. Belief must have evidence, things or facts, and hence true faith in the true God,

4. Is *based* on a *threefold ground*, or a trinity of reasons.

(1.) His works, the visible universe, marvellous creation. Here reason comes to the aid of faith. All existence must have a cause. No cause, no results. The eye and the hand, the wisdom and power, are essential for construction. The earth and sea, the heaven and stars; so great, so grand, and so harmonious, indicate creative effort, therefore a divine Creator.

(2.) The Word of God sustains this, the genesis of all

things is told clearly, distinctly, and claims the belief of the understanding, judgment, and will. Bible testimony, if not exhaustive, is sufficient.

(3.) The universal consent of mankind. I say, universal, for the opposite is the exception. Heathen nations of all ages may have been cloudy, confused, exaggerated, or gone into polytheism; but they had a god, or gods. So, as extensive as man, is this belief.

(4.) Then there is the *inner conciousness* of our own souls. We feel in ourselves the touch of His moral hand, and the light borrowed from Himself. The works of God, the Word of God, and divine kindled light within, compel us to believe "God is." This, so far, is undeniable, irresistible, but not sufficient, and—

**II. In this Divine Being we must place our trust.**

"As the rewarder of them," &c. Our moral consciousness inquires about God. Our universal moral need moves us to seek Him.

1. If we seek to know His essential attributes, His works display them. Self-existence, independence, omniscience, ubiquity, knowledge, wisdom, &c.

2. If we seek to know His moral perfections, the Scriptures give us ample testimony. He is good, impartial, just to all, compassionate, full of mercy, of great long suffering, a gracious Monarch, a kind Master, a loving Father. The blessed God and fountain of blessing to all His creatures. He rewards all who diligently seek Him, and He has revealed the way to Himself, and given us a map and guide, where and how he may be found.

3. If we want to see God as *thus represented*, we gaze on the Divine image *in His Son* our *Saviour.* Here we have all that is good and tender and kind and gracious. We see God incarnate, breathing, speaking, acting, and

we know that those who came to Him found every
blessing they required. The blind, sight; the deaf,
hearing; the leprous, purity; the possessed, deliverance;
the deceased, life; the lost and perishing, salvation.
Such then is the faith without which we cannot please
God, nor obtain the blessing of His favour. I ask then
in conclusion—

1. Do you believe in God?
2. Feel your need of God?
3. Diligently seek Him? And—
4. Having found Him, obtained the great reward;
"the pearl," &c. Restoration to His heart's love, and to
the hope of eternal life.


# X

## FAITH AND WORKS

"What doth it profit, my brethren, though a man say he hath
faith and have not works? Can faith save him?" "Even so faith,
if it hath not works is dead, being alone."—JAMES ii. 14 and 17.

GOOD men have stumbled at the Epistle of James.
Luther would not admit that it was a part of canonical
Scripture: yet it does not require much skill to recon-
cile Paul and James.

Paul's declaration, By grace are ye saved, &c., refers
to the act of faith, receiving the gift of salvation. Faith
alone must justify, for there are no good works till we
are accepted and renewed; the tree must be made good
and then only is the fruit good. But mere belief does
not save, &c. "The Devils believe," &c. The faith
that saves is described by Paul, Rom. x. 9, 10, and this

is the faith of which James speaks, not dead, "but living, working, fruitful.

Now in reference to faith, notice—

**I. It is called a work.**

I. Thes. 1-3, and Gal. v. 6.

To know the course of the heavenly bodies the believing astronomer works—the believing navigator works —the believing explorer works—the wrecked mariner works till he gains the life boat. Sometimes it is anxious work, the Syro-phœnecian woman; and agonizing work, as in the case of the father of the child, "Lord, I believe," &c. It is the work of the ear, of the eye, of the foot, of the hand, of the heart.

Observe—

**II. How the fruits or work of faith are exhibited by the Apostle.**

1. Of *Abraham*, verse 21.

All the processes attending the offering of Isaac, were by faith, but it was faith in exercise and working.

2. The case of *Rahab*, verse 23.

Faith believed the spies, received them and actively delivered them. Believing and working.

Then we see—

**III. How all Christian works and faith are connected.**

Works, without faith, are self-righteous, as the Pharisees; or dead, or nominal; cannot please God, Heb. xi. 6. Some instances of faith's working will illustrate and establish the subject. See it—

1. In *works* of *devotion*.

Prayer, praise, meditation; in hearing the Word, &c.

2. In the *ordinances* of *religion*.

Baptism, the Lord's Supper,

3. *Self-denial* and *cross bearing*.

4. In the *action* of the *living soul*, as we see it in the body, heart, lungs, &c.

5. In *maintaining* the *Christian warfare.* Light of faith's shield, &c.

6. In the *persistent progress* of the *Christian* towards *eternal life.* We stand, walk, run, &c., by faith.

7. In the *final struggle* and *last battle.* All these died in the faith, Heb. xi. 39. Kept the faith, &c. So how clear is the text that faith and its works go together—inseparable. The subject should lead us—

1. To *examine* ourselves. Are we in the faith and the faith in us?

2. To *seek* its *growth* and *vigour.* Strong faith, invincible, abiding. To hold it fast.

3. It is the *antidote* to *all* evils, to fears, to troubles, &c. "Let not your heart," &c.

4. Christ is the great object of Christian faith. "Believe in me," John vi. 29. True faith is faith in the Son of God, &c.

# XI

## PERSISTENT PRAYER

"Continue in prayer."—COL. iv. 2. (See Rom. xii. 12.)

IT has truly been said that prayer is the evidence of spiritual life; the necessary result of regeneration; the fruit of the indwelling Spirit; a glorious privilege of the sons and daughters of God; and a solemn duty obligatory on all the saints of the Most High. But there are many things opposed to its steady, fervent exercise, and many things by which prayer may be hindered, or

become formal, or be interrupted, or cease; so the necessity of feeling the force of the text, to "Continue in
prayer." See—

**I. What this continuance in prayer involves.**

1. *That* the *exercise* of *prayer* has *begun*. It is not to
commence prayer, that is assumed as a fact, a reality,
but still to cultivate it and to attend to it. Then it
signifies—

2. To *continue in* the *habit* of *prayer*. Cherish it as an
essential condition of spiritual life, as breathing is to the
natural life, or the heart's motion is to continuance of
existence, or as eating is, &c.

3. Continuance in the *spirit* of prayer. There may be
the form, the words, &c., and yet no spirit. All may be
cold and merely nominal; the corpse without the soul.

4. To *continue* in *all* the essential parts of prayer—
in adoration, confession, pleading, supplication, intercession with thanksgiving.

5. To continue in the *various kinds* of prayer—secret,
or closet devotion, family, or household prayer, &c.

Notice—

**II. How we may obey the injunction.**

1. By *cherishing* a *sense* of our *constant need*. No
prayer without this; this will ever lead to prayer.

2. By *seeking* the Holy *Spirit's quickening aid* in *prayer*.
Thus we shall be stirred up, and inflamed, saved from
drowsiness and apathy.

3. By *remembering* the *great* and *precious* promises in
*relation* to *prayer*. They abound everywhere in the sacred volume, especially in the Psalms, Gospels, Epistles,
and Matthew vii. 7-12.

4. By *setting before* us the *illustrious examples* of persistent prayer; as Jacob, Moses, Elijah, David, Daniel,
&c., the Disciples, especially Jesus.

5. By a *recollection* of the *good* things we have *realized* by *prayer*. Our own experience at the commencement of the Christian life, in various seasons of need, trouble, perplexity.

Observe—

**III. Why we should continue in prayer.**

1. It is a *Divine obligation*. We are called to it, exhorted, commanded. Not to do so, would be disobedience, rebellion, &c.

2. *It is linked with our very safety*. We only can stand, or advance, or labour, or avoid the perils around us, or overcome our foes by prayer. See chap. xi. 8.

3. It is *indispensable* to *our happiness*. The renewed soul must pray; it would be gloom, sadness, misery, without it. It brings us to God's gracious presence, smiling face; it banishes clouds, surrounds the soul with joy and sunshine and heaven.

4. It is an *essential* of *salvation*. "Whosoever shall call," &c. We cannot conceive of a soul being saved without it. Prayerlessness would be a sign of self-reprobation and destruction.


APPLICATION

1. A word to the prayerless.

2. Exhortation to God's people as to unceasing prayer. Praying always with all prayer, &c.

3. As to the sweetness of the exercise, and greatness of the privilege.

4. As to its being a test of our true spiritual condition.

## XII

## THE SPIRIT POURED OUT

" And it shall come to pass in the last days, saith God, I will pour out My Spirit."—ACTS ii. 17.

BY the Spirit is meant the Holy Spirit of God, the Third Person of the Blessed Tri-unity. The personality of the Spirit is as constantly taught as the personality of the Father or the Son; He is invariably spoken of as a person; He is associated with the Father and the Son in the work of creation, providence, and redemption; and yet in the economy of our salvation, He has a distinct office and work, as distinct from the gracious purposes of the Father, or the mediatorial work of the Son. Jesus, in concluding His mission on earth, indicates the coming of the Holy Ghost as His special gift, as the Convincer of sin and the Comforter of His people, and assures them of the absolute certainty that He will come unto them. And now the way is opened for His wondrous descent. Jesus has died, risen again, and ascended to the Father, the disciples are waiting for the promised Paraclete, and on the fiftieth day, the Pentecost, the Feast of Weeks and of Harvest, the Spirit descends in all His plenitude and power. The account is most minutely given, and as the abiding Divine Presence in the Church, He becomes the guide, the sanctifier, and consolation of believers.

Notice,

**I. The Divine Spirit has executed His Divine power from the beginning.**

(1.) He wrought with His strong operations in the preaching of Noah.

(2.) He was eminently manifested in raising up God's

servants to do His special work—as Moses, Aaron, Caleb, Deborah, Samson, Gideon, Jephtha, Saul, &c.

(3.) He inspired the holy men of old to reveal the will of God in the Holy Scriptures. Heb. i. 1.

(4.) He endowed men for great and extraordinary duties—as Elijah, Elisha, Zerrubbabel, Nehemiah, Simeon, Anna, the Baptist, &c.

(5.) He inaugurated the Saviour, and testified to His Divine person and work. Matt. iii. 16, 17.

(6.) By His might He vanquished the Devil in the wilderness. Matt. iv. 10.

(7.) So Jesus, also, in His miracles put forth the power of the Spirit of God that dwelt fully in Him. Here we have the distinctly marked course of the Holy Spirit from the earliest records of Bible times. But now,

II. He was given to the New Testament Church.

And thus,

(1.) Ancient prophecies were fulfilled.

(2.) The wants of the Church supplied. The holy oracles had long been silent, the Messiah had ascended, and the Holy Spirit came down to supply the bereaved and sorrowing Church.

(3.) The Messiahship and glory of Christ were thus attested; here was the sign, the witness, the seal of the divinity of Jesus, and of His finished earthly work.

(4.) By Him the needful gifts and power were bestowed on the apostles and disciples of Jesus. Thus they had burning flaming tongues, power for their arduous and onerous work. He came to inspire with knowledge and wisdom and zeal and courage and eloquence.

(5.) By Him success was given to the Divine means employed. For conviction—for conversion, sanctification. He is the illuminator, the regenerator, the indwelling witness, the guide and leader to eternal glory.

## XIII

## THE HOLY SPIRIT — IN HIS DIVINE OPERATIONS

" And it shall come to pass in the last days, saith God, I will pour out of my Spirit upon all flesh : and your sons and your daughters shall prophecy, and your young men shall see visions, and your old men shall dream dreams."—ACTS ii. 17.

WE have considered briefly the Holy Spirit in His Divine personality, His general work, His miraculous operations, &c., and in His free and universal influences. We shall be much assisted if we look now at some special aspects of the Holy Spirit given to us.

I. As the result of the Saviour's sacrifice and work.

Hence, Jesus was to send the Holy Ghost. He was to baptize with the Holy Ghost and with fire. He was given and poured out as the result of Messiah's work. Hence the magnificent passage—"He hath ascended on high, and led captivity," &c. Hence the Holy Spirit took Christ's place in the Church, and was to abide for ever. The ascension of the one, the descent of the other. The going away of Christ, and the coming of the Spirit.

II. Notice the blessings the Holy Spirit brings to believers.

He is poured out, given, sent. But He must be received—accepted, and become ours. This only by faith and prayer. "If ye," &c.

(1.) He is the Spirit of Holiness to sanctify, so constantly called the Holy Spirit, as He cleanses, transforms.

(2.) He is the witness within of our acceptance with God. " The Spirit bears witness," Rom. viii. 16.

(3.) He is the seal of our sonship.—See 2 Cor. i. 22.

(4.) He is the pledge of all good—called "The earnest," 2 Cor. i. 22.

(5.) He is the anointer for all Christian offices, 2 Cor. i. 22 ; 1 John ii. 20, and v. 27.

(6.) He is the perfecter of the Divine work in the soul—establishes, builds up, teaches, guides, &c., makes us meet, &c. Hence, "He is the Spirit of worship, of prayer," of praise, Jude xx. Let us see,

III. Some of the symbols by which the Holy Spirit is represented.

1. As the *vital air* or *wind.* "Valley of dry bones," &c. Christ to Nicodemus. No life without it. So the winds scatter miasma, &c.

2. As the *rain* and the *dew.* I will be as the dew, &c. Where no rain there is no fertility—beauty, &c. "Showers" come down as the rain. "He that believeth in me." "So I would have given," &c. "Let Him take of the waters," &c.

3. As the *fruit* of the *vine,* and as *milk,* Isaiah lv.

4. As *oil.* "Oil of gladness." The consecrating oil of the king and of the priest. Softening, beautifying, cooling, healing, &c.

5. He is compared to *fire.* "Holy Ghost and fire," so an Old Testament prophecy, Isaiah iv. 5. Quench not the Spirit." "Stir up the gift." "Fire on the altar," &c. Observe,

IV. The Spirit we should cherish with regard to the Holy Ghost.

1. Deep humility. How unworthy. What condescension, &c.

2. *Entire dependence.* He is to be our light and strength, our defence, guide, guard.

3. *Constant believing* prayer. Pray for Him. By His aid we pray, &c. Seek His presence, &c.

4. Holy *tranquility* and *joy.* Righteousness, peace, and joy in the Holy Ghost.

5. Our abiding Comforter in all our *trials* and *sorrows*, &c.

6. Ever to be *extolled* and *glorified* by us. Exhort to a closer recognition, &c., of the Holy Spirit. We all need it—the whole Church, &c.

# XIV

## THE IMPORTANT ENQUIRY

"How many are mine iniquities and sins? Make me to know my transgression and my sin."—JOB xiii. 23.

THE text is the language of Job, but may well be uttered by us all. Let us see its significancy, and how it may become the utterance of every one of us.

Notice,

**I. The Question.**

"How many are mine iniquities?"

1. The *question* is *personal*. Not about others, but himself. "Mine." "My."

2. It *concerns* his *moral state*. His evil conduct towards God. And the words take in all sorts of moral delinquencies, iniquities, transgressions, sins. These words would include secret, open, and all kinds of evil.

3. The question relates to *their number*. "How many?" No one can tell this, not even the best, but God knows, and he can reveal the iniquities and sins of heart, lip, and life. Every one—and all—and under what circumstances committed. Psalm xc. 8; Jer. xvi. 2.

Notice,

**II. His expressed object in presenting the question.**

That he "might know," &c.

1. By a *consciousness* of them. Time obliterates, effaces, &c.

2. By a *penitent sense* of them. So as to sorrow, and grieve, and repent on account of them.

3. By a *gracious removal* of them. To know in order to confess. Bewail, and accept God's mercy. To know their heinousness. Just penalty, and then God's remedy of mercy, through the one Mediator, the Lord Jesus Christ.

Let the subject,

1. Lead us to self-examination as to our moral state.

2. To true and unfeigned repentance, and faith in the Saviour. 2 Chron. iii. 14; Acts ii. 38.

3. To absolute trust in the blood of Christ for justification, sanctification, and eternal life.

4. How deplorable to be ignorant of our state, and to be without concern for its final consequences. Our message is, repent, and believe the Gospel message of the Lord Jesus Christ.

## XV

### THE APPEAL TO GOD TO WORK

"It is time for thee, Lord, to work; for they have made void Thy law."—PSALM cxix. 126.

Our text contains,

**I. A painful declaration.**

"They have made void Thy law."

This has been true of man in all ages.

(1.) God's law is pure and just and good.

(2.) It ever includes the welfare of man as well as the glory of God.

(3.) God's law is revealed so that men may know it.

(4.) It is obligatory on all men, for all are under sub:—jection to God, yet

(5.) The majority of men make God's law void by disregarding it—by violating its precepts—by contempt of its authority—by open and frequent transgression. The violation of God's law is often followed by fearful results, as in the case of the antedeluvians—Pharoah and his host—Sodom and Gomorrah—the Israelites in the wilderness, &c. &c., and the final penalty is death. "The soul," &c. "Wages of sin," &c. In the text,

**II. There is an affecting appeal.**

"It is time for Thee to work."

Notice,

1. The *appeal* is *made* to *God*.

It belongs to God, His honour and glory, &c.

2. The *appeal* is for *God* to *work*.

No doubt it is in mercy and graciousness that the appeal should be made, as such,

(1.) That God would work by opening men's eyes to their evil doings.

(2.) By converting their consciences and awakening their fears, as on the day of Pentecost. Jailer, &c. Saul.

(3.) By translating men from darkness to light, &c.

(4.) By bringing them into His church and kingdom.

(5.) By the overthrow of the powers of evil, &c.

3. *The appeal* is *made* by *God's people*.

From their love to God and of holiness. By their compassion for souls. By their interest and desire for the glory of Christ. And by their zeal for the spread of the truth and the up-building of His church.

**III. God has various ways of responding to this appeal.**

1. By the *overthrow* of the *adversaries* of *religion*.

Canaanitish nations. Priests of Baal, &c., &c.

2. By *raising* up eminent *agencies* to do His work.

Moses. Joshua. David. Daniel. Baptist. Apostles. Martyrs. Reformers. Puritans and Wesleys.

3. By the *plenteous pouring* out of His *Holy Spirit.*

Pentecost. Various revival seasons. Let us feel, and pray, and labour for this. "Not by might," &c.

## XVI

## ATTENTION TO READING

" Give attendance to reading."—1 TIMOTHY iv. 13.

THIS command of the Apostle to Timothy might refer to the importance of his being intellectually acquainted with the Scriptures. He had known them from a child. Early taught, hence that beautiful passage, 2 Tim. i. 5, 6, and yet Timothy had not exhausted the Divine word. But as teacher and bishop, he must know the Scriptures fully. Or if Timothy in conducting the Divine worship, it was essential he should give attention to what he read and how, so that the Christian assemblies might be edified. Now let us

I. Look at some of the readers of the Divine word presented to us in the Bible.

(1.) The grand servant of God, and type of Jesus—Moses, Exodus xxiv. 7.

(2.) Then Joshua, viii. xxxiv.

(3.) Ezra and the elders, Neh. viii. 5.

(4.) Then Jesus, the Saviour, Luke iv. 16.

The reading of the Scriptures always has been a prominent part of Divine worship, see Acts xiii. 26, 27.

Observe,

II. There is the social and private reading of the word of God.

(1.) This is implied in the command to Israel, Deut. vi. 6.

(2.) So the Psalmist speaks of His acquaintance and meditation in the Divine word, Psalms i. ; cxix. 35, 47, 92.

(3.) The dignified treasurer on His way from Jerusalem, Acts viii. 27.

(4.) So the letters of the Apostle were to be read to the Christian churches, Cor. iv. 16, 1 Thess. v. 27.

Observe,

### III. The attention to Scripture reading demanded.

1. *Attention as to what* we *read*. "All Scripture," &c., but all not equally important or edifying. Especially in families great discretion necessary. There are deep mysteries. Ezekiel. Revelation. Some Psalms, &c.

2. The *spirit* in which *they are to be read*. With humility, docility, teachableness. Solicitude to know. " Thy words were found, and I did eat them," &c.

3. The *prayerfulness* that *should attend* the reading of Scripture. "For light," &c. " Open thou mine eyes."

4. The *great design*—to obtain *saving knowledge*, to know God's will, to be wise to salvation.

5. To be *helpers* to *others*. Shew men the way of salvation. See Apollos, the mighty orator, and yet Priscella and Aquilla taught him the way of the Lord more perfectly. And now

### IV. The Scriptures are not to be read exclusively.

1. There are *helps* to us in *reading* the *Scriptures*— Eastern usages, explanatory works, expositions, dictionaries, marginal bibles.

2. There are books of evidences of the Scripture truth and authenticity.

3. There are books *exhibiting* the *influence* of the *Scripture*—biography, the ancient fathers, the learned, &c.,

the Reformers. Puritans, &c., Wesley, Doddridge, the
Henrys, and Watts, &c.

4. There are *works* as *auxiliaries to the Scriptures*—
periodicals, weeklies, monthlies, for all classes, ages, &c.
All prices. Now, religious information, &c., how common, how cheap. How God is ruling the world and
the church.

5. *General literature*—poetry, science, &c., natural history, &c. Taking in all this and the daily papers,
giving the events of the hour.

Observe,

**V. Some reasons for attending to the injunction of the
Apostle.**

1. Most of our *knowledge must be attained* by *reading.*
Ignorance the result if neglected.

2. *Reading* not only *fills* but *enlarges* the *mind.* It is
to the soul what eating is to the body—gives growth,
strength.

3. The *unspeakable pleasure* it *affords.* I say unspeakable—it surpasses expression. One of the soul's luxuries
of this life.

4. The *abiding* profit *it secures.* It gives treasures,
that thieves cannot steal. It gives moral vigour, that
sickness cannot impair. It gives joys, that misfortunes
cannot destroy. It gives influence, that makes us pre-
eminently blessings to others. It gives hopes, that
eternity can only meet. Then give attention to reading.
Secure books. Redeem time. Be in earnest. Especially give the pre-eminence to the highest, holiest kind
of reading. "Search the Scriptures," &c.

## XVII

## A REMEMBRANCE OF GOSPEL TRUTH

" Remember that Jesus Christ, of the seed of David, was raised from the dead, according to my gospel."—2 TIMOTHY ii. 8.

THE Gospel only saves when it is received by faith, and when it is kept in memory or remembrance. It may be despised, rejected, or temporally received only, and so in vain. Let us see in the text

**I. The designation the Apostle gives to the Gospel.**

" My Gospel." That is the message, tidings, good-news, which he designated as Gospel. The Apostle's term " My " Gospel, might refer

1. To the *Gospel he received*. When smitten to the earth. When Christ arrested him. Revealed his purpose of mercy, Acts ix. 6 and verse 15. See also Gal. i. 11.

2. To the *Gospel* he had ever *preached*, 1 Cor. xv. 1, 4.

3. To the *Gospel* he had *opposed*, to that of Judaizing teachers. See Gal. iii. 1, to end.

Observe,

**II. The leading truth in this Gospel of the Apostle Paul.**

1. The *subject* of it *Jesus Christ*.

The anointed Saviour. Gospel of Christ. Good news concerning Jesus, who came into the world to save sinners. No other Gospel than this. He refers, to

2. The *lineage* of the *Saviour*.

"Of the seed of David." This was predicted, promised, according to this promise Christ came. Hence, He is the son of David. See Luke ii. 4. While the offspring of David, He was also David's root, and Lord.

3. That the *Saviour died*.

This is clearly involved in the text. This the basis of the Mediatorial scheme. Slaughtered victims had prefigured it. Prophets had predicted it. Jesus himself declared it. Evangelists attested it. The solemn fact of the Gospel is, "Christ hath died"—died for sinners, &c.

4. That Jesus who *died* had been *raised* from the *dead.* This also had been both predicted and prefigured. Jonah in the belly of the fish. Statements of David and other prophets. So also of Christ again and again. Then verified by the missing body of Christ. The averment of the women. Of Peter and John—of the eleven, &c. See 1 Cor. xv. 3, 8; Acts ii. 23, 36.

Notice,

**III. How the retention of this great truth is urged.**

"Remember"—keep distinctly in mind,

1. The *essentiality* of this *truth.* If Christ is not risen, then the Gospel is vain, and our faith is in vain also. This is the key-stone of salvation.

2. The *vital power* of this *truth.*

Evincing the power of God. Messiahship of Christ, and the veritableness of Scripture truth. It is the truth that vitalizes the Gospel, and the believer that accepts it.

3. The *practical influence* of this *truth.*

In raising us from death. In providing us with a living intercessor. In imparting power to all believers for the Christian service and warfare. Christ liveth in us, and by Him we live and labour and overcome.

4. The *comforting assurances* it *conveys.*

As to Christ's headship. As to the world to come. As to our resurrection and immortal life. As to the cheering hope of living with Christ for evermore. John xiv. 1, &c.; 1 Cor. v. 8.

### APPLICATION

1. How needful to understand and receive the essentials of the Gospel truth.

2. To retain and hold them fast to the end.

3. To seek a sanctified memory, by which they may be treasured up in our souls.

4. How the word and ordinances are adapted to help us in the continued remembrance of these saving verities of the Gospel,—especially pre-eminently the Lord's Supper.

# XVIII

## UNCHANGEABLENESS OF JESUS CHRIST.

"Jesus Christ, the same yesterday, and to-day, and for ever."— HEB. xiii. 8.

AMONG the various proofs of the Divinity of Christ, is that of His eternal immutability, or unchangeableness. God alone is so. Angels had a beginning. Some of them became apostate, and all are mutable. But Jehovah is the same self-existent One, and besides Him there is none else. So that either Christ is not eternally immutable, or He is manifestly Divine. I know of no way of evading one of these conclusions.

Observe,

**I. The person.**

"Jesus Christ." The person is the Lord Jesus Christ.

1. In *His office* He *is* "*Jesus*." Because He shall save. He is the one and only Saviour, as to the redemption of mankind : Joshua was a deliverer. So the rulers and judges, but their work was limited. Christ is the Saviour of the race of the world. His name, Jesus, was divinely given—is divinely consecrated—is of Divine majesty and power—is the only name essentially connected with salvation. No other, &c. "Whosoever shall call," &c. Is to be universally preached. That

repentance and remission, &c., be preached in His
name.

For this office,

2. He was *anointed, and then* He is *Jesus Christ;* consecrated a great high priest for evermore. How? See
Heb. i. 8, &c.; Matt. iii. 13. Here was the anointing
and mandate, "Hear ye Him." Jesus is the anointed
consecrated Saviour. See Heb. i. 12; Rev. i. 4.

Observe,

II. The declaration of the text.

" The same."

1. In His own *Divine essence.* "Yesterday"—in past
eternal ages. "Word was with God, and was God."
Hear Him speaking. Prov. viii. 22, &c.

2. In His *saving work.* All the saved, past and
present and future, are saved by Him. See this exhibited, Isaiah xliii. 11; and xlv. 21, 22. No reference
to any other.

3. In His *boundless grace.* His saving purposes origin-
ated here, His declarations, promises, provisions, &c.
So as the past, is the present and the future. An eternal fathomless ocean.

4. In His *exhaustless sufficiency.* Able to save to the
uttermost. Nothing too hard, ever. Now and for ever,
His fiat made the worlds. All power in heaven and
earth is given, &c.

5. In His *final designs.* His plans are partly revealed.
He is working them out, will complete them, so subject
the moral universe to God. Reign till He hath put all
things, &c. 1 Cor. xv. 25; Phil. ii. 9. He shall reign
for ever and ever.

Notice,

III. The conclusions deducible therefrom.

Observe,

1. We see the *difference between dispensations* and *Jesus Christ*. Several successive and progressive dispensations, but Christ was in them, and with all of them. They changed, but He did not.

Observe,

2. We see the *difference between* the *Saviour* and *His servants*. All they were fragile and dying. Noah, Abraham, Moses, David, the Prophets, the Baptist, and the Apostles; but the Saviour is the immutable Jesus Christ, &c.

3. We see the *difference between Christ's kingdom*, and *those* of the *world*. Fashion of this world, &c. Look at the past—dynasties, empires—gone. They attained their meridian—declined, perished, not so Christ. "Thy kingdom is an everlasting kingdom," &c.

4. We see the *difference between* the *blessings* of the *Saviour*, and *those* that are *earthly* and *secular*. Their riches, and honours, and enjoyments, all fail and decay. Christ's peace, the joys, &c., and dignities, are for evermore.

### APPLICATION

Observe,

1. Christ's claims are ever the same.

2. So Christ's connection with His people. Jesus Christ the Saviour of our parents yesterday—Jesus Christ the Saviour of us to-day—Jesus Christ the Saviour of our decendants for ever.

3. We invite every class of sinners to the one unchanging Redeemer.

4. The subject affords matter for constant confidence, and peace and hope, &c.

## XIX

## DIVINE TRUTH AND ITS ACKNOWLEDGMENT

"The acknowledging of the truth which is after godliness."—
TITUS i. 1.

TRUTH is important always, in all things, at all times.
Divine truth is especially so. The world is full of fiction and errors. Truth has often been compromised,
adulterated, and often it has been sold. Semblances
and counterfeits abound. Early in the Christian Church
false teachers began to add human conceits and vague
utterances, instead of the pure solid truths of the
Gospel. So Paul, in writing to Titus, speaks of the
faith of God's elect, and "The truth," &c.

Notice,

I. The subject of the text—" Truth."

Obviously there is a reference to the Gospel, and its
sacred revelations, doctrines, principles, &c., and so it is
called, by way of emphasis, the truth. As such it is
distinguished,

1. From the *types* and *shadows* of the old *dispensations*.
These abounded from Adam, the first type of the Saviour, up to Zerubbabel, including Abel, Isaac, Joseph,
Moses, Joshua, Samson, David, &c., and also typical
sacrifices and things, all prefiguring the coming of the
Christ. Such were the various offerings, &c. Now
the Gospel was the fulfilment, the substance of these
types, &c., and therefore "the truth," the substance, &c.
The Gospel was,

2. The *truth* of *prophecies* and *promises*. All the good
things predicted, &c. The great person of the Saviour.
The great blessing, salvation. The great dignities and
privileges.

3. The *truth*, as being the *dispensation* of the *Spirit of*

*truth*. The Gospel, not only of the Prince of truth, but of the Holy Ghost, sent down from heaven. Such truth was Divine, pure, full, perfect.

Observe,

**II. Its special characteristic.**

"According to godliness." Gospel truth is,

1. *From God*, the *source of godliness*. Godliness is the possession of His likeness and spirit, &c., and is immediately from Him, and this is revealed in the Gospel of truth.

2. It is the *truth that produces godliness*. Regeneration is by the word of truth, the incorruptible seed, &c. So sanctification—"Sanctify them by Thy truth," &c. So is Divine growth, &c. The truth of the Gospel is the instrumental agency of the Holy Spirit.

3. It is the *rule* of *godliness*. In the Gospel it is defined, illustrated, fully stated, in all its phases, virtues, graces, spirit, life, fruits, &c. Only here do we know all the traits of godliness.

4. It *exhibits* the *blessedness* of *godliness*. The gracious accompaniments. The distinguished enjoyments. The final glories.

Then see,

**III. The acknowledgment of the truth.**

1. By *faith* in *its revelations*. Credited—accepted as revealed.

2. By open *profession* of *it*. Demanded by Christ. Evidenced by His disciples, and the confessors. Rom. x.

3. By *abiding attachment* to it. Holding it fast. Cleaving to it. Abiding in it. Permeated by it.

4. By *its visibility* in our *spirit* and *life*. Christians, living epistles, true witnesses, real embodiments, children of the truth.

This subject,

1. Is *doctrinal* in its bearings.
2. *Experimental* in its realization.
3. *Practical* in its exhibition.

# XX

## CONTENDING FOR THE FAITH

"It was needful for me to write unto you, and exhort you, that ye should earnestly contend for the faith which was once delivered unto the saints."—JUDE i. 3.

CONTEXT, &c. Writer and design. See Matt. xiii. 55.

**I. The subject of the text.**

The faith; v. 20—meaning the system of Christian truth. The Gospel, or revelation of Divine grace. Now this faith,

(1.) Is clearly presented to us in Holy Scripture.

(2.) It is Divine, being God's record of His will.

(3.) It is one in opposition to the various creeds, &c., of men. One Gospel.

(4.) It is saving to all who are partakers of it.

(5.) It has been deposited in the Church of the Lord Jesus Christ. Pillar and ground of the truth. Delivered to the saints for their illumination and guidance—for the foundation of their trust—for propagation to the ends of the world.

Notice,

**II. For this faith we are to be devoted champions.**

But not bitterly, blindly, in the spirit of wrath. Contending,

1. As the *consecrated soldiers* of Christ.
2. With the *whole panoply* of *truth*.
3. With *burning zeal* for the *honour* of Christ.
4. In the *loving spirit* of our *great* commander.

III. The motives by which we should be influenced.

1. For the *faith's sake.*

As against scepticism, credulity, perverted faith, &c. Against all mere opinions, dogmas, &c.

2. For the *sake* of our *brethren* in the *faith.*

To establish them—preserve, &c.

3. For the *sake* of *those without.*

Who are in unbelief. Far off, &c.

In our application, there are some things to be suggested,

1. A distinct clearness in our mind as to faith.

2. A full acquaintance with Scripture teaching.

3. An ardent supplication for the Spirit's aid.

4. A single eye to the Lord's glory. Have we this faith? Is it precious to us? Are we jealous concerning it? In some seasons, special calls are made on us to exemplify the text in spirit and letter.


## XXI

## ONE WITH GOD AND ALL SAINTS

"That they all may be one : as thou, Father, art in me, and I in thee, that they also may be one in us ; that the world may believe that Thou hast sent Me."—JOHN xvii. 21.

VERY great value is attached to this prayer of the Saviour. It is the longest recorded. It is the last comprehensive one. It takes in His whole Church, and the glory of His saints for ever. Thoughts so sublime and grand.—Its spirit so pure, &c.—Its petitions so majestic and imperative; v. 24. "I will," &c. Observe, the unity of the Church is the chief subject of Christ's prayer. The grand end—the final end—the mighty irresistible end, &c.

Observe,

**I. The character of the persons referred to.**

Here we cannot mistake.   They are,

(1.) Given out of the world; v. 6.

(2.) They have a personal knowledge of God and His will; v. 7.

(3.) Believers of Christ's words; v. 8.

(4.) Given to Jesus of the Father; v. 9.

(5.) Nonconformists to the world; v. 14.

Now these traits belong to all saints.

Observe, nothing is said,

1. Of their opinions.

2. Nor of their creeds—nor of,

3. Their mode of worship.

4. Nor of their nationality.

It is all experimental, practical.   Now here is the wide basis of the Christian Church—the catholicity of Christ's kingdom.

Observe,

**II. The nature of Christ's prayer for them.**

"That they also may be one in us."

Observe,

1. The *unity* in *Tri-unity* of *God* is distinctly stated.

Pre-existent glory; v. 5. "Even as we are one;" v. 22.

2. Then their *unity* in *God* is *asked*.

"One in us."   One in acceptance—one in adoption—one in sanctification—one in likeness—one in harmony with God's will—one in spiritual union and fellowship. As the member in the body—as the branches in the vine—as the spirit in material man.   Observe, the plurality expressed, "In us"—in the Father—in the Son—in the Holy Ghost.   But, notice,

3. Their *unity* with *each other* is *sought*.

(1.) The intimacy; vs. 21, 22.

(2.) The universality. "They all;" v. 21.

All orders, ages, conditions. Jews and Gentiles. Every and each saint or believer.

(3.) The *visibility* of *this unity*.

World believe; v. 21. Then the world must see it— observe it. So Christ. "By this shall all men know," &c. Now let us see,

**III. The grounds on which we should be found in harmony with the text.**

1. The Divine model. "Unity of the Godhead." One absolutely. No dis-union. Father, Son, and Holy Spirit one.

2. One unity *in the Tri*-unity. The Divine works give and exhibit, variety in unity. Seven colours making the unity of light. Three gases. Unity of the vital air. Two also giving the unity of water. The ocean one with its multitudinous drops; the earth one, with its unnumbered atoms; the heavens one, with its countless orbs, planets, stars, suns.

3. *Unity* of *the spiritual life*. Phrases may differ, ideas and notions, conclusions, &c., but the same elements and experiences have to do with all Christian life. Illuminating, quickening, renewing, reconciling, sanctifying, no exception, yet the phraseology may be as different as the languages of the human family.

4. *Unity* in the *blessings* of *the Gospel*. One holy calling, holy forgiveness, holy experiences, joy, hope, holy privileges, faith, prayer, communion.

5. *Unity* in the *final felicity of the glorified*, v. 24. With Christ. Beholding, &c. One temple world, one holy city, one river and tree of life, one song of Divine praise, one eternal life.

APPLICATION

1. Disunion is unlikeness to God.

2. Opposed to God's holy will.

3. Displeasing to God as an element of evil.

4. Injurious to us.

5. Prejudicial to the Gospel.

6. Fruitful of evil.   Union and church prosperity. Triumphs of the truth.   Conversion of the world, "that the world may believe," &c.

# XXII

## THE CHERUBIM AND THE GLORY

"The cherubims of glory shadowing the mercy seat."—HEBREWS ix. 5.

THE Levitical dispensation was one of types and shadows and sacrifices, all pointing onward towards the person and work of the Lord Jesus Christ.   The pious Israelite here had a pictorial representation of the great scheme of redemption.   So we see how clearly and fully the Epistle to the Hebrews is the key to the book of Leviticus, and this chapter especially, bears out that grand idea in the text.

Notice,

**I. The Divine law.**

The tables of the Covenant.   The Covenant made with Israel, engraved on stones, and enshrined in the sacred ark.

Here is,

1. The *law* in its *Divine sacredness*.   Of God, from God, like God, holy, just, and good.   Nothing severe or oppressive—but good and godlike.

2. The *law* in its *twofold relationship*.   To God—to man.   On these hang all the law and prophets—every thing here included.

3. The *law* in its *unchangeableness*. It abides—its claims ever the same—obedience ever the same—Christ did not come to annul or destroy. It is of everlasting obligation. Like its Author, Immutable, and Eternal.

4. The *Divine law*. Treasured up—in safe keeping. To be ever referred to. Exhibiting God as Lawgiver, man as subject. But man is a transgressor—under its penalty—curse. The law, therefore, can do nothing for him, but exhibit his guilt, and pronounce its malediction, "cursed is every one," &c. It knows nothing of pardon, of grace, or of mercy. Its character and office is one—to bless obedience, or to curse transgression.

So now we have to see in the text,

**II. Divine mercy.**

Mercy seat, the covering of the ark—the propitiatory. Observe,

1. It is the *mercy* of the Lawgiver, but *not the law*. A new manifestation of the Divine character.

2. It is *mercy* in *harmony with law*. Not superseding, or in conflict, and therefore must be a propitiatory. One who can be the meeting place of both law and mercy—God and man. Here we have exhibited the Lord Jesus Christ.

(1.) Made under the law.

(2.) Obedient to the law. Perfect, &c., cheerful.

(3.) Bearing the penalty of the law for law breakers. See Gal. iii. 10-13. And now,

(4.) Comes the proclamation and exercise of mercy to the guilty. "God can now be just, and yet," &c.

3. It is *mercy* now *taking* the *place* of *the law*. The law was given by Moses, but grace and truth came by Jesus Christ. Now is the dispensation of the Gospel. Now, not under the law, but grace. Now Sinai receded,

Zion and Calvary in sight. Now no curses, but to the rejectors of the grace of God. "Christ came not to condemn the world," &c. Now God is, in Christ, reconciling, not imputing, &c. Such is the mercy seat and its lessons.

### III. The wondering angels.

"The cherubim of glory," &c. Now the cherubim evidently are the celestial ones, unfallen, and holy, and blessed. A passage in Peter will, I think, give the meaning. "Which things the angels desire to look into." The sufferings of Christ, and the glory," &c.

Now just observe,

1. The angels *have exhibited* great interest in the *world* we *inhabit.* Job. "When the foundations," &c.— The morning stars viewed it with delight and benevolent concern.

2. The *angels* were *convened* at the giving of *the law, which was placed* in the ark. Ex. xix. 16; Deut. xxxiii. 2; Acts vii. 53; Heb. ii. 2.

3. The angels sang *Christianity's anthem.* At the *incarnation,* the Heavenly host burst forth, &c.

4. Angels *ministered* to the *Saviour.* Temptation— agony—resurrection—ascension.

5. They rejoice in the *restoration* of *perishing sinners.* "When one sinner repents," &c., "joy," &c.

6. They are united with *the redeemed* in the celebration *of the praises of Christ* in the celestial temple. Rev. v. 11.

Now see how "glory" is connected with the whole scene,

(1.) The cherubim are glorious, holy, unfallen.

(2.) The law is glorious.

(3.) The mercy seat is more glorious.

(4.) Future and eternal glory is the result of the Divine ministrations.

Now this representation of the Divine mercy seat, &c.,

1. Should be our study as well as of angels.

2. This is especially the Christian minister's theme. The sufferings of Christ, and the glory, &c. The law of God in its claims and penalties. And the Divine Mediator for purposes of grace and mercy.

3. Our personal duty and interest. "Let us come boldly to the throne of grace," &c. Here is the propitiatory—here is our reconciliation—at-one-ment of men with God. Our salvation with eternal glory. The holy angels are our friends, and will be our companions for ever. "Ye are come," &c. Finally, legalism is of the past, and gone. No longer written, do and live, but believe and be saved. "Not by works of righteousness." Ours is not Sinai, and Moses, and the tables of the law, but Zion, Jesus, and the Gospel. But with these observe the exceeding glory of the Christian system, Paul presents fully its nature and influence. 2. Cor. iii. 7, &c.

## XXIII

## VIGILANCE AND SOBRIETY

### (A MIDNIGHT SERVICE SKETCH FOR THE LAST EVENING OF THE YEAR.)

" Therefore, let us not sleep, as do others; let us watch, and be sober."—1 THESS. v. 6.

THIS is a very solemn chapter; v. 2, 3. Full of admonitions, cautions, exhortations. The text is referring to God's people, for he says, v. 5, "Ye are all the children

of the light, and the children of the day; we are not of
the night nor of darkness;" "Therefore," this is the
practical deduction, "let us not sleep," &c.

Observe,

I. **The two classes spoken of in context.**

"Children of light" and "of the day." Children of
the night and of darkness; v. 5. Here are the two
classes—the righteous and unrighteous, saints and sinners, the godly and the wicked. Take into consideration

1. The *children* of *the night* and *of darkness*. In ignorance, unbelief, wrath. In the regions of civil rebellion
and imminent peril. Then there are the opposite class.

2. *Children* of *light* and of the *day*. Enlightened by
the word and Spirit of God. Transformed, brought
out of spiritual Egypt. Translated from the kingdom
of darkness and Satan. Renewed, adopted into God's
family, &c. See Eph. ii. 1-12; Acts xxvi. 18; 1 Peter
ii. 9. They have Divine light within them. The citi-
zens of the kingdom of light have knowledge, love,
and holiness. In their path is light, shining more and
more, &c. Heirs of the inheritance of light. Shine as
lights in the world. Not in darkness of ignorance, unbelief, open rebellion, or condemnation.

II. **The obvious course of the children of the day.**

"Therefore, let us not sleep, as do others," &c.

Notice,

1. *What* is *to be avoided*. Moral sleep—soul lethargy
—conscience slumbering—spiritual drowsiness. This
sleep is a state of moral unconsciousness—vague and
illusory dreams—real perils—helplessness—wasted opportunities, &c.

2. *What* is to be *attended* to.

(1.) Vigilance. "Let us watch," &c. Against the
evils that surround us. Against the snares of the world,

the stratagems of the evil one, the deceitfulness of our
own hearts. As the sentinel at his post. As the mariner
looking for day. As the wise virgins. As Peter and
the disciples should have done. As all are exhorted
to do.

(2.) Sobriety. "And be sober." Physical sobriety—
avoiding revelling, and banquetting, and drunkenness ;
v. 7, and all tendencies to it ; abstaining from the very
appearance of evil, &c. Mental sobriety—walking in
humility and self-abasement, not intoxicated with vanity
and the praises of men. Moral sobriety—seeking even
lawful things with moderation, not inebriated with love
of the world, pleasure, riches, &c. Sobriety of mind—
of spirit—of conversation—avoiding foolish excite-
ments, and vapid and silly conversation. Such sobriety
as includes a well-balanced mind, a serious spirit, and a
becoming walk before God and men. Now this sobriety
is to be real, entire, and constant.

Now notice,

III. The motives by which this course may be urged.

From a consideration of

1. The *enemies* and *perils which surround* us.

2. *Our* own *weakness* and tendency *to evil.* Evil
heart. Constitutional leanings. Liability to err. Violence of our passions. Influence of others, &c.

3. The *sad consequences which* may *result.* Spiritual
declension. Degradation. Open apostacy. Misery,
woe, death.

### APPLICATION

Let the text be solemnly considered and pondered.

1. In the light of our Christian profession.

2. In connection with our peace and happiness.

3. With our usefulness and honour.

4. With our final acceptance and salvation.

## XXIV

## CHILDREN NOT TO BE DESPISED

"Take heed that ye despise not one of these little ones," &c.—
MATTHEW xviii. 10.

THE words of the text take in two classes,

1. Literally, children; v. 2 and 3.

2. It takes in God's spiritual children. The lowest of
those who believe in Christ; v. 6. We apply the text
to-day literally to children, to the young, &c., those who
are still minors, under age, &c., and I look at two things
in this view of the text.

I. **How we are not to despise children.**

To despise is to undervalue, contemn, seem to treat
with neglect. We despise,

1. *If we under-estimate* their *worth.* What is the value,
father, mother, of your child in money currency? Look
at their form, face; hear their prattle, questions. Think
of their souls, undying, immortal souls. Reflect, what!
It may be their capacity of progress, and for enjoyment,
for distinction, glory. Sir I. Newton. Sir D. Brews-
ster. Faraday, &c. For usefulness. As patriots, philan-
thropists. Christian missionaries. We despise them,

2. *If we neglect them.* How dependent. For many
years. Body, mind, soul. We are to mould, impress,
train. We despise,

3. If we do not *bring adequate means* and *agencies to
bear* upon *them.* The communication of knowledge.
The force of example. The influence of love. The
resources of prayer. Bible. Christ. Holy society, &c.
Then,

II. **The why we are not to despise them.**

1. They are God's creatures. Gems. We do not

despise pearls, flowers, trees, stars, animal creatures. Who can despise the faithful dog, the noble horse, the soaring eagle, the royal lion, the subtle elephant? How much more precious and superior are the children! For

2. *They are* of *our nature*, &c., fashioned as we are. Senses, instincts, faculties, our lesser brethren and sisters.

3. By the *recollection* of *our own* past *history.* Look back to childhood, youth. How loved were we! How cared for and prayed for! Where had we been and what, but for the love and care of others?

4. By the *implanted instinct* of our *own nature.* How deep, &c., how unquenchable. How it awakens, and lives, and burns in us. "As a *father* pitieth," &c. "As one whom his *mother* comforteth," &c.

5. By the *noble examples*, the Scriptures *supply*— Abraham and Jacob, Moses and his parents, David and his, &c.

6. By the *conduct* of our *blessed* Lord, "they brought children," &c. He is asked by a nobleman for his son, the ruler for his daughter—the father for his child—the Syrophenician for her daughter. Did Jesus despise children? &c.

7. *By the express commands* of *God*—to love—to teach —to provide—to train—promises are given, Divine aid supplied.


### APPLICATION

1. See how the words of the text are addressed. "Take heed." Watch, judge, remember.

2. Our accountableness in this matter. Several tribunals—bar of public opinion. We should respect that —bar of the child's conscience—bar of our own—bar of God; now, and at the last day.

3. The blessedness of recognising the text. How great our satisfaction. Hope, joy, reward.

4. To all we speak. Parents—teachers—ministers—all Christians—all persons, &c.

## XXV

## SUPERABOUNDING GRACE

"But where sin abounded, grace did much more abound."—ROMANS v. 20.

How grand this chapter! But it requires careful attention. Full of antithesis, therefore, needs great care. It is evident all human sin is to be traced to one man; v. 12. That death, obviously spiritual as well as natural, flows from that one sin; v. 12. The fearful result to many by that one man and his one sin; v. 15. Then we have the bright side. There is another one man; v. 15; the second Adam—Jesus Christ. By this one man came the grace; v. 15. That this grace was to many persons; v. 15. Then it is added, the grace is to many offences; v. 16. But the climax is this: the gift or offer of life to all men; v. 18. And, finally, by the law the offence did abound in all, and over all; and our text is the antithesis. But where sin did abound grace &c., did much more abound. This is the grand climax of the whole—grace did superabound.

Now observe,

I. What superabounds?—"Grace."

Favour to the unworthy—favour to the guilty—favour to condemned sinners—transgressors—dead in sin, and dead by law.

II. Whose favour superabounds?

"God's"; v. 15. The grace of God. God the Father —the fountain—source—author.

**III. Through whom did this grace superabound?**

By Jesus Christ; verses 15, 17, 21—Christ, the Mediator—the channel—God's flowing love.

**IV. To whom did this grace superabound?**

To many; verses 15, 19—to all; v. 18—the fallen world—all, every one, &c. But,

**V. In what respects did grace superabound?**

Surpass, go beyond, exceed, for so it means. Now grace superabounds

1. In the *greatness* of *our covenant head*—Second Adam —Lord Jesus—God's Son. How much more exalted is He over the first Adam! First Adam great, but Jesus greatest. First Adam lord of earth, Jesus, Lord of glory. First Adam holy but fallible, second holy and infallible—higher than the angels—"Brightness of the Father's glory," &c.

2. In the *ability grace supplies*. First Adam stood in his native goodness and personal sufficiency—we stand in the infinite righteousness, and grace and power of the Lord Jesus. Adam in his own righteousness—we in the obedience and righteousness of the Lord Jesus Christ. Adam in himself—we in Christ Jesus. Grace superabounded,

3. In the *blessings we receive*.

(1.) We lost the Divine image, it is restored in Christ.

(2.) We lost innocency, we regain holiness.

(3.) We lost Eden, we obtain the kingdom of Heaven. We lost life here, we obtain life eternal. We forfeited the earthly inheritance, we gain the kingdom of God's eternal glory. We fell from a state lower than the angels, and are raised to be equal to them and their

companions for ever. We lost the Divine image, but
are made partakers of the Divine nature.

4. In the *number* of *the subjects* of *grace*. Sin's abounding have ruined untold myriads of every age and nation.

(1.) But grace has always superabounded. We see
this in the salvation of all infant children. These will
form one-half of the human race. All beyond these will
give Christ the majority of the saved. Now just look
at the saved of all generations—all nations, &c.—Look
at the promises as "sands" of the seashore, "stars
of heaven," &c.—look at the earth filled with the redeemed—look at the multitude that no man can number, &c.—look at Christ's soul satisfied, &c. Now thus
it is evident "That where sin," &c., "Grace did," &c.
May we ask,

**VI. If there are any reasons to be given why grace did
superabound?**

We venture to think there are three.

1. *The glory* of *God*. Redemption is the highest glory
of Jehovah—the work of grace is the greatest. Shall it
not exceed the abounding of sin? The work of the
devil—the triumph of evil. Is the vile rebel to triumph
over God?—evil over good?—hell over heaven?

2. *The reward and honour* of *Jesus*. His voluntary
work is to be rewarded—his designs accomplished—his
kingdom set up—his seed to fill the earth—his joy completed—his crowns many. Shall the devil baffle our
Lord, and exalt sin, and slavery, and death above holiness, liberty, and life? Christ must triumph—"Be the
conquerer."

3. The *lessons* of holiness and *love* to be set *before* the
*universe*. All intelligent and holy beings are interested
in this conflict; and it would be a scene of horror to see
hate, envy, malignity, and rebellion in the ascendant.

Satan would rejoice—hell be jubilant. But God has said, and it shall be, that where " Sin abounded, grace shall much more abound."

## APPLICATION
1. Man has really gained by the fall.
2. The reign of grace is for us.
3. Are we recipients of it ?  Should we not
4. Joyously anticipate its final victory ?


# XXVI
## VOLUNTARY LIBERALITY

" Freely ye have received, freely give."—MATTHEW x. 8.

THIS is a part of our Lord's address to the twelve. What a commission—endowment; v. 7, 8, &c.  What credentials, what powers, &c.  Now the text is capable of universal Christian application—to all ministers—to all Sunday school teachers—to all labourers—to all Christians.  Jesus reiterates this to us all.  Enjoins it on all.

I. See the declaration.
" Freely ye have received," &c.
It will apply,

1. To the *privileges* and *blessings* of the *Gospel*.  The good news.  Like a fountain, freely flowing.  Like the air—ocean.  No restriction—limitation.

2. To our *spiritual bestowments*.  Pardon, justification, regeneration, sanctification, grace, &c.

3. To *our gifts*.  Knowledge, wisdom, speech, teaching.

4. To *our influence*.  God must give it—in means, money, tact, energy, &c.  In all these there is the readi-

ness, plentitude, &c., of God's gifts. Grace for grace, &c.

Now this free receiving,

(1.) It applies to all.

(2.) To all gifts.

(3.) Involves our consciousness of it.

Then see,

**II. The outcoming duty.**

Freely ye have received, "freely give." Now, then, it is to freely give,

1. The *heart* to the *Lord* and His *service*. "My Son." "Who is willing."

2. The *life* to His *open service*. Confession before men. "Cross-bearing."

3. Our *talents* to His *cause*. See 1 Cor. xii. 6-11.

4. Our *means* to advance *His kingdom*. Not a step without money. Scriptures, translating, printing, missions, pastors, teachers, the labourer worthy of his hire, buildings, houses of worship, schools, &c. Now our pecuniary means are needful, absolutely, &c. How the women ministered to Christ in His travels and toils.

5. *Our prayers* for the *Divine blessing*. Free, hearty, earnest, united, &c.

Now notice,

6. This *duty comes* out of our *ability*. Is in proportion to our ability, must be in the same spirit. Freely, our motives are manifold—our spiritual good—our usefulness, reward—Christ's favour, the blessings of those we serve, harmony, and, with God, felicity for ever.

Now apply the text,

1. Each one individually.

2. Every one to the Lord.

3. The claims of the world.

4. Glory of the Lord Jesus.

# XXVII

## THE ROBE OF CHARITY

" For charity shall cover the multitude of sins."—1 PETER iv. 8.

THERE has been much disputation about this passage; as to whose sins. The Romanist says, ours. By charity we merit and obtain forgiveness. Totally opposed to the tenure of Scripture. Faith in Christ alone can put our sins away, by looking for the Divine mercy in Christ Jesus. No, it hideth or covereth, &c., the sins of those towards whom we exercise it.

See,

**I. What is enjoined—" charity."**

Now charity means "love," not almsgiving, &c. Here it is the love of the Christian brotherhood. "Among yourselves," &c. See chap. i. 1, &c.

1. There is love *of commiseration* for all.

2. Love *of sympathy* and *heart union* for God's people. This is often enjoined as "brotherly test of Christianity." The sign of the Christian dispensation. And,

3. This *love* is to *be "fervent."* Not cold, not luke-warm, but hot, intense, thorough, genuine, unmixed.

4. It *obviously takes* in *all* God's *children.* Of course those with whom we mingle, &c., but love of the whole brotherhood. Every order, condition, young, old, weak, strong, ignorant, wise, &c., holy, frail.

This love,

5. We *are* to *keep in stock.* Have it on hand. Have it in our mouths—hearts—spirits, &c.

6. It is to be *practically exemplified.* Not in profession only, but deed. To live in actions, pitying, helping, praying, bearing, &c.

7. It is to *have* the *highest place* in *our estimation.*

"Above all things"—above creeds, names, parties—
above faith—or hope—or ordinances. It is the highest
—greatest—"best" of all the principles of true religion.
It is of God, &c.—like God—from God, &c.—never
faileth—will be immortal as the soul.

**II. The reason assigned.**

"For love covereth," &c. "Hatred and envy," the
opposite of love, expose the sins of men—aggravate the
sins of men—and denounce the sins of men,—are unfeeling and bitter, &c. "But love covereth," &c. Prov. x.
12; xvii. 9.

1. It does *not delight* in conversing on their sins.

2. If *constrained* to do so, it never *magnifies*, but *dimin-
ishes* them.

3. It seeks to *find* all *possible excuses*.

4. It would desire to *cover them over* that *others* might
*not see them.* As the sons of Noah—their Father.

5. It would *seek* the *Divine forgiveness*.

6. If personal sins, would forgive, as God does.

7. Would not *unkindly refer* to *them* again—"covered,"
as a stone by the waters of the sea.

Observe,

**III. Why these reasons should influence us.**

1. Because *God's love* has *done so with* us.

2. Because Christ has *exhibited* this in *His own* example. Towards all His disciples—Thomas, Peter.

3. Because *we need* this *from our brethren.* Our sins.
"He that has no sin," &c.

4. Because of the blessedness of this state of mind.
It is Heaven on earth, and the way to Heaven for ever.

Now let us,

1. Examine, and see if we have this fervent charity.

2. Cherish and embody it.

3. Thus we shall honour religion, and recommend it, and greatly please our Father in Heaven.


## XXVIII

## CAPERNAUM

"And thou, Capernaum, which art exalted unto Heaven, shalt be brought down to hell: for if the mighty works, which have been done in thee, had been done in Sodom, it would have remained until this day."—MATT. xi. 23.

THE treatment the Saviour received in His eventful ministry is most striking and instructive. On account of their worldly loss, the Gadarenes request Jesus to depart out of their coasts—the religious mob of Nazareth attempt to hurl Him from the brow of the hill, &c. —while the Samaritans entreat Him to abide with them, and He tarries among them several days. He dwelt very much in Capernaum, and He receives no rude treatment—no bitter scoffs—no cruel attacks on His person or name. But they did not receive His spiritual teaching, nor did they repent of their sins. So the solemn warning and fearful prediction the text contains.

Let us look,

### I. At Capernaum's exalted privileges.

Their privileges were three-fold.

1. Christ's *special presence among them.* Matt. iv. 13. When the people sought Jesus, they came to Capernaum to find Him; so that this was His usual residence. See Mark ii. 1. Called His own city. Matt. ix. 1.

2. It *was* the *chief sphere* of *His teaching.* Mark ii. 2. Many of His discourses were delivered here. They had seen Him—beheld Him daily—heard Him constantly.

3. But they had *witnessed* His *most extraordinary miracles.*

(1.) The healing of the Centurion's servant; Matt. viii. 5.

(2.) Peter's wife's mother; Matt. viii. 14.

(3.) Seen all sorts, &c.; Matt. viii. 16.

(4.) So again; Matt. ix. 1, 2.

(5.) Ruler's daughter; Matt. ix. 18.

(6.) Woman with bloody issue; Matt. ix. 25.

Surely these signs and miracles were enough, &c., to distinguish Capernaum above all other places.

Then see,

**II. Capernaum's obdurate impenitence; v. 20.**

Now this excess of light, and privileges and blessings did not lead them,

(1.) To a knowledge of their sins.

(2.) To feel their spiritual misery.

(3.) To realize their peril.

(4.) To confess and turn to God.

(5.) To accept Christ as their Divine Saviour. However civil, or kind, or respectful, or outwardly acquiesing in what Christ said or did, they did not repent, or accept Him as the Messiah.

And therefore, observe,

**III. Their final and fearful doom.**

"Brought down to hell," &c.—from the heights of Heaven, to the abyss beneath—to Hades, the region of the departed. Our Lord's solemn predicted sentence has been most awfully fulfilled in reference to Capernaum.

I. It *has* been *blotted* out of *the cities* of the world. The doom of Sodom—Babylon—Nineveh—swept away utterly.

2. The *very site* of *Capernaum* was unknown for ages.

It is even uncertain yet—mounds and ruins, &c., but the exact spot is doubtful.

3. Its *history stands* out in *contrast* to *many* other *places.* The site of Jericho, Bethany, Bethlehem, exist. So the New Jerusalem on the ruins of the Old. So even murderous Nazareth—so Cana—so Tiberias—so Magdala :—not Capernaum.

Hence the great lesson the subject suggests.

1. The different degrees of privilege that persons or places may possess. The Jews, as a nation—different places—so Capernaum—so Britain—so some of you as to residence, parents, &c.

2. Great privileges involve great responsibility—where much is given, &c. How reasonable is this—how exactly just!

3. Great privileges are not always productive of the designed effects. Special ends to be attained. "Repented not."

4. Whatever other results may be produced, God will not be satisfied. Moral restraints, outward prosperity, order, intelligence, &c., nominal religiousness.

5. The final award and penalty will be proportionate. To Heaven exalted—to hell abased. How important and solemn the enquiry, as to our mercies and their results!

## XXIX

## THE PROMISED PRESENCE

### (A NEW YEAR'S SKETCH)

"And he said, My presence shall go with thee, and I will give thee rest."—EXODUS xxxiii. 14.

WE can sympathise with the deep anxieties of Moses. See the sublime revelations of this chapter. Then

Moses' address to God; v. 12; and the Divine response in the text. Many points of resemblance between Israel and ourselves. Delivered from Egypt—on the way to the Promised Land—yet in the wilderness surrounded with difficulties and enemies, and therefore, entirely dependent on the protecting care and blessing of God. So, then, these solicitudes are natural at all times, especially on entering on a New Year.

Observe,

### I. The presence spoken of.

Not the presence of illustrious men, or of holy angels, but God Himself. "My presence," &c.

Now notice,

1. *There* is the *omnipresence of God.* "Do not I fill Heaven and earth?" &c. The Heaven of Heavens cannot contain, &c. But this is grandly expressed; Psalm cxxxix. 7, &c.

2. *There* are *the symbolical signs* of the Divine *presence.* The voice in the garden—the call of Moses out of the flaming bush—the bright cloud in the Tabernacle and the Temple—the tongues of fire—Day of Pentecost.

3. The *providential and gracious presence* of God in *our* daily life. See the case of Jacob; Gen. xxviii. 10-15. Joseph in prison; Gen. xxxix. 23. Moses; Ex. iii. 12; xxiii. 20, 21. A Divine guide.

Now observe,

4. There is the *spiritual presence* of God, with His *disciples* and all His people; Matt. xxviii. 20.

### II. The special purpose of the promised presence.

See in yourselves what, as His people, you need. Sustentation, food, water, shelter, guidance, protection, deliverance, &c., all these are distinctly met by clear and abundant promises. But the text specifies "one" —it is "rest."

Now this promise is,

1. *Conscience rest* in the Divine favour. Rest from guilt—condemnation—apprehension of peril and woe. Rest in God's pardoning and accepting grace.

2. There is *heart-rest* in the *Divine love.* Affections brought back to God, and loving Him supremely. Like John, resting on His bosom.

3. There is *trusting rest* in the *confidence* of the soul. Deliverance from alarms, dread, &c. "Fears gone." Leaning on the Lord. As Mount Zion, &c. Mind stayed on God, &c.

4. *Satisfying rest* with our *choice* and *portion.* "Satisfy us early," &c. "The Lord is my portion, saith my soul," &c. "Happy," &c. "Whom have I in Heaven?" &c. Psalm lxxiii. 25.

5. *Hopeful* and *joyous rest,* as to the eternal future. Psalm lxxiii. 26. "Thou shalt guide me," &c. "I know whom I have believed," &c. "He that hath begun," &c.

Now notice,

### III. The characteristics of this Divine promise.

1. It is *unequivocal* and *clear.* Not ambiguous—not involved—not misty—but presented in a way most easily to be understood—no mistaking it.

2. It is *certain* and *positive.* "My presence," and "I will," &c. Nothing higher—nothing stronger—nothing to hinder or frustrate. God's will is supreme, unchanging, invincible.

3. It is a *promise* to *all* His *people.* Every child, saint, believer, pilgrim, of every class, position, &c.

4. It is a *promise* for *daily use.* This first day of the year, and each and every one to the end of life. We must keep it in memory—in our hearts and in our constant belief, and connect it with our prayers and work.

In conclusion, we may,

1. Congratulate God's people.

2. Ask others to go with us.

3. No substitute for this rich and gracious promise. "If Thy presence go not with us, carry us not up hence." This involves every good.　All else insufficient.

## XXX

## THE PERPETUAL ALTAR FIRE

" The fire shall ever be burning ; it shall never go out."—LEV. vi. 13.

IT is remarkable that we have traditional records of the perpetual fire of the Persians and modern Parsees ; the eternal fire so-called of Rome ; and the inextinguishable fire of the Greeks at Delphi.　We assume that in each of these instances the idea had been adopted from the Jewish altar.　The Hebrew altar symbolised the human heart, from which was to ascend the holy flame of perpetual devotion.　In this light let us see how we can consider the text to our spiritual profit and edification. Let us look,

### I. At the symbolism of the altar.

This was both of Divine appointment and of Divine arrangement.　Nothing was left to priestly skill or expediency.　The heart, that is the moral nature of man, especially his emotional powers, must

1. Be *separated from sinful* uses, and then *consecrated* to the *Divine service*.　And this is to be in connection

2. With *sacrifices* and *blood-shedding*.　For without these no deliverance from bondage—no forgiveness nor acceptance with God—no sanctification or adaptedness

for holy service. Religion begins with the presentation of the whole man to God—a living sacrifice, and as his reasonable service. Now, it is this holy consecrated nature, this sanctified heart, which constitutes the true altar for God and His worship. Then see

## II. The symbol of the fire.

This fire was Divine, purifying, with its hallowed smoke or incense ascending to Heaven. The true spirit of devotion,

1. Is *Divine*. Of God's enkindling by His gracious spirit. It reflects the Divine nature and character, as fire was the frequent sign of His presence and symbol of His purity. So the fire is not natural, but supernatural.

2. It is *from Heaven*. Of God, like God, and from God. It descends, with every other good and perfect gift, from above. Every thing in connection with New Testament religion is heavenly. The Saviour—the Lord Jesus. The Holy Spirit sent down by the ascended Christ. The kingdom is the kingdom from heaven. The laws, the principles, the graces, the conversation of citizenship, &c.

3. It *is purifying*. Consumes dross—hay, stubble, thorns, briars, &c., makes holy—transforms all it touches into the pure. Its essential elements are love and zeal, or zealous love, burning with holy fervour within the soul.

Observe,

## III. This fire is to be inextinguishable.

"It is ever to be burning upon the altar, and never to go out." Religious conversation is to be perpetual, abiding, everlasting.

1. It is *to burn* in *all places*. Wherever the Patriarchs

went they reared their altar. So this altar is ever to be our accompaniment wherever we sojourn and dwell.

2. It is *to burn* at *all times.* Every day and every night, and at all seasons.

3. It is to *burn under all circumstances.* In prosperity or adversity—health or sickness—life or death.

4. The *devotional* fire, with hallowed loving *enflamement,* is to *burn* for *ever.* Hence the striking representations and symbols in the visions of the Apocalypse ! To secure this perpetual fire on the altar,

1. *Vigilance must guard* it. It must be watched with unsleeping and untiring attention.

2. *Prayer* must *ever* be *stirring* it. All prayer—praying always—without ceasing.

3. *Faith must* realise the *power, gifts,* and *presence* of the *Holy Spirit.* We live by the faith of the Son of God, and all holy love and consecratedness are sustained and perpetuated by it. Very many reasons why this devotional fire should not go out—as our own security, progress, comfort, and meetness for the future life— God's willingness ever to hear, and answer, and give tokens of His love and favour, and because only thus are we fitted for the Divine service and glory.

APPLICATION

The subject is of,

1. Individual importance — essential to personal piety.

2. It is of universal importance—to all believers everywhere, and under all the varied conditions of their lives and labours.

3. It is important to the Church of Christ. Personal fervid devotedness is the vitalism and power of the Church.

4. It is of importance to all phases of personal religion—inward piety—closet devotion—sanctuary worship—work in the Church—of labour and toil in the world without. A cold professor, a fireless altar, will neither glorify God, nor honour the Saviour, nor bless mankind.

## XXXI

## THE TEACHING OF THE PEOPLE

" Hearken now unto my voice, I will give thee counsel, and God shall be with thee : Be thou for the people to God-ward, that thou mayest bring the causes unto God : And thou shalt teach them ordinances and laws, and shalt shew them the way wherein they must walk, and the work that they must do."—Ex. xviii. 19, 20.

OF some very great persons very little is said in Scripture. An instance of this, in the case of Jethro, the father-in-law of Moses. His general information, his wisdom, his aptitude for government, are all signally indicated in this chapter. The meeting is most interesting; v. 5, 6—their mutual salutation, conversation, &c. He sympathises with the onerous work of Moses— gives him counsel; v. 13, &c., v. 18. Then the text. Equally important is it now for Christian ministers and pastors.

I. The beautiful exhibition of the pastor's work.

" Be thou for the people to God-ward," &c. That is be God's mouth—God's servant—mediator—really, for so Moses was, revealing God's will—bring to God their wants and interests. See xx. 18. Then we have,

II. The pastors and churches.

Encouragement—" God shall be with thee." Repeated by the Lord Jesus : " Lo, I am with you," &c This presence of God is,

1. Essential—no substitute, &c.—essential to all, and for all.

2. Is *pledged*. Promise upon promise.

3. Has *never failed*. All God's servants can testify, &c. In regard to Moses. See Deut. xxxi. 1.

4. *Belongs* to the *entire Church* of God. He is in it—its foundation—light—glory, &c.

**III. The pastor's duty to the people ; v. 20.**

Observe,

1. He is to *teach them*. Being taught of God—teach them what God reveals—teach them things about religion. Not science; but the fear and service of God.

2. *Teach* them *ordinances*. The services God had fixed—instituted offerings, sacrifices, &c.; of course God's ordinances, and His only—all of them—not to abate, or add, or change. So now Christ, &c. Ordinances.

3. *Moral precepts*. " Laws:" God-ward laws first, man-ward laws next, self-ward laws also. All the Divine precepts. Practical religion, as well as ceremonial and doctrinal—all conjointly.

4. The *exhibition* of *public religion*. "Called the way" —open. Observe the right way, old way, good way, way of life and salvation, way to Heaven.

5. *Religious work*. " The work that they must do." Now religious work

(1.) Is very diversified. Various kinds—public—home, &c.

(2.) Religious work is obligatory—must be done—no evasion permitted—no neglect excused.

(3.) Religious work must be done by all God's people. For their own sakes. It is their health, happiness, &c. For the sake of the Church. Every member of the body. Of the family. For the world's sake. The Church has a message and mission to the world, and

God's people must fulfil it. You see the word, "Must walk," "Must do."

1 Christianity has its instituted teachers, established ordinances, holy laws, public profession.

2. Christian people must be taught, shewn, and told.

3. Christian work is for all believers—to cheer us.

4. God will be· with us, and to sustain, qualify, and bless.

## XXXII
## THE IMPORTANT QUESTION

" Who is on the Lord's side ?"—Ex. xxxii. 26.

THE chapter gives a fearful account of the gross *apostacy* and folly, and misery of the *Israelites*. Even *Aaron*, &c. Senselessness of the *sin*. The wrath of God. Judgment, &c. Then the appeal of the text,

I. **What is meant by the Lord's side?**

*Jehovah*, the Lord, is the *Creator, Governor, Lawgiver,* Bountiful Provider, *Redeemer,* &c.

1. The *Lord's side* is *that of holiness.* He is the pure God, &c. "Be ye holy," &c. Iniquity he hates.

2. It is the side of *righteousness.* Equity is the rule of the Divine conduct. His claims are just. There can be no iniquity in Him. Righteousness towards men is *acting* according to justice and truth. All mankind *have claims* upon us, which cannot be ignored. It is the side,

3. Of *knowledge.* God is light. *Divine* saving knowledge. Spiritual intelligence. By religion the mind is *illumined.* Men know God and the way of eternal life. It is the side,

4. Of *truth*—reality—sincerity—guilessness.  It is the side,

5. Of *goodness*—right emotions—benevolence—beneficence—kind actions—compassion, &c.  It is the side,

6. Of *mercy*—*kindness* to the bad and evil—to enemies, &c.  Such is God's religion.  His side,

Observe,

**II. The side that is opposed to God's.**

The side or cause of sin : Moral evil, rebellion, &c.

1. This is the side of *Satan*.  The enemy—the destroyer—the daring foe of God and man.

2. It is the side of *open treason* and opposition to God. An attack on God's prerogative and authority.

3. It is the side of *darkness, ignorance,* and *superstition.*

4. Of *misery* and *woe.*  " Woe unto the wicked," &c.

5. Of *ruin* and *death.*  Destruction is the end.  Wages, death; Psalms vii. 12, ix. 17, xcvii. 2 ;  Malachi iv. 1. &c. ;  Matthew ix. 43.

Observe,

**III. These sides are directly and totally opposite.**

No *union*—no agreement—no *compromise.*  So that the two sides are *eternally hostile.*

1. The devil seeks to *seduce* and *destroy.*

2. God sent *His Son* to *destroy* the *works* of the *devil,* and to *save.*

3. All *men* belong to the one side or the other.  No neutral ground.  It is sin and pollution, or grace and holiness.  Only two kingdoms.  Of God and darkness.

**IV. How this important question is to be answered.**

If on the Lord's side we are changed, renewed, &c., we shall know this,

1. By the *examination* of our *hearts.*

2. By the *profession* we *make*. General—openly professing Christ.

3. By the *tenure* of the life—devotional and obedient.

4. By the *bearings* of our *general conduct*—seeking the things of God, glorifying God, &c.

Now let the answer be pressed on all.

1. Who are on the Lord's side? certainly, distinctly.

2. Who will be?

3. "Who will be on the Lord's side now?"

## XXXIII

## PARENTAL SOLICITUDE

"How shall we order the child, and how shall we do unto him?"
—JUDGES xiii. 12.

ON well ordered families depend the glory of the Church, and the prosperity of nations. Neglected, reprobate children are the burdens of society, and the source of Church weakness and declension. The duty of parents to their children runs through all the Books of Holy Scripture. We have examples, modes of training, results of religious education, and pious examples. We have proverbs, maxims, and precepts in abundance. We therefore hail with delight the solicitude exhibited by Manoah and his wife in reference to their child of the future, as to "*how* they should *order* him, and what they should do unto him." All the circumstances connected with this extraordinary child, Samson, are deeply interesting. The visit of the Divine angel—the dread of Manoah lest he should die, "having seen the Lord." The cheering counsel of his wife, &c.

But our text leads us to consider,

**I. The subject of their enquiry; v. 7.**

It was in relation to a child, then unborn, but who
was promised of the Lord. So far it was special and
peculiar, but in all cases a child is well worthy of our
attention and concern.

1. As one *of the human family.* Of our species. Not
a flower, or gem, or star, or some inferior creature, but
our human relative, flesh of our flesh, spirit of our
spirit, &c.

2. A human being in *childhood.* Helpless, dependent,
exposed to all the ills and perils of infantile life.

3. A *human* child *committed* to *us.* Ours, from our
loins, born of us, and for us, to bear our name, dwell
with us, &c.

4. For *whom we are largely responsible.* Extensively
for its health and comfort, its education and moral culture—a responsibility most intimate and inseverable—a
connection exists never absolutely to be dissolved.

In the light of these remarks then, notice in the text,
**II. The solicitude displayed.**

A solicitude most proper, evidently very deep and
earnest, yet not beyond the important thought and care
it demanded. It evidently comprised,

1. The *child's physical condition.* The food it should
eat, and the drink it should use. Dietetics should be
a household study—what to give children, and what to
withhold. Due care for its corporeal health, vigour, and
existence.

2. The *child's mental development* and *education.* Not
to be left to the ignorant influences that may surround
it. To let the child have light, and knowledge, and
training, to the development of all its faculties and
powers.

3. The *child's religious culture.* To be taught all the

lessons of moral truth. Its accountability—fear of God —evil of sin—way of life—the Divine claims—God's love—the person and work of the Lord Jesus, and the blessedness of a religious life, and the glory of the world to come. Now to these questions, so natural and apposite, and so important and momentous, we ask,

III. **What is the reply Scripture supplies.**

In the text,

1. The *dietical enquiry* is *met*. This takes in the conduct of the mother before the child is born. She is not to eat of anything unclean, nor that cometh of the vine, neither let her drink wine or strong drink; vs. 4, 14. So the child is to follow in the wake of the mother, and to be a Nazarite from the womb to the day of his death; v. 7. No question, improper food, and intoxicating drinks, are often the insidious precursors of disease, vice, mental weakness, and premature death.

Observe,

2. He *was* to be *devoted* to God. And this involved all due preparation for so onerous a position—and here comes in the employment of instruction, discipline, example, prayer, and continued paternal and maternal influence for the salvation of the child. And all these influences must commence early. Be continuous, and employ the constant assiduous labour to secure the great important end.

### LEARN

1. The absolute responsibility of the parental relationship. It is innate, fixed, cannot be transferred, and will have to be met at the last day.

2. The necessity of a Divine preparedness for so great a work.

3. How important to care for the neglected children of irreligious parents.

4. The necessity for the Sabbath School institution.

## XXXIV
## GOD READY TO PARDON

" But Thou art a God ready to pardon."—Neh. ix. 17.

It is right to consider God in all the aspects He has revealed himself. Creative, in law, governmental, in judgment, but especially in His mercy and grace This suits our fallen state. Well, the text is full of cheer and encouragement to fallen apostate sinners.

Notice,

I. God can pardon.

So He has proclaimed this, &c. "Forgiving iniquity, transgression," &c.; Ex. xxxiv. 6 ; Psa. ciii. 8. No hope for man without it. He can punish, but He can also forgive.

II. God only pardons in His own appointed way.

He does not pardon so as to violate His holy laws or truth. He pardons through a law magnifier. A penalty bearer. So it is by and through the Lord Jesus Christ. Remission of sin through His name, through His blood, by His intercession, &c.

III. God thus can pardon any and every sinner.

Young or old. The best and worst. " All manner of sin," &c. No exception.

IV. God is most willing to pardon.

It is His good will and pleasure. Not reluctantly, but freely—heartily.

V. God is always ready to pardon.

His unchanging heart ever delights in it. Ready in all places—at all times.

**VI. God has given abundant evidences that He is ready to pardon.**

Look at individual cases—Manasseh—the penitent woman—the dying thief—the jailer, &c. Look at bodies of men—the Ninevites, Jerusalem sinners, the defiled Ephesians, superstitious Athenians.

**VII. God pardons all and every one only through the Lord Jesus Christ.**

Christ is the one Mediator—"No other name," &c.— through His person—work—and efficacious grace—only by Him—through Him.

**VIII. God pardons all who will receive pardon.**

Faith is the gracious condition. "Believe," &c. . That is, receive as true God's declaration of mercy. Receive so as to rely on it. It is represented by the open eye —looking to Christ—open ear—open hand—open heart. That is, have it—accept it—as it is proposed.

**IX. God's pardon is followed by restoration to His favour.**

He restores as well as pardons—to His favour, family, &c. Such become His subjects—sons and daughters, &c.

**X. All impediments are removed to our pardon.**

The Divine way opened.

**XI. God is grieved when men reject his pardon.**

"Why will ye die?" &c. Jesus was grieved for the hardness of their hearts. "Tears over Jerusalem," &c., "I would," He said, "but ye would not." Now if these propositions are true, then

**XII. There is increased guilt in not accepting pardon.**

Base ingratitude, &c. Infatuated stubbornness.

**XIII. In such cases punishment is the only alternative.**

It must be one or the other.

1. And thus punishment must be *increased*—"greater" as sin resists and rejects God's love and grace.

2. Then the *condemned sinner* is *absolutely without excuse*. God willing and ready—the sinner not. Here will be the chief source of bitter remorse. We now proclaim this pardon to all, and to all in God's name, through the Lord Jesus Christ, who came that men might not perish but have eternal life.


## XXXV

## THE TEMPORAL BLESSINGS OF RELIGION

" Bless, Lord, his substance, and accept the work of his hands."—
DEUT. xxxiii. 11.

OBSERVE in connection with the text, Moses blessing the children of Israel. His final interview. The Divine Spirit guiding him. Begins with Judah, the royal Messianic tribe. Then the priestly tribe of Levi; v. 8. That the Thummin, Urim might abide. Holiness and knowledge—light and perfection. Then the text. They had no lot. All the tribes gave a tenth—no worldly greatness—a competency.

I. **God's people are the spiritual priests of the Lord.**

1 Peter ii. 5, 9. As such, no earthly abiding inheritance. Have their substance in the wilderness, day to day. Food and raiment. Yet this substance is to be recognised, &c. Observe, the apostle Paul affirms that godliness is profitable to all things, and under the Old Testament dispensation, the blessings of Divine providence are constantly promised and exhibited. The Land of Canaan, &c. So the blessings to the obedient; Deut. xxviii. 1-12. Now let us see how this is distinctly illustrated and true.

II. **God gives His people their substance in this life.**

This is a distinct sign of Divine providence. He

chooses for us—appoints our lot—fixes the bounds of our habitations, just as a wise and good father does that which is best for his children. So God, only with perfect knowledge, and wisdom, and foresight.

Now it may be,

(1.) A substance of wealth—as in the case of Abraham, David, Solomon, &c.

(2.) Or a substance of mediocrity—as Jacob, and the great mass of God's people.

(3.) Or of homeliness and poverty, as is extensively the case. The poor widow—Lazarus—chosen the poor, &c.

**III. God blesses the substance He gives.**

Some striking cases in Scripture—Joseph, David, Job, Daniel. He does this in various ways,

1. By *preserving their substance* for their *use*. Accidents, contingencies.

2. By *making* their *substance sufficient*. Bounding their desires—limiting their wishes. So Paul, "I have enough, and abound."

3. By *implanting true contentment* of *spirit*. "I have learned, in whatsoever state I am, therewith to be content," &c. The Shunamite woman did not want the luxuries of the royal palace. "I dwell," &c. So the beautiful instance of Barzillai; 2 Sam. xix. 31, &c.

4. By *adding* His *special* blessing *thereto*. The blessing of the Lord, &c., on his person, house, seed, worldly affairs, "so long as he sought the Lord," &c. "Whatsoever he doeth shall prosper;" Psalm i. 3.

Then notice,

**IV. God accepts as well as blesses.**

"And accept the work," &c.

1. *Hands* are *made to work*. Their cunning, skill, &c.,

these can open and receive, but they should first labour. Working hands are honourable—idle hands a disgrace.

2. *There* is *work* for *all hands to do*. Secular, social, religious, &c. World a field—a sea—workshop, &c.

3. We should *feel* the *obligation of work*. To do it— our own special work, in the right spirit. Motives, &c., Willingness of heart, cheerfulness, patience, perseverance.

Then observe,

4. God *will accept* the *work thus done*. This acceptance involves approbation, satisfaction, reception of the work, and, of course, the suited reward. How express is this; Heb. vi. 10, &c. "Recompense every man," &c. Work cannot be in vain, &c.

### APPLICATION

See the advantages of religion over irreligion in this life.

1. In the union of man with God.

2. In the specific advantages. Those of the same class. Personal, domestic. Father, mother, household influences, &c. Especially in poverty, affliction, bereavements, &c.

3. In Christ we have this blessing fully exemplified. He is our Brother, Friend, Sympathiser, Helper, and all in all. He, too, our example of submission to God, incessant toil, and hopeful expectancy of His Father's smile and reward. "I have finished," &c. "Glorify Thou me," &c.

## XXXVI

## DOMESTIC CLOUDS AND HOLY SUNSHINE

" Although my house be not so with God; yet He hath made with me an everlasting covenant, ordered in all things, and sure: for this is all my salvation, and all my desire, although He make it not to grow."
—2 Sam. xxiii. 5.

Last words, how solemn, affecting, instructive. Jacob's, Moses', David's, Christ's. No life more chequered than David's. Morning on the mountains of Bethlehem. Day of valour and glory. Noon of anxiety and conflicts. Evening serene and hopeful.

Observe in the text,

**I. A mournful lamentation.**

"My house"—family. "Not so with God."

1. As *God would have had it.* Discord, jealousy, strife, evil passions, rebellion. Much like a cage of unclean birds, &c.

2. Not so as *David had desired.* Intelligent, godly, united. One wife a mocker—one son a rebel—another incestuous. How sad and sorrowful!

3. Not so as the *nation might have expected.* The palace or court a glory or shame—joy or grief. Surely David's honour—his influence—his talents—piety and prayers.

4. Not as the *Church would have prayed for.* David one of the first and highest. Prophet, king, singer, type, &c. His family should have reflected all these, but it was not so, &c.

But observe,

5. It *might have been worse.* Some bright spots—one noble wise son. There was a family altar—family religious associations, &c. Such is the mournful lamentation, and how very common it is. First family—Noah's,

Abraham's, Jacob's, Aaron's, Eli's, and how much to be lamented—humbly confessed.

But observe,

## II. A bright recognition.

"Yet he hath made with me," &c. It was a recognition,

1. Of a *Divine covenant*. God had covenanted with Israel, through Abraham, Isaac, and Jacob, to be their God—to bless them—to save them, &c. Full of all sorts of blessings for both worlds.

2. His *personal interest in it*. "With me," &c.—of Israel—by faith—my portion—my interest in it—my God, &c.

3. Its *perpetuity*. "Everlasting," as it existed in the Divine heart and eternal purposes, as it would exist to the future eternity, even everlasting life.

4. Its *inviolability*. Ordered in all things and sure. Drawn out and specified. Signed and sealed. Available by the death of the Chief Testator; Heb. ix. 16. Sure, confirmed by the Divine oath; Heb. vii. 20.

5. As *including perfect salvation*. "All my salvation." Now and onward for ever. Salvation of body, soul, and spirit.

6. As *comprehending all he could desire*. Not a thought or wish left out. More than he could ask, wish, or even conceive. Beyond his loftiest thoughts, &c.

Observe,

## III. The lessons the subject presents to us.

1. The imperfection of the best things on earth. Who does not feel the force of the text? &c.

2. The temporary character of earth's institutes, dignities, wealth, homes, &c.; all terrestrial, all perishing.

3. The best things have to do with the future—Heaven, Immortality, &c.; these secured to us, by the Divine

mercy, the Divine gift, &c.,—of the sure and good covenant, &c.

4. How much better we fare than we deserve.  Our
folly and sins, the chief sources of our sorrow and tears.
The two words, "although" and "yet," how significant.


## XXXVII

## GOD THE OBJECT OF PRAYER AND PRAISE

"I will call upon the Lord, who is worthy to be praised: so shall
I be saved from mine enemies."—PSALM xviii. 3.

DAVID begins this Psalm with a holy resolve to love
God.  He enlarges on what God is to Him.  His rock,
fortress, deliverer, strength, buckler, and the horn of
salvation; and then adds, "my high tower."  He now
devotionally turns to God in the language of the text.

Observe,

I. His prayerful resolution.

"I will call upon the Lord," that is, I will pray to
God, tell my need, and supplicate His good and gracious
help.  "I will call, &c."

1. For Divine *guidance*, that I may not err.  "Lead
me," &c.  "Thou shalt guide me," &c.

2. For Divine *aid* in my *daily necessities*.

3. For Divine *strength* for *holy service*.

4. For Divine *protection* from *personal enemies*.

5. For the Divine *blessing* on all I *am* and *have*.  To
rest upon Him, in his person, family and kingdom, to be
his inseparable joy and safety.

6. For the *acceptance* of his *person* and *work* of the
Lord—as Abel, &c.  Only thus can our religious life be
really blessed.  Accepted of the Father, in the Beloved,
by the Holy Spirit.

Notice the declaration,

## II. Of God's worthiness to be praised.

Worthy, &c.   Hence,

1. All *God's works praise* Him; Psalm cxlviii., cxlix., cl.

2. All *God's people praise* Him.   This has been the heartfelt offering of all ages and dispensations.   We cannot separate a happy godly life from the service of praise.   So in the Tabernacle and Temple and Christian assemblies.

3. All *holy intelligences will praise* Him for ever.   See the veil drawn aside, and hearken to the services of holy angels and redeemed saints, before and around the throne; Rev. iv. 9-11; v. 9-14; xv. 3.

## III. The confident assurance as to the future.

"So shall I be saved from mine enemies."

1. God's *people have their enemies*.   Within, without, the whole empire of sin is against them—the world, the flesh, and the devil.   Their enemies are material and spiritual, subtle and malignant, persistent and terrible, numerous, and ever at hand to distress and to destroy.

2. God *alone can save from these enemies*.   His wisdom and skill, His almightiness, His ubiquity.   He is the ever present shield and buckler, and is ever at hand as the fortress and strong tower.   He is the faithful loving Saviour of His people.

3. *Prayer* is the appointed *medium of safety*.   "I will call."   "So shall I be saved."   God has said, "Call, and I will deliver thee," &c.   Prayer does not inform God of our peril, for He knows it.   Nor does it move Him to sympathize with us, for He does this always.   Nor does it move Him to come to our help, for He is ever near and never afar off; but it brings us to His presence—places us beneath His wings, and lays hold of His helping and delivering arm.   The Psalmist speaks without any doubt

or misgiving. "So shall I be saved." For He can save—has saved—will save—does always save, those who call on His name.

APPLICATION

In our subject, we have,

1. The union of prayer and praise. They must ever be linked together. See Philip. iv. 6; 1 Thes. v. 16, 18. Prayer obtains material for praise. Praise extols the victories prayer has achieved.

2. The subject also prescribes to us both enemies and our deliverance. All God's people, in all ages, have had their enemies; but equally so deliverance from them.

3. The subject inspires with an assurance of salvation —"So shall I be saved." For it is the Lord's will. He has made provision. He is saving now, and will complete His work in salvation and glory everlasting.

# XXXVIII

## REMARKABLE CONVERSIONS

### RAHAB

"By faith the harlot Rahab perished not with them that believed not, when she had received the spies with peace."—HEBREWS xi. 31.

THE history of this woman is found in two chapters of Old Testament history: but if we had only looked at that record, we might not have placed her among the Bible converts. But when we find her held up by Paul as one of the illustrious heroines of faith, and by James as one whose faith was living and true, followed by good fruits, then we see that the Holy Spirit has designed that she should stand among the seed of God's chosen, and as an extraordinary convert of Old Testament times. Observe,

**I. Her character and condition before her conversion.**

1. She was a *pagan.* Jericho was devoted to gross idolatry, and its manners were little better than the cities of the plain. Think of a residence in the midst of such blackness and evil!

2. She was as the word *signifies,* a "taverner." Kept a house on the wall, for the entertainment of travellers, and for the reception of the revellers of the city. Her occupation unfavourable to morality. Just as such a business is now. Our occupation has much to do with our personal moral state.

3. It was *intimated* that she was a *harlot.* Much dispute about this. But the idea is not improbable. Our Lord did not exclude such from His mercy. Now no person humanly speaking, could be further from the kingdom of God.

But notice,

**II. The means of her conversion.**

She had

1. Heard of the *wonders* of the *God of Israel.* Joshua ii. 8-11.

2. She was *favoured* with the *mission* of the *servants* of God. "The spies." No record of this; but, no doubt, they had to reveal all the particulars to her of the Divine purposes and providences.

3. They *presented* to her a *striking sign* of the Divine *covenant;* v. 18. "The scarlet line." She accepted this—acted upon it—and was delivered, &c.

Notice,

**III. The evidences of her conversion.**

1. She *preserved* and *delivered* the spies—" text." Thus

she allied her interests with theirs. Here was an entire severance of herself from idolatry.

2. She did this at the *hazard* of *all she possessed.* Her house and home were in Jericho. They would all perish in the destruction. Her own life, if detected, would be destroyed by the vengeful authorities of the city. She absolutely risked all, and forsook all for God and His cause.

Observe,

**IV. The glorious results of her conversion.**

1. *Adoption* into God's *covenanted* family. One of the true seed, &c. of Israel. Wild olive grafted into the true vine. Once alien, outcast, rebel, idolator—now of Israel, and the true faith.

2. She *obtained* the *Divine mercy* and *favour.* Her sins all forgiven—now a reconciled daughter of the Lord— having peace and joy in her new life and profession.

3. She was *favoured* with *all* the *blessings* and *privileges* of *Israel.* Sacrifices—priests—spiritual covenant —promises, &c.

4. She *had* a *lot* in the *goodly land.* Her house and home came back manifold.

5. She *became* one of the *Messianic mothers* of Israel. Of her lineage Christ came; Joshua vi. 25; Matt. i. 5.

6. She *died* in the *true faith*; Heb. xi. 34.

7. She *stands ennobled* in the gallery of godly *women* to all *generations.* Paul's portrait; James ii. 25. Now observe the infirmities this converted Rahab evidenced; Joshua ii. 2, &c. Here were the remains of cunning, deceit, falsehood, and so far positive sins. No vindication can be given—no apology presented in the Bible— no justification but what would dishonour God.

But remember,

(1.) This was in the crisis of her conversion.

(2.) These were fruits of her old religion, and not the new.

(3.) See the contrast, as soon as the covenant was ratified, how she felt for her father and relatives, &c.

(4.) How could perfect holiness be expected. If Abraham through fear, and Isaac also, were guilty of a similar sin, it would be cruel to cast stones at this extraordinary Pagan woman. But how dishonourable to religion to vindicate and defend it. Now

1. The lessons are many. We see God's infinite mercy—His sufficient grace.

2. The worst are not excluded.

3. Jesus gives hope to all. Let us read Luke vii. 36, &c.


## XXXIX
## MANASSEH

" Now the rest of the acts of Manasseh, and his prayer unto his God, and the words of the seers that spake to him in the name of the Lord God of Israel, behold, they are written in the book of the Kings of Israel."—2 CHRON. xxxiii. 18.

WEALTH, rank, and power, have their very special and imminent perils. No doubt the extremes of condition are unfavourable to religion. Extreme riches or extreme poverty. Hence, that wise and beautiful prayer—"Give me neither poverty," &c.

Observe, in reference to the subject of the text,

I. **The advantages Manasseh possessed.**

1. He was the *son* of the *good* king *Hezekiah*.

As such, interested in the Divine goodness and providence. Favoured with a pious example. Instructed in religion, in early life. The subject of special prayers and promises.

2. He was *witness* to the Divine *dealings* with his father's *house*—kingdom.

Hezekiah had exposed himself to God's displeasure: chap. xxxii. 25; 2 Kings xx. 12. Now, here was need of the Divine discipline. But, observe,

3. He had known of the *healing* and *restoring mercy* of God. 2 Kings xx. 1. But, observe,

**II. The perils to which Manasseh was exposed.**

1. He was *early* deprived of his father's *presence* and *counsel.* A sad irreparable loss.

2. He *ascended* the *throne* at a time of youthful *inexperience.* Only twelve years, &c. What a situation for a youth! Luxuries and pomp, &c. No condition of greater peril. Then observe,

**III. The extreme wickedness he exhibited.**

1. He *abandoned* the *service* and *worship* of God.

2. He *restored* gross and God-*defying* idolatry; v. 3.

3. He wantonly *polluted* the *Temple* of the Lord; v. 4, 5.

4. He *impiously* set up a *defiant* idol *against* Jehovah; v. 7.

5. He *offered* his *children* in idolatrous *sacrifice;* v. 6.

6. He *leagued* himself *with* wizards and soothsayers; v. 6.

7. He was *guilty* of *cruelty* and *bloodshed.* 2 Kings xxi. 16. It is said he murdered the aged and seraphic prophet, Isaiah, by having him sawn asunder. Now, here is a portrait of moral blackness, probably without a parallel.

8. He *rejected* the merciful *interposition* of Heaven; v. 10. Observe,

**IV. The circumstances connected with his conversion.**

Now observe,

1. God *arrested* him and *sent* him into *exile;* v. 11.

2. He placed him in a *condition* of *great suffering;* v. 11.

3. He graciously *sanctified* his *affliction;* v. 12.

4. He *elicited* a spirit of *penitence, repentance,* and *prayer;* v. 12.

5. And thus he was *savingly brought* to the *knowledge* of God; v. 13.

6. The *evidences* of his *conversion* are *strikingly* given; v. 14-16.

7. He *enjoyed* the *benefits* of his *conversion;* v. 13.

Restoration to his kingdom—usefulness of life—honourable death; v. 20. "Slept with his fathers," &c.

1. How extreme may be the aboundings of human wickedness.

2. How greater still the mercy of God.

3. Reasons for hope with regard to all.

4. No ground for presumption. See his son; v. 21, &c.

# XL

## WOMAN OF SAMARIA

"There cometh a woman of Samaria to draw water. Jesus saith unto her, give me to drink."—JOHN iv. 7.

A WOMAN of Samaria! No narrative can be more instructive or interesting than this. This is unquestionably one of the most extraordinary conversions of Scripture. Observe how the narrative will bring this out, by giving us a series of pictures, striking and suggestive.

Notice,

**I. The wearied traveller; v. 6.**

Wearied, not of His labour, but in it. Christ was an

itinerant preacher—went about, &c.—walked—no account of riding, except when He entered Jerusalem.

**II. The noon-tide rest; v. 6.**

Sixth hour—twelve, noon.  Heat excessive.  Christ and His disciples came to the famous well of Jacob; Gen. xxxiii. 19.  The well was about fifteen minutes walk from the city—is still called Bir-Jacob.  Here Jesus rested—here the disciples were to bring the food for the noon repast.  Observe, while Christ rests, the approach

**III. Of the woman of Samaria; v. 7.**

Of her it is clear that,

1. She was a *person* of *low habits;* v. 18.

2. Yet she was *not ignorant* of *religious truth;* v. 19, 20 and 25.

3. She was evidently *trusting* in the *rites* of her *national religion.*  No consciousness of her sin—no sense of her misery.  Inwardly dark, hard, and wretched.

Observe,

**IV. The extraordinary and blessed meeting.**

Jesus resting—the woman coming.  How providential—how gracious—how blessed!

Now notice,

**V. The conversation of Christ and the woman.**

(1.) Jesu's request for water, v. 7.

(2.) The woman's bigotted expostulation; v. 9.  Not refusal, but evasion.

(3.) Christ's spiritual appeal; v. 10.

(4.) The woman's inward darkness; v. 11, &c.

(5.) Christ's explanatory answer; v. 13, &c.

(6.) The woman's unmoved ignorance; v. 15.  Only thought of material water.

(7.) Christ's searching solicitation; v. 16.

(8.) The development of her religious condition—

Ritualistic. Yet a glimmering of faith and hope; v. 25. Then we come,

**VI. To the grand crisis in her experience.**

1. The *revelation* of Christ to her.
2. Her *obvious faith*; v. 28.
3. Her *public avowal.*
4. Her *great success;* v. 30.

### APPLICATION

1. Learn the misery of human nature until restored by Divine grace.

2. See how this grace was displayed by Jesus.

3. The wondrous trophy of Christ's love and mercy.

4. The influence of the heart on the voice and life. She the first Christian preacher to the people of the city.

5. Invite all to come, &c. Christ is here waiting, &c.

## XLI

## THE WOMAN SINNER

" And, behold, a woman who was a sinner," &c.—LUKE vii. 36-50.

OUR subject will illustrate most fully how true the declaration that Jesus Christ came into the world, not to call the righteous, but to save sinners, even the chief.

Observe,

**I. The person presented to our notice; v. 37.**

It is obvious that this woman was one of the lowest— debased condition—one of the unhappy fallen of her class. Here then, we see

(1.) Hers was a moral state of great pollution.

(2.) A state where all the associations would be degrading and wretched.

(3.) Where she would be abandoned by religious and moral people, and then

(4.) Left to sink lower and lower without sympathy or help.

But,

**II. The circumstances under which she is brought before our notice.**

(1.) A Pharisee entertains Christ; v. 36.

(2.) This woman hears of Christ being there. "When she knew;" v. 37. No doubt had seen Christ and heard Him, and felt the power of His compassion.

(3.) She ventures into Christ's presence. What an ordeal!—To go into the Pharisee's house—here moral courage was needed.

(4.) She took with her a token of liberal affection; v. 37.—Perfumes essential to hot climates—some very costly—in this case very likely the best and most precious she had.

(5.) She humbly goes behind the Saviour. At meals they recline on couches, the feet would be at the back of the couch. No boldness—no irreverence—but deep humiliation.

(6.) Her eyes stream with penitential tears. Not a few—not constrained—her head like a fountain, they gush forth—run down—fall on Christ's feet.

(7.) She abases herself by the attentions she pays to Christ. She takes her hair, &c. The glory of woman —the pride and adorning, and of this she makes a towel, &c. She kissed His feet, and then anointed them with the precious fragrant perfume. What a picture! sufficient to have attracted angels to the scene.

Now,

**III. Let us look into the inner man of the host—"Pharisee."**

He was astounded—felt himself compromised, &c., and now doubts Christ's character and purity; v. 39. His reasoning was in harmony with his views and profession. Well, he is passing judgment on both, but "secretly," in his heart.

Observe now,

**IV. The case Christ presents for his consideration; v. 40.**

Now Christ so puts it that he is fairly shut up to one verdict; v. 41-43.   And now

**V. Christ vindicates both the woman and Himself.**

Jesus now "turns to the woman"—pointed to her—and contrasts her with the Pharisee, for he had omitted several of the usual courtesies of hospitality. "No water"—her tears. No kiss of salutation—she kissed His feet. No cooling ointment for the head—she, the precious ointment for the feet. In one word, his deficiencies how striking, when contrasted with this woman's persistence and love.

Jesus now

(1.) Pronounces her pardon. Full, free, entire; v. 47.

(2.) He extols her love.  "Loved much;" v. 47.

(3.) Proclaims her faith; v. 50.

(4.) Gives His benediction, "Go in peace."

Observe, we learn

1. The worst is welcome with Christ.

2. True repentance will be most manifest.

3. The Saviour's person and mission must be believed.

4. Faith works by love.

5. Love will make any sacrifice.

6. Jesus will honour and reward such faith and love.

## XLII

## ZACCHEUS

"And Jesus entered and passed through Jericho," &c.—LUKE xix. 1-9.

ZACCHEUS was altogether a different person to some of the notoriously wicked converted by the grace of God. Not a profligate—not blood-thirsty—not an outcast— but a Jewish worldling, the most difficult of all to convert. A sordid money getter, given up to the realization of riches, &c.

Now let us notice,

I. Zaccheus, and what is said about him.

1. His *profession*—"Publican." Farmed out a district for taxation, one in direct contact with the civil authorities at Rome. He would have other persons to do the details of his profession. He was a chief. Now this was an odious calling among the Jews. Our occupation much to do with our moral character and religious condition.

2. He *was rich.* Such often made fortunes—he probably had done so—much of it might be the gain of ungodliness.

3. In his *person* he *was of small stature.* Some of the greatest men in the world have been so—Dr. Watts, Wesley, many others. It is the head and mind, not size, length of legs, or corpulence, that makes the man.

Observe,

II. The favourable providence recorded.

" Jesus passed through Jericho." The place of his residence. Now this was the great tide of mercy in his life —the golden opportunity—the special season of hope. Most persons have such.

### III. The strong desire he felt.

"He sought to see Jesus." Had no doubt often heard of Christ—now He is passing through he is anxious—it might be mere curiosity, but he acts wisely and promptly.

But notice,

### IV. The difficulties in his way.

A great crowd, and he was low of stature; there seemed to be no chance. Well, he had probably tried to see Christ in vain, so now his wits come to the timely help. But are there not always difficulties in the way of coming to Christ?

### V. The course he adopted.

1. He *ran* in *advance* of the *crowd;* v. 4. Repenting sinners must always do this—be in advance of others.

2. He *climbed* up a *tree* by the *way.* But this would seem to be rather strange for a respectable man—an official—and one of wealth. But he had an object in view, and he resolved to attain it. And now observe him in the tree, waiting—looking—hoping.

### VI. We now hear the marvellous address of Jesus; v. 5.

1. The *look* of Christ. One of interest, compassion and grace.

2. The *personal address* of Christ. Called him by name, so that Jesus knew all about him and within him.

3. The *kind command* of Christ. "Make haste and come down." He had made haste to climb up—now he must descend, and quickly. "The king's business," &c.

4. The *friendly self-invitation* of Jesus; v. 5. "To-day I must abide," &c. Christ invites himself—how affectionate, condescending and gracious.

### VII. See how Zaccheus acts; v. 6.

1. He immediately *came down.* No delay, &c.

2. He came down *joyfully*—gladness of heart.

3. He *heartily welcomed* Christ. "Received Him" with open heart and arms.

Now notice,

**VIII. The murmuring crowd; v. 7.**

Astonished—confounded, &c. Always, &c. Sinners by the Pharisees.

**IX. The open confession of Zaccheus.**

1. His *implied guilt;* v. 8.

2. His *ready restitution.*

And now

**X. The Saviour's loving and saving declaration; v. 9.**

"Salvation." Christ was salvation—God's salvation. But this salvation He imparted—how clear—how open —how He refers to his race. "A son of Abraham"—one of the lost sheep of the house, &c.

#### APPLICATION

1. Jesus is with us in His Gospel.

2. We need His saving grace.

3. We must seek to see and hear Him by faith.

4. Now is the very season.

5. He will say to you, if you invite Him, &c., "salvation has come," &c.

## XLIII
## THE PENITENT THIEF

"And he said unto Jesus, Lord, remember me when thou comest into thy kingdom. And Jesus said unto him, Verily I say unto thee, To-day shalt thou be with me in paradise."—LUKE xxiii. 42-3.

OF all extraordinary conversions this is the most astounding. No doubt designed as an exhibition of the infinite mercy of God—the boundless grace of Christ—and the illimitable influence of His merit and power.

Observe,

### I. The character of the man.

Matthew and Mark call him a thief. No doubt he was one of a banditti, like the brigands of Italy. He lived by robbery and violence. Very likely guilty of blood-shedding. He was a lawless, desperate transgressor—an outlaw, and, therefore, doomed to ignominious death. Darkness, hardness, recklessness, and ruin, might be written over his cross.

Observe,

### II. His extraordinary conduct.

He is now hanging on the tree. A companion on one side, and Jesus in the midst. His companion joined the railing mob; v. 39. And now the penitent malefactor shews,

1. His *right appreciation* of Christ.

He confesses his own guilt; v. 41. He is religiously impressed; v. 40. He avers his belief in Christ's innocency; v. 41.

2. He *offers* an *extraordinary* prayer; v. 42.

Now see what this prayer recognized—

(1.) Christ's Messiahship—" Lord." Yet Jesus was treated as a seditious blasphemer. Dying by public execution.

(2.) Christ's kingdom. Obviously of the future world. In eternity, &c.

(3.) He recognizes Christ's authority as having power to grant favours,—What! the dying one on the cross having such power ? &c.

(4.) He recognizes the mercy and grace of Christ, that He would even look upon a wretch like himself.

Now, observe,

III. The striking character of this extraordinary prayer.

We have seen what it took in, &c. But look at the attributes of this prayer.

1. How *direct*. No tedious prefatory remarks. Not long, elaborate, but a few words—like an arrow, &c.

2. How *brief*. A sentence only. How often we meet with these! The publican—the Syrophenecian woman —Peter, &c. Long prayers are never commended— look at the model prayer, &c.

3. How *expressive*. "Remember me!" The three ideas : Christ—his soul—a future gracious recognition.

4. How *humble*. Specifies not one particular—leaves all to Christ—His own word—names nothing, and takes in everything.

5. How *strongly believing*. A malefactor to address a king, and to refer to his kingdom. A dying man, believing and hoping as to the future. Death, darkness, and horror, and yet his eye of faith pierces through the whole. He sees the light—a kingdom. He sees Christ on a throne, and all by faith, and he hopes and asks for it.

6. How *efficient*. Christ hears, attends, feels. His bleeding heart throbs, &c. Look, then,

IV. At Christ's remarkable reply—" Verily " &c.

The answer of Jesus,

1. Was *immediate*. No delay—no hesitation—at once. Paul prayed thrice, &c.

2. It was *infinitely gracious*. To be with Christ. The trophy of grace. No upbraiding. To be with Him in paradise,—the place of the blessed departed spirits, where Christ went till His resurrection. Not Heaven. How rich the grace! How effectual to pardon—sanctify —make meet!

3. It was *explicitly assuring*. "Verily"—truly—cer-

tainly. I say, &c. The truth, &c. No doubt—no delay—no cool words; but, "verily," &c.

Observe,

1. The worst in this life are not in a hopeless condition.

2. Christ can save the chief of sinners. None need despair.

3. The conversion of the dying thief is not to be looked upon as a precedent, but rather unique and peculiar. No other ever was or ever will be in that extraordinary condition.

4. Death-bed repentance is not to be trusted to.

## XLIV

## JERUSALEM SINNERS

" Now when they heard this, they were pricked in their heart, and said unto Peter, and to the rest of the apostles, Men and brethren, What shall we do?" &c.—ACTS ii. 37-42.

IN this text we come to showers of blessings and multitudes of converts. The day of Pentecost had come, the fiftieth day—the day Christ had intimated again and again; especially Acts i. 4, &c. Now the grand jubilee of the Gospel had arrived—now the Holy Spirit had been given, and the door of the kingdom of Heaven was to be opened to the Jews in Jerusalem.

Observe in connection with our subject,

I. The immense congregation; v. 6.

"A multitude," of various countries. Not only residents, but those who had come to the Jewish services from the lands all about; see v. 9, 10. They were chiefly religionists—"devout men," believers in God, in Moses, and in the prophets.

Notice,

## II. The distinguished preacher—"Peter;" v. 14.

As Christ had said, "I give thee the keys," &c. He was to be the one great Apostle of the kingdom— "rock," &c., or instrumental basis. He had been restored after his foul fall—He had been reinstated—"Feed my sheep," &c. Peter had with him his brethren, as his coadjutors, and other disciples as his fellow witnesses.

## III. The sermon he delivered.

(1.) His exordium—vindicating himself and brethren; v. 15.

(2.) Fixing the Pentecostal event on the word of prophesy; v. 17-21.

(3.) Exhibiting Jesus as the true Christ; v. 22.

(4.) Referring to the gracious decree of Heaven concerning Him; v. 23.

(5.) Charging them with the atrocious murder of God's anointed; v. 23.

(6.) Attesting that Christ had risen from the dead; v. 24, 32.

(7.) Assuring them that Jesus was the only Messiah; v. 36. Such was the discourse of Peter. Now see in reference to this sermon,

## IV. Its extraordinary influence.

(1.) Their consciences were convicted. The arrows of the King went right into the hearts of His enemies.

(2.) They became anxious to obtain salvation. Their sins, especially the blood-guiltiness of slaying Jesus, filled them with extreme terror.

(3.) They now seek counsel how they shall escape from their sins; v. 37.

And, observe,

**V. The saving directions given to these anxious enquirers.**

(1.) A change of heart is essential. "Repent," &c.

(2.) Profession of Christ is demanded. "Be baptized." Own Christ—profess Christ—put on Christ.

(3.) And this is to be personal and universal. "Every one of you," each and all—the best and worst—the whole.

(4.) The great promise of the Spirit is proclaimed; v. 38. "Ye shall receive the gift of the Holy Ghost," &c. Observe,

**VI. The evidences of their conversion.**

1. They *believed* the Gospel preached.

2. They did this *gladly*, and at once.

3. They did it *openly* and were baptized.

4. *Three thousand* did it, and thus the first Christian Church was formed. How extraordinary!—how the arm of the Lord was made bare; see Psalm cx. Think of the persons—the number—and in Jerusalem. Here is hope for all—a Christ for the greatest of sinners.


# XLV

## SAUL OF TARSUS

"And as he journeyed, he came near to Damascus; and suddenly there shined round about him a light from heaven," &c.—ACTS ix. 3-6.

GOD can work by what instruments He pleases. He generally pours contempt on the great and imposing things of this world. He selected fishermen chiefly to be His Apostles, &c.; but He had an extraordinary agent in reserve. He was one of the bitterest foes of Jesus that ever lived, and on him the eye of mercy rested, with the purpose of making him the brightest star in the Christian firmament, and the most noble trophy of Divine grace, that should preach His gospel to mankind. Saul of Tarsus is the subject of the text.

Let us,

**I. Look at him in his unconverted life.**

Observe what he was not. Not ignorant—nor profane—nor irreligious. He had,

(1.) A most religious ancestry. Philip. iii. 5.

(2.) He had been highly educated. Acts xxii. 3.

(3.) He belonged to the most strict sect of the Jews. Acts xxii. 3.

(4.) He had been employed officially to oppose Christianity.

(5.) He was most bitter in his attacks on the disciples of Christ. Acts vii. 58.

(6.) He was even guilty of the blood of the saints. Acts viii. 1, &c.; xxii. 4; see xxvi. 9-11. Here is the portrait of Saul before his conversion. Look,

**II. At the circumstances of his conversion.**

(1.) His engagement as the official persecutor. The avowed, open enemy of Christ.

(2.) His intensely vehement spirit; v. 1. His life—his being—his very breath—his spirit and office one.

(3.) His journey—near to Damascus; v. 3. One of the oldest cities of the world—beautiful plain.

(4.) The supernatural light; v. 3: "about noon." The light was overwhelming—"sudden." He felt, &c.

(5.) Then the Divine appeal; v. 4. "Saul," &c. How pointed the question! The declaration, "It is hard," &c. The ox kicking against the goad.

(6.) Saul's recognition of the appeal. He knew it was supernatural—he knew it was Divine—yet he knew not whose special voice spoke; v. 5. "Who art thou?" &c. Now,

(7.) Jesu's proclamation of Himself—"I am Jesus," &c. Here is revelation and proclamation.

(8.) Saul's intense spiritual agony; v. 6. " Trembling and astonished." Alarmed and conscience smitten.

(9.) Then his heart felt anxiety ; and question, "Lord, what wilt thou ? " &c.; v. 6. Observe,

(10.) His soul is not immediately delivered ; v. 6. Blind—helpless—dependant; v. 8.

(11.) Three days' darkness and fasting ; v. 9.

(12.) The messenger of comfort sent him; v. 10. Notice,

**III. The results of his conversion.**

(1.) Bodily light; v. 18.

(2.) The gift of the Spirit; v. 17.

(3.) Open profession of Christ ; v. 18.

(4.) Inauguration in the great evangelistic work; v. 15.

(5.) His immediate proclamation of the Lord Jesus; v. 20. He was about thirty years' old when converted. Lived and laboured about thirty years more. Beheaded at Rome.

How free the salvation, and rich the grace! 1 Tim. i 12-16. How efficacious ! Paul a pattern sample.


# XLVI

## THE PHILIPPIAN JAILER


"And they said, Believe on the Lord Jesus Christ, and thou shalt be saved, and thy house. And they spake unto him the word of the Lord, and to all that were in his house."—ACTS xvi. 31, 32.

PHILIPPI, the scene of this remarkable conversion, ought

to be especially interesting to us, for it was in this city that the very first Christian Church was set up in Europe. Then the apostolic visit was paid under very remarkable circumstances; v. 9. The vision—and now Paul and Silas promptly obey. The results are described—the demonized girl—the persecution—the imprisonment of the Apostles.

Observe,

I. A prison scene.

Apostles in the stocks—scourged, &c.; v. 23—singing; v. 25.

II. Now there is a terrific earthquake; v. 26.

Its effects threw back the gates and opened the doors. Then,

III. The alarm of the jailer.

See his sense of honour; v. 27. His intended self-destruction—suicide—fearfully common among Pagans, especially when pride of office, &c., prevailed.

But observe,

IV. His still greater astonishment and anxiety.

(1.) The appeal of Paul; v. 28.

(2.) The safety of the prisoners.

And now,

V. His spiritual concern for his soul's salvation; v. 29.

Here observe,

(1.) His intense alarm—"trembling."

(2.) His prostration—"fell down."

(3.) His momentous question—"What must I do?" &c. Various subjects had rushed on his mind—now his soul was everything. How weighty and solemn this question about salvation—about his salvation—what he was to do to secure it?

VI. The direct answer given.

"Believe," &c. Here is an answer,

(1.) Which belonged to the Gospel specially.

(2.) To all places.

(3.) To all persons. Christ is the Saviour—faith receives Him—and thus salvation is secured. How clear, short, positive ! Then the answer was followed,

**VII. By Scripture teaching; v. 32.**

No doubt there would be narratives, expositions, prophecies, explications, &c. For this teaching the whole household were convened—children, servants, &c.

**VIII. The evidences of the jailer's conversion.**

(1.) He rejoiced in the good tidings of salvation.

(2.) He believed in Christ Jesus with his heart.

(3.) He exhibited the change of heart by his mercy—kindness, &c.; v. 33.

(4.) He professed his Christianity by Baptism.

(5.) And his home all shared in the blessings of salvation.

Now learn,

1. The efficacy of the grace of God.

2. The one way of salvation.

3. The fruits of conversion exhibited. The same message we proclaim to every perishing sinner.

## XLVII

## THE FIRST LIE

"And the serpent said unto the woman, Ye shall not surely die."—
GENESIS iii. 4.

SIN entered our world by falsehood. Satan, through the medium of the serpent, turned away from truth and holiness the first woman of our race—Eve, the mother of all living. To this the apostle refers ; 1 Tim. ii. 13,14.

As sin was thus introduced, so it has been very mainly sustained and propagated by lies, so says the apostle John, and gives evidences of its truth. Lies may be conceived in the mind and heart, and laid up there—or they may be uttered with the lips—or they may be acted in the life. That which presents the unreal as true—that which deceives by what is said, or unsaid, is a lie.

Now let us look,

**I. At the author of this first lie.**

Satan—the devil—the deceiver, are the titles given him in Scripture, and Jesus says of him, "He is a liar, and the father of lies;" John viii. 44. No doubt this was scenic or dramatic, with the tree in sight, as the conversation was held. Here is the earthly fountain of falsehood, and the author of the first lie.

**II. The nature of the lie uttered.**

"Ye shall not surely die." Observe, it was the direct falsification of God's threatening, in absolute contradiction of God's own word; Gen. ii. 17.

**III. It was a most daring and presumptuous lie.**

The height of desperate effrontry. A challenge of the Almighty. Bold collision with the God and Creator of the universe.

**IV. It was a most malignant and envious lie.**

There can be no doubt that Satan saw and envied and then hated the first human pair in their innocency and blessedness; and now, serpent like, he fascinates, and throws his horrid spell with fatal accuracy, over the ready listeners, and then inserts the poisonous and venomous iniquity and ruin into the soul.

**V. It was a destructive murderous lie.**

So Jesus connects the first lie with the murder it effected. It slew our first parents—destroyed their innocency—blinded their minds—defiled their consciences—and overspread the soul with leprous defilement and guilt, and as God had said, death not only arrested our first parents, and bound them with chains and fetters as guilty and condemned before Him.

**VI. It was the germ of all unrealness and deception that should curse mankind.**

Now crookedness, illusion and deceit began their career. The false, in all its forms and shades, is traceable to this first lie. All ignorance—all error—all superstition—all base fear—all inward treason of heart, took their rise here. It poisoned the moral blood, degenerated the race, and introduced every hideous deformity and foul impurity into the human family and species.

**VII. It was a lying entanglement from which humanity could not extricate itself.**

Man could rush into darkness, but could not find his way back to light and day—he could fall, but not restore himself—he could die, by choosing to do so, but he could not resuscitate or raise himself again to life. The Divine image was effaced—the Divine Spirit exorcised the soul, in its original glory destroyed.

**VIII. Jesus, the Divine Truth, came to deliver us from this lie and its results.**

He was immediately promised as the woman's conquering seed—He came, and was manifested to destroy the works of the devil—He overcame him in the wilderness—cast him and his demons out of the bodies and souls of men—He overthrew him on the cross—entered his domains of death, and opened a royal passage through the tomb, and opened the gates of the second paradise to all believers.

Hence, observe,

**IX. The Gospel is the delivering power from Satan's falsehoods.**

Christ is the Author and Prince of truth—His word is truth—He makes this word His own power to salvation. This is the remedy for Satan's falsehood and malignity. By the Spirit and word of truth He regenerates, sanctifies, and makes meet for eternal glory. By this His saved people defy Satan, and overcome his machinations and lies. The Kingdom of Christ is the kingdom of truth—this truth of Christ is to destroy the kingdom of Satan, and renew the world in true holiness, and bring down the Tabernacle of God from Heaven to earth.

APPLICATION

1. Truth and falsehood are the characteristics of the two kingdoms of God and Satan.

2. All men are the subjects of one or the other of these kingdoms.

3. Falsehood invariably destroys, murders mankind, as it did our first parents.

4. Truth lifts up, exalts, purifies, saves with all the power of an endless life.

XLVIII

## THE GOODLY HERITAGE OF THE RIGHTEOUS

"The lines are fallen unto me in pleasant places; yea, I have a goodly heritage."—PSALM xvi. 6.

THE land of Canaan was divided by lot, and thus apportioned to the various tribes of Israel. Of course it would follow that there would be great diversity in the heritages possessed. Some would be more pleasant and fertile than others. We may suppose those with the choicest portion would gratefully adopt the [sentiments of the text. David, too, the writer of the psalm, might with the highest sense of thankfulness, know it was true of God's goodness to him. Raising him from the sheepfold to a palace—from a shepherd's condition to be king of Israel. But how true the text is of all God's people, in its spiritual application. Brought from a state of alienation and misery and bondage, to have a place and portion in God's Church, and with His people. Eph. ii. 12. Observe how the text may apply,

**I. As to the temporal condition of many of God's people.**

Godliness blesses men in every state of life. It exalts the poor. Prospers the toiler. Helps up those born for adversity. And as a rule religious persons have a better portion even of earthly things than those that live in rebellion against God. How often we see,

1. The *godly exalted* in *life*. We need only refer to Moses, Joseph, and David, as most striking instances.

2. The *possessions* of the *godly* are often greatly *increased*. Here we have evidences in the wealth and prosperity of Abraham. The contrast in Jacob's condition,—going out a solitary wanderer and returning with great abundance. So Jacob's history forcibly illustrates this.

3. True *happiness* is *connected* with the *heritages* of the *pious*. God makes his people happy in poverty, in bitter adversity, &c. But when His favour is added to their earthly good—when His smile lightens up the dwelling —and when there are the abiding tokens of His love— how every gift is doubled, and every earthly good is surrounded with joy and sunshine.

But see,

**II. The spiritual realization of the text.**

1. The *pleasure* of a *goodly heritage* of the Divine *word*.

How the Psalmist exulted in this! let the 119th Psalm testify. How truly blessed are they who have the word of God! Contrast these with Pagans and their lying Shasters. With Mahommedans and their fanciful and frivolous Koran. With the dupes of the Papacy, to whom the Divine word, in their own tongue, is denied. And let us contrast our condition with that of our forefathers three centuries ago, when only the rich could possess the Word of God.

2. The *pleasure* of a *goodly heritage* of Divine *ordinances*. The weekly ordinance of the Lord's Day—the frequent ordinances of Christian assemblies—the sacred ordinance of the Lord's Supper—the often presented ordinances for prayer and praise and holy fellowship. God's house being the centre and rendevous of most of these. Psalm xxvii. 4; lxxxiv. 1—12.

3. A *goodly heritage* of Divine *blessings*. God's blessing is upon the righteous. And it is with them and around them and within them. The blessing of holy light and peace and joy and hope. The blessing of forgiving mercies—adopting love—and sanctifying grace. The blessings of a benign providence — heavenly care — and heirship to life eternal. "All are yours," &c. 1 Cor. iii. 21—4.

4. The *goodly heritage* of *prospective glory*. Grace in possession—glory in reserve, and also in prospect. Looking towards it and for it. Hoping, expecting, and seeing its glory dimly outlined and foreshadowed. Having the earnest—first-fruits—pledge, and foretaste of bliss immortal. 2 Cor. i. 21—24.


APPLICATION

1. Such a heritage and such pleasant places should ensure holy joyfulness and praise.

2. Should excite to an entire consecration to the Divine service.

3. Should produce an earnest striving for meetness for the future glory.

4. Should induce us to invite all around us to be partakers of our blessings and joy.


## XLIX
## THE ATTENTION OF CHRIST'S HEARERS

" For the people were very attentive to hear Him.—LUKE xix. 48.

ALL sorts of persons listened to Christ's teaching. Self-righteous Pharisees, sceptical Sadducees, and critical Scribes. Some of the great and rich, and many of the low and the poor. On the occasion to which the text refers, the state of the congregation is most beautifully described. The religionists, the enemies of Christ, were perplexed, not knowing how to deal with the preacher; v. 47. "For all the people," &c.

Notice,

I. The general congregation.

1. No doubt comprising *persons* of all *ranks*, but chiefly the *common people*.

2. Persons of varied *mental distinctions*. The cultivated and taught, but chiefly the unlettered.

3. Persons of every *moral* grade, but most probably chiefly *publicans* and *sinners*.

4. No doubt the congregation was *large*.

5. Evidently under considerable *excitement*. Of joy; v. 37. Of anxiety; v. 42, &c.

Notice,

II. What is said concerning this congregation.

1. They had evidently *come* to *hear* Christ.

2. To what Jesus said, they *paid marked attention.*

3. This *marked attention* was evidenced by *them all.* "For all the people," &c.

4. And this attention was *distinctly observable.* "They were *very*" &c.  Exceedingly, unusually, markedly.

We ask,

### III. The probable reasons for this general attention.

1. Surely it was to be *found* in the *preacher*—the Lord Jesus Christ.  Their Messiah, Saviour, the great preacher, to whom all their prophets had given witness

2. Was it not to be traced to His *solemn theme?*  A prophetic sermon respecting the destruction of their city, and ruin of their nation.

3. Was it not the result of His *intense pathos* and *overflowing sympathy?*  His heart—His bowels—His tears of mercy all intensely telling, in His words and eyes and voice.

#### APPLICATION

1. Here we have the true model for the Christian preacher.

> "'Tis not a cause of small import,
>    The pastor's care demands;
> But what might fill an angel's heart,
>    And filled a Saviour's hands."

2. Here we have a model congregation.

Attentive to the preacher—all so, and all very attentive.  What a reproof to the dull, sleepy, formal, listless hearers, often present in Christian assemblies!  "If any man hath ears," &c.

3. The adaptation of subjects to times and seasons· Aptness in teaching involves subtle themes, adapted topics to times and places.  How Jesus excelled, and is our pattern in this way.  His were not general, loose addresses, but subjects meeting express emergencies,

and adapted to the places and times of His ministry. How much so on this occasion.

4. The importance of fidelity in preaching. Read the whole chapter. See this expressly, v. 11 to 27, and v. 44 to 46.


## L

### SYMPATHY WITH THE POOR

" Was not my soul grieved for the poor ? "—Job xxx. 25.

THE piety of Job was broad and full, not only ascending to God in worship and holy service, but to man in kindliness and beneficence. He could appeal to God as to this trait in his character, and does so in the text. " Was not my soul," &c.

Observe,

I. The objects of his sympathy.

" The poor."—Those not fully supplied with the necessaries of life. No man is poor who has food and raiment, however plain. But where there is occasional want and always a condition below sufficiency, such are poor. There are,

1. Different *degrees* of *poverty*. Some absolute—others occasional. Some born and reared in it. Some fall into it by misfortunes and calamities. Losses, sickness, bereavements, &c.

2. Different *occasions* of *poverty*. As where it is the result of causes over which they have no control, and as the result of extravagance, idleness, vice, and crime.

3. Different *moral states* of the *poor*. God has His poor. Often many of His children are so. Scripture gives us many instances. But wickedness and poverty are often allied. Sin is often most expensive and ruin-

ous.  The Prodigal wasted all, &c., then began to be in
want.  Some vices speedily swallow up an estate.

Observe,

**II. The nature of his sympathy.**

It was not mere feeling, but grief—soul grief, as the
text expresses it.  Such sympathy,

1. Is Divinely *wrought in us*.  It is the development
of the emotions, which belong to our nature.  God has
made us capable of this, and elicits it, draws it forth, &c.
God maketh the heart soft.

2. Is *most pleasing* to God.  He views it with delight.
It is resemblance of Himself.  Obedience to His command.  Exhibition of His spirit.  "Pure religion," &c.

3. Is *most profitable* to *us*.  Such outgoings of goodness are evidences of moral excellency.  Will tend to
our fruitfulness.  Is an imitation of our Divine Saviour.
A fruit of the Holy Spirit, and is connected with many
great and precious promises.  Psalm xli. 1; cxii. 9.
Prov. iii. 9; xix. 17.  Isa. lviii. 6; vi. 11.  Acts xx. 35.


APPLICATION

Let the text be: A test of character.—An incentive
to goodness.—As supplying an appeal in adversity, as
in the text.


# LI

## JOSHUA'S DYING APPEAL

"And, behold, this day I am going the way of all the earth: and
ye know in all your hearts, and in all your souls, that not one thing
hath failed of all the good things which the Lord your God spake concerning you," &c.—JOSHUA xxiii. 14.

THE speaker, Joshua, was an extraordinary man; full

of faith and holiness; earnest, devout, decided, per-
severing, magnanimous—the successor of Moses—a
type of Jesus—same name—led Israel into Canaan.
His work is now drawing to a close—he delivers his
farewell dying appeal, and it is worthy of universal
remembrance.

Observe,

**I. What he recognizes as concerning himself.**

It is the closing of his earthly career. So David; 2
Kings ii. 2.

Now here is,

1. The *universal fact.* "Way of all the earth"—that
is, the way to the grave—way of mortality.

(1.) Nature teaches this—everything dies. Flowers,
grasses, trees, even the cedars. Observation teaches
this. All around are advancing towards the tomb; we
see the signs, evidences, mile-stones.

(2.) History teaches it. Read the Bible; Genesis v.
1; the Prophets, &c. Moses, David, Solomon, Daniel,
the Apostles, &c.

(3.) Our family reminiscences teach it. Son, where
is thy mother? Daughter, thy father? Parents, where
your children? Friends, &c.

(4.) Our Church books teach it. Our statistics have
a column marked for mortality. Every Church, &c. So
it applies to all classes, ages, and nations, &c.

2. Joshua's *recognition* of the *fact* as *relating* to himself.
Behold, this day "I go." No doubt he had reasons in
his body, and the mental consciousness, and the moral
sense. Many won't personally recognize it—not allow
death to be mentioned—won't think, &c. Queen Eliza-
beth. This personal recognition is wise—it may be
profitable—admonitory to others. Joshua did not re-

pine—he was not sad—as a man and saint he expresses
it with magnanimity.

**II. The appeal he makes to Israel.**

He speaks,

1. Of the *good things* God *had spoken.* Not the heart,
purposes, or thoughts of God, but uttered—spoken in
prophesy or promises. How rich, and varied, and numberless!

2. He *refers* to the *fulfilment* of the *good things spoken.*
Promises fulfilled — cheques honoured — engagements
realized. The fidelity and truth of God.

3. Of the *fulfilment* of *every one* of *them.* Not one
failed, large or small, of any kind or time.

4. He *speaks* of *their knowledge* of all this. "Ye know
in all your hearts and souls." Really—obviously—
manifestly—experimentally. They had seen—heard—
tasted—and handled. Not some of them, but every one
—"all."

Notice,

**III. The great design of this appeal.**

1. To *awaken gratitude.*

2. To *excite* to *continued obedience.*

3. To *induce holy fear;* v. 15, 16.

4. To *establish loving confidence* in their hearts; v. 11.
Now, how directly this appeal should come home to our
hearts to-day—this season—(last Lord's Day of the
year.)

1. A *greater* than Joshua of old appeals—"Jesus."

2. He can refer to a more *momentous death*—that of
Calvary—death for us.

3. He can speak of *richer blessings.*

4. Demands a *higher service.* Ye are not your own,
"therefore glorify God," &c. "I beseech you, brethren, by
the mercies of God," &c.

## LII

## THE GOOD MAN'S RECOGNISED INHERITANCE

" Thou hast granted me life and favour, and Thy visitation hath preserved my spirit."—Job x. 12.

AND this grant to Job, and acknowledged by him, was not peculiar to the patriarch, but is the inheritance of all God's people.

### I. Life is God's grant.

Natural life.—In its origin, preservation, and continuance. In all its enjoyments and privileges. In Him and from Him we live, &c.

Intellectual life.—Mind-life, of thought and reason and mental power, and activity and soundness.

Spiritual life.--The new life of the inner man. That which is quickened by the Spirit and Word of God. All the capacities and powers of life are of God.

### II. He grants us also favour—or grace.

Deals with us in mercy, and not according to our desert. Life itself is a favour, and so all its privileges and enjoyments. But God's favour continues life— sanctifies life—makes it a blessing—prepares us for the life to come. God's favour sweetens its joys—consoles its sorrows, and delivers from its troubles.

### III. God's visitation preserves the spirit.

Observe this visitation,

1. Is by God's *gracious* Spirit—in us, with us, for us.

2. It is this visitation that *preserves* us from apostacy and ruin. Keeps us in safety. Delivers from dangers, &c.

3. This visitation is our *essential security*. We cannot preserve ourselves—nor can our fellow-men keep us. God's Spirit alone can do this.

4. The preservation must be *acknowledged.*—As in the text. Gratefully—joyously—hopefully—humbly.

5. We are to be *co-operators* with God's Spirit in our preservation. Hence the admonitions—cautions—exhortations. "Building up yourselves," &c. "Keep yourselves," &c. Jude, v. 20, 21. By vigilance—diligence—prayer—faith—self-denial, &c.

The subject,

1. Should produce holy fear. Preservation always supposes peril, &c.

2. Holy watchfulness. "Watch," &c.

3. Prayer and thanksgiving.


## LIII

## GENEROUS DEVOTEDNESS TO GOD AND HIS HOUSE

"Now therefore, our God, we thank thee, and praise thy glorious name," &c.—1 CHRON. xxix. 13—15.

THE text relates to David and his great zeal and liberality for the intended House of the Lord. God did not permit him to build it, but he was allowed to make great preparation for it, and both he and his people did so. Our text utters the holy and sublime views he entertained, and the resolves on which his soul was set. He is now in the congregation of the Lord; v. 10, and after his ascriptions to Jehovah, v. 11, 12, comes our text.

Notice then,

I. **The service he presents ; v. 13.**

Observe in regard to this service,

1. To *whom* it is *presented*.—" God "—only Being, &c. "Our God." Revealed to us. Believed, loved, devoted. Ours by covenant—realized by faith. Observe,

2. The *service itself*. "Thanks." Acknowledgment

of blessings—all blessings from Him. " O give thanks !" &c. " In every thing," &c. " Bless the Lord !" &c. Praise. Celebration of His glories. Titles, works, ways. His name especially. Good, great, merciful. " He passed by," &c.

Notice,

**II. The gifts he offered.**

See v. 2, 3, 7, 8. Now, notice, the various particulars expressed.

1. These *gifts* were for the *House* of the *Lord*. Other objects good—this pre-eminently. God's glory. Man's best interests. Soul, &c. Numbers interested. Generations connected with it. Gate of Heaven, &c. No object so excellent—so dear to God. " He loveth the gates of Zion," &c.

2. His *gifts* were *rich* and *generous*. Not the pareings —not the fragments—not small tithes, but large and munificent.

3. The *spirit* in which these *gifts* were *devoted*.

(1.) With profound self-abasement; v. 14. " Who am I?" &c. He falls into the dust, &c., He and His people, &c. One ray of self-glory spoils all. "A fly in the ointment," &c.

(2.) With great voluntariness. Not extorted—not given by constraint — " willingly," desiring God to accept, &c. The gifts of the heart—flowing. This is the greatest element, &c., in beneficence.

(3.) His acknowledgment of God as the Source of the ability; v. 14. "All things come of Thee." The means—all means—of every kind, disposition—to will and to do, &c.—"all of God." Talents, worship, gifts and everything—every mite, &c.

Notice,

III. The solemn considerations by which he had been influenced.

See v. 15. "For we are strangers," &c.

1. *Man's pilgrimage condition.* "Strangers and sojourners," &c. Why then be absorbed in the world? Why captivated with this day's scenes? We are ever moving on—no rest for the sole of the foot—no continuing abode—we brought nothing into this world, &c.

2. That *all we can do* for God and religion must be *done now.* So our predecessors, they had their generations' work, but as shadows they have passed away —all the great and good men, even Noah, Abraham, Moses, David, &c. So the prophets, and so the apostles, so all the good. "Their day"—their work, &c.—"none abiding." How important to remember the fathers, &c. How solemn!—we should be earnest and self-consecrated, &c. Now every word and idea in the text is applicable to us.

(1.) The God of David is ours.

(2.) The House of God is dear to us.

(3.) Liberal support is necessary now as ever.

(4.) The spirit of liberality should be as great, yea, greater. Our obligations greater—blessings richer.

(5.) The motives as solemn. And now let this day have your best praises, thoughts, gifts, &c.; and so make this day a great and glorious realization.

## LIV
### SAMSON'S RIDDLE IMPROVED

"And he said unto them, Out of the eater came forth meat, and out of the strong came forth sweetness. And they could not in three days expound the riddle."—JUDGES xiv. 14.

SAMSON was a most extraordinary character. The

Hercules of the ancient world—his parents eminently godly—an angel announced his birth—he was to be an abstainer from wine and strong drink. See also the counsel to his mother; v. 4, 5. He was raised up to judge Israel, which he did for twenty years. His course began by his receiving the Spirit of the Lord for the work; chap. xiii. 25. No Old Testament saint more frail than he—his achievements were by his personal prowess, extraordinary physical strength. One instance recorded; chap. xiv. 5-8. Now there was the week's wedding feast, and the oriental custom of tales and riddles. Samson told one—none could solve it; see v. 8, 9, &c. Now let us see what important moral truths may be got out of this riddle, and

**I. At the sin-destroying lion and eater.**

First parents holy, happy. The tempter came—sin entered—man fell. Now this in itself was an unmixed evil; but does not God, by His rich grace, give us meat and sweetness out of it? We have,

1. *Brighter revelations* of God. Before great, holy wise, and good—now gracious, merciful, &c. We see the superabounding grace—no such manifestation could be given before. Here the whole Deity is known "Out of this eater," &c.

2. Came *higher blessings* to man. Innocency was blessed—holiness more.

(1.) He becomes closer and higher related to God. From a creature to a son—heir. Humanity exalted by and through Christ.

(2.) His security greater. He stood in his natural goodness—now in the sufficiency of God's grace.

(3.) He has greater joys as a saved sinner. Joy of deliverance—health—pardon.

(4.) He has sweeter songs to sing. Of infinite love

—sovereign mercy—Christ's precious person—and grace
of the Lamb slain.  Now eternal song.

(5.) He has a higher destiny.  Not earthly—not Eden;
but Heaven—glory—eternal life.  Read of the two
paradises, Genesis and Revelation.  So that in regard
to man and his ruin, by the grace of God came meat
and sweetness.

Observe,

**II. How the riddle is illustrated in the providential disci-
pline of life.**

Afflictions and troubles come and assail us—terrify
us—put us in peril.  Losses—bodily sufferings—mental
—family, &c.  But see how these, instead of killing and
devouring, absolutely are for our benefit.  In themselves
they are medicines, and not poisons—corrections, not
destructions; see Rom. v. 3; Heb. xii. 9.

(1.) When sanctified they lead us to God.  Flee to
Him, &c.

(2.) Wean us from the world.

(3.) Strengthen all the Christian graces.  Make us
valiant, heroes, victors—more than conquerors.

We see it,

**III. In reference to the roaring lion—death.**

His name appalling—king of terrors—and last enemy,
&c.  But through the grace of Christ death is now,

(1.) Placed among our blessings.  Death is yours—to
die is gain.

(2.) It opens a happy door out of this world of sorrow
and sin.  "Lord, now lettest Thou, Thy servant," &c.
"I have a desire to depart," &c.

(3.) It brings us to our Father's house and home.

(4.) It ends all sorrows and calamities.

(5.) It introduces us to life eternal.  "Blessed are
the dead," &c.  So that death, the roaring lion, yields
immediate honey and eternal sweetness.

We learn,

1. The supremacy of God. He can do all this. His wisdom, power, and grace.

2. All this honey and sweetness came by the Lord Jesus Christ.

3. Heartily adoring and grateful praise is our obvious duty and privilege.

4. The Gospel offers its blessings to all.

## LV

## EVERY MAN BY HIS OWN STANDARD

"And the children of Israel shall pitch their tents, every man by his own camp, and every man by his own standard, throughout their hosts."—Numbers i. 52.

THE various tribes of Israel had to be placed in order, and the whole to be put under a strict regulation. This was needful for encampment—for march—for worship—for battle; without this, confusion, &c. The number and special circumstances of the various tribes are given. Some large, some smaller; v. 17, 18. Of the children of Ephraim, 40,000—Asher, 41,000—Dan, 62,000—the whole, 603,000; v. 46. Then comes the matter of order, &c., in the text—particulars given in next chapter. Israel in many things typical of the Christian Church. We see it in this also,

**I. The One Israel.**

Observe,

1. Their *real oneness* of *descent*. The children of Abraham.

2. Their *original condition*. All bonds-men.

3. Their *Divine deliverance*. Brought out of Egypt, &c.

4. In *one Divine covenant*—promises, &c.

5. Journeying to the *one inheritance*.

6. Under *one command*. See how this all applies to the Church of the Saviour. All the children of God by faith—all heirs—all pilgrims—all of one covenant—one Saviour, &c.—essentially one—one in Christ Jesus.

**II. The various tribes.**

Observe,

1. Their *different names*. Necessary for distinction—recognition.

2. Their *different positions* in the camp; see next chapter. East side; v. 3—South side; v. 10—West; v. 18 —North; v. 25.

3. The various tribes were in *one general accord* and *union*. All one religious confederacy—absolutely one —worship one, &c.—in perils one—in warfare one—in prospects one.

**III. The special directions to the different tribes.**

1. Each tribe had their *own standard* or *banner* to distinguish it from the rest—no order without.

2. Each man was to be *by his own standard*. Not a wanderer—not a visitor to all—but his own fixed legitimate position.

3. Thus the *duties* of every tribe would be *regarded* and *fulfilled*.

4. Thus the *interests* of all would be *sustained*. Now, if this was important and necessary in the camp of Israel, how much more in the Church of the Lord Jesus. The thousands there—millions here.

But let us see,

**IV. The spiritual lessons the subject presents to us.**

1. We see now the *denominational tribes* in the Kingdom of Christ. Christians of different conditions—education—training—leaders, &c.

2. Christians have a *special interest* in *their own camp.*

3. To *devote themselves* to these, &c., is the first *duty* and *privilege*. Just as families are constituted—so Churches, &c.

4. All the *various denominational camps* constitute the *one Church* of the Saviour. Only one Israel—one body —one army, &c. For particular purposes, every man by his own camp—for general purposes, all acting in conjunction and harmony. How absurd jealousies and envyings—how ridiculous isolation—how oppressive— assumptions are priestly dictations—how suicidal strifes and contentions—how monstrous exclusions and anathemas. The great Tabernacle of God is built four square, and includes all the tribes. Christian denominations have special standards, and we serve the whole best, by every man being by his own standard. The glory of God is identified with the unity of the whole. "Christ's prayer to him," &c.


## LVI

### MANLINESS

"Let us play the men," &c.—2 SAM. x. 12.

SEE the context. Difficulties—perils, &c. So manliness was essential. In a better cause than of battles between nations is equally important. "Quit you like men" says Paul. Children are not destined for hardship and the fight. Woman must stay at home and mind the stuff; but the young and strong must exhibit manliness of spirit, and be good soldiers of Jesus Christ.

**I. God's people must have the intelligence of men.**
Knowledge and wisdom and prudence and skill.
**II. The vigour of men.**

Not feebleness and weakness.

**III. The decision of men.**

Not irresolution and vacillation.    A man of two minds, &c.

**IV. The enterprise of men.**

Projecting and devising, and aiming at great things.

**V. The persistency of men.**

Without wavering, or halting, or turning aside, going back.

**VI. The heroism of men.**

Valour, unflinching courage.

**VII. The trust and faith of men.**

Like Samson, Gideon, Barak, David, &c.

Observe,

1. We can do little without this manliness.

2. Cause great.

3. Enemies mighty.

4. Results momentous.   Then ourselves, and the cities of our God.


## LVII

## GOD'S FOREKNOWLEDGE OF THE SINNERS REJECTION OF HIS WORD

"Therefore thou shalt speak all these words unto them; but they will not hearken to thee: thou shalt also call unto them; but they will not answer thee."—JEREMIAH vii. 27.

AN infinitely perfect God must know all things—because He is the Creator of all, and the Governor of all.   Ignorance, therefore, is incompatible with His originating and governmental power.   This must be true, not only of material things, but of the minds, thoughts, and actions of all His intellectual and moral creatures; so that all who can think and act, and do so most freely, are known to Him, and His government is adapted to all such creatures. Now the prophet Jeremiah is to tell Judah God's will, and make known His word, and yet it is added "they will not hearken." We understand their condition as described v. 23, 24, and also Ezekiel ii. 7; but there is a peculiarity in telling them, and yet knowing they will not hearken or answer.

Now we will,

**I. Seek for instances illustrative of the text.**

Where God knew His word would not be regarded, nor His messages answered.

We go back,

1. To the *original transgression* of our first parents. God's words were clear, easy, distinct—no mist, &c.— yet God knew how Adam and Eve would act—He saw their hearts—noticed all their emotions—and beheld sin developed and committed.

2. Take the *old world*. He saw the rise of evil—its progress—its wide-spread guilt and pollution. Yet Noah preached 120 years—built ark—spirit strove, &c.

3. Take *Pharaoh*. Moses and Aaron are sent—miracles wrought—God's message proclaimed, and His demand urged and enforced. But God knew that Pharaoh would harden his heart, and sin, in the midst of various repentant relapses, to his destruction.

4. Take the *Jews* as a nation. How prophets and holy men went to them—the Baptist—God's own Son —and yet God knew their unbelief, wickedness, cruelty, &c. Christ referred to this as to His own ministry, &c. He declared their obstinacy and ruin. So the text is only one of innumerable cases given in the Word of God.

Well now, observe,

**II. How this can be explained and defended.**

Unless God did know results such as we have described,

1. He would be *imperfect*. Not the all-wise, infallible God, and He could not govern the world.

But this perfect knowledge of the future,

2. Does not make Him the *cause* of the rebellion that He foretells. He does not predestinate it, but foreknows it—just as He foreknew Noah's sin, and yet did not make him drunk—and Lot's incest, but did not fill his veins with unnatural fires—He foreknew the murder of Abel, but did not impel Cain to the deed—He foresaw the shipwreck of the Atlantic, but did not steer it on to the rocks—so of all evil that ever existed. The astronomer, by calculation, foreknows every visible and invisible eclipse of the year, but does not produce them.

3. He *never influences* men to do *wrong* because He foresees it; see Acts ii. 23. Now this is a case fully to the point. God designed His Son to be the Saviour, and hence the sacrifice for sin He purposed, and He foresaw the conduct of the Jews, but they freely and wickedly crucified Him.

4. There are *many ends* to be *attained* by God. God speaking, &c., though He knows men will not hearken, &c.

Notice,

(1.) God exhibits His true desire for their salvation. He truly, earnestly calls, &c.

(2.) He thus treats men as reasonable and responsible beings.

(3.) He thus leaves them without excuse. I called—I sought—I commanded—sent My servants, &c.—My spirit.

Observe, in conclusion,

1. Man's free agency is his glory, not only before the fall, but after. God's address to Cain; Gen. iv. 6, 7. "If thou," &c. God does not interfere with it.

2. God's infinite goodness is undoubted. His love to all—His mercy.

3. Our duty is most manifest. To hear—believe—obey, &c.

4. Thus men will be finally inexcusable, having had means employed for their restoration to holiness and God.

## LVIII

### THE CONSTANT PSALM

" I will bless the Lord at all times."—Psalm xxxiv. 1.

David was pre-eminently the saint of holy song. It comported with his sanctified musical soul. In harmony with his joyous, grateful spirit. He evidences this in every conceivable form, and he exhausts human language in his fervid utterances of praise.

Notice,

**I. What the Psalmist engages to do.**

"To bless the Lord." To praise Jehovah, the God of Israel. This includes,

1. Having exalted views of God.

2. Feeling the most grateful emotions.

3. Expressing these emotions of praise in the loftiest strains he could suggest.

Notice,

**II. The extensiveness of this resolution.**

"At all times." In times of trials and comforts—health and sickness—sorrows and joys—life and death

—time and eternity. So in private, and in his royal household. When at home, or in exile. Especially in the public services of God's house.

### III. The grounds on which he would do so.

1. God at all times worthy. "The blessed God."
2. God at all times good and gracious.
3. This service at all times pleasant and comely.
4. At all times profitable.
5. As it will connect all time with the everlasting future. The service of earth and heaven.

## LIX

## ABUNDANT PEACE

" Peace be multiplied unto you."—DANIEL vi. 25.

WE may take a lesson from a royal proclamation. Darius was a noble king, sincerely attached to Daniel, but was under the tyranny of an imperial law and usage. Compelled to consign Daniel to death, yet he did it with reluctance. God interposes—Daniel delivered. And now he issues a royal proclamation, and our text is one part of it, "Peace be multiplied." It is just a motto for the New Year.

### I. What is the peace?

The peace we recognize is much more than that of Darius.

1. It is God's *peace*. Towards you in Christ—for you in the Gospel—in you by the Holy Spirit.

2. It is *your peace*. Peace of conscience—harmony of all powers, &c.—Peace in every faculty—Divine, full, constant, increasing, perpetual.

3. It is *peace* with *mankind*.

(1.) With God's people—all—of every name; Rom. xii. 18.

(2.) With all men.

(3.) Even with your enemies; v. 20. Peace includes all good—God's blessing.

## II. Its multiplication—"be multiplied."

1. In your own *experience* of it. Deeper, fuller, daily, &c.

2. In your *homes*. Dwellings of peace.

3. In your *religious circles*. Meetings, labours, &c. Church associations.

4. In your *neighbourhoods*.

5. In your *nation*. All classes—orders.

6. In the *world*. All lands. Wars cease—brotherly love binds all in one girdle of amity and goodwill; Luke ii. 14.

Now notice,

## III. Its desirability.

No personal happiness without the Divine peace—no Church prosperity without the spirit of peace—no national progress without it—it is good for all—the labourer and the employer—the rich and the poor—the ruler and the subject. The world's blessedness depends on it.

Now this multiplied peace is,

1. One of the *distinct features* of the Gospel dispensation; Psalm lxxii. Prince of peace, &c.

2. Of the *prophecies* and *promises*; Micah iv. 1, &c. Messiah shall make wars to cease to the ends of the world; Psalm lxxii.

3. This *peace* of the spirit we must *cultivate*. "As much as lieth in you," &c. "Follow peace" with all men.

4. *Prayer* should ever be *presented* for it. The Father,

is the God of peace—Jesus, Prince of peace—Holy Spirit, Spirit of peace. So prayer must be in harmony with God and His Divine purposes.

In conclusion, let us enquire,

1. Have we this peace?—are we the sons and daughters of peace?

2. Not content with past or present realizations—it is to be multiplied—flow as a river.

3. It must be cherished and exhibited. Say to one another, to-day and every day, "peace be multiplied." Observe, there is no peace in rebellion—no peace in perdition. There is peace in religion—in Christian life—in death, &c. All peace, with godly joy, and eternal praise in Heaven above, where all the saints enter into peace.

## LX

## THE SAINT'S HOPE

" Hope thou in God."—Psalm xlii. 5.

HOPE ever essential. More so in seasons of darkness and depression and weakness. See context.

**I. What is urged in the text—"Hope."**

That is, expect all needful future good of every kind, and for religious work and enjoyment. No limit to the region of hope.

**II. The object of hope is presented—"In God."**

Not in self, or men, or angels, but in God. In the Father, the "God of hope." In Christ, the Son, who is our hope. In the blessed Spirit, the inspirer and sustainer of hope.

Notice,

**III. The various phases of Hope.**

Similitudes are employed. The anchor of the soul, in storms and perils. The light of the soul in darkness. The elasticity of the soul midst renewed trials, &c.

**IV. The many reasons for this Hope.**

1. God's ability and all-sufficiency.
2. His willingness to do all we need.
3. God's changeless love.
4. God's sworn covenant.
5. God's provided sacrifice.
6. God's precious promises.
7. The Holy Spirit's work in us—for us. This Hope in God is an imperative, glorious privilege, and an unspeakable duty and joy.

# LXI

## GOD, AND HIS WONDERFUL DOINGS

" He is the living God, and stedfast for ever, and his kingdom that which shall not be destroyed, and his dominion shall be even unto the end. He delivereth and rescueth, and he worketh signs and wonders in heaven and in earth."—DANIEL vi. 26, 27.

THESE are the sublime words of Darius, on the preservation of Daniel, in the den of the lions. Words as true as they are sublime, and words representing the most momentous principles of intelligent religion. Let us examine them, ponder them, and see what fruit they will yield, both for our mental and moral nature.

Now it is evident,

**I. That here we have a personal God.**

He does not refer to chance, or accident, or mere laws. He does not refer to nature, or to natural causes and results. According to these, Daniel would have speedily been devoured by the hungry lions. But he speaks of a Divine Being—a glorious person—one possessing wisdom, power, and dominion. In other words —a supreme ruler—a personal God.

But, observe, with this view of a personal deity, is also given a representation,

**II. Of His certain present existence.**

" The living God." Not a superannuated deity—not a grand effigy—not a wondrous idol or image, but a personal God, having " life." Without life theɩe would be no available attributes of knowledge, or presence, or influence, or power. A living God is,

1. *The God of nature.*

A being without conscious life could produce nothing. Not a clod of earth—not an atom of matter. But there is life in nature. Living plants—vegetable life—living animals—organic life ; and to these existences of life, a living God is indispensable : so also not only to give life, but to preserve and to sustain it.

2. *A living* God is *our* God.

We are endowed with the breath of lives. We have a living materialism. A mind having mental life. A soul having moral life, and these must have a living sire—a living source of being—and this is what is truly said, " In Him we live and move, and have our being."

3. *A living* God *only*, can be the *object* of *worship, confidence,* and *hope.*

Our knowledge and faith and reverence, must have respect to a living God. So praise and prayer and trust. So hope of continued life and future glory, must look up to a living God.

4. *A living* God is *essential* to the idea of *immortality.*

Only a living God can be "stedfast," or abide, as in the text. Only a living God can perpetuate His kingdom, and keep it from destruction. What could the

most heroic of the ancients do, after their death ?
Nimrod—the mighty Nebuchadnezzar—the magnificent
Solomon—the wise and illustrious! So our God is the
being having in Himself unoriginated life, and who has
absolute changeless being and immortality.

Then see in the text,

### III. The operations of this living God.

Notice,

1. His *providential interpositions.*

"He delivereth and rescueth." Now the incident
of Daniel being preserved in midst of roaring, hungry
lions, was a striking illustration ; and here fraud and
collusion were impossible : see chap. vi. 16-18. So all
history teems with instances of God's delivering and
rescuing providences. As in the case of David—Jonah
—the three Hebrews, &c. There is reference,

2. To the Divine *wonders* and *signs.* "Worketh signs
and wonders." Now these words convey the idea
of miracles and their evidences. Such as the miracle of
Daniel safe in the lions' den. It was not a natural
result of natural laws, but a supernatural interposition,
staying the natural appetites, and fury of hungry and
ravenous lions. Now, miracle is not so much a suspension of natural law as the over-ruling by supernatural
intervention. Bringing in a direct law immediately,
diverting or over-ruling the lower natural laws. As in
the burning bush, the flame would have naturally con-
sumed—the supernatural power preserved it though in
the midst of the flame. Now, supposing material for
the creation of a world had existed for unnumbered
ages, and those material forces had been acting and re-
acting on the existing atoms,—yet is it not evident that
when a new state of things is to be produced, order,
beauty, harmony, and life ?—then the supernatural

must give the mandate, and raise to higher laws than those in operation before. So creation is obviously a stupendous miracle, and hence the solicitude of Atheists and Pantheists to drivel and dream about, the unbeginning eternal part of the universe.

All Bible revelation is built on what is implied in miracle; and the very existence of the Lord Jesus Christ, as the Son of God, rests on this basis. So says Peter in his pentecostal sermon: "Jesus of Nazareth, a man approved of God, among you by miracles and wonders and signs, which God did by Him in the midst of you," &c. Acts ii. 22, &c. Now we see the wondrous work of Christ, in stilling the tempest on the Galilean lake, and the evident sign or evidence in its immediate tranquil condition. So in expelling the legion of demons, and the sign in the composure of the man's spirit as he sat at Christ's feet. In the production from a few fishes and loaves food for thousands; and in the sign given by the multitude, that they were perfectly satisfied and filled.

3. To the *moral transformation* and evidences given in the renewal of man's *nature* and *spirit*.

Observe the numberless instances around us of men and women who had been slaves of vice, bound in fetters of corruption and misery. Left to the courses of nature they would have waxed worse and worse, and never would have been changed either in heart or life. But, Jesus, by His holy word and by the spirit of His grace, brought them under higher and holier influences, and now, they are new creatures, "washed, sanctified, justified," and the sign is immediately manifest in a life of purity and goodness.

Now this is the moral standing miracle of our Christianity, and is as extraordinary as any physical miracle that was ever wrought.

### LEARN

1. How glorious the Divine Being in whom we believe and trust. " The living God," &c.

2. How our faith and confidence are fully justified. "He delivereth and rescueth and worketh signs," &c.

3. How stable should be our trust, and reliant our hope, in so glorious a Being.

4. What room for all the services of worship, and exercises of devotion.

## LXII

### THE RELIGIOUS RACE

" So run, that ye may obtain. "—1 COR. ix. 24.

ALL men by nature are in the wide way of death and destruction. By Divine grace men are translated and renewed, and brought into the way of peace and life. To such, and such only, is the text addressed. " So run," &c.

**I. In the religious life there is a course in which we are to run.**

Specified in God's word, and in which all the worthies were found. Into this course we are brought by faith, and also kept in the course by faith. Only one Divine course—the way of life, &c.

**II. For this religious race there must be preparation.**

Enrolment—putting off unsuitable costume—laying aside every weight.

**III. There must be holy self-denial.**

Training—suitable diet—avoiding luxuries—bracing up the mind—rigid sobriety—strict mortification.

**IV. This religious race must be with spirit and holy resolution.**

**V. In the exercise of lively hope and joy.**

Looking to the goal.

**VI. With invincible faith in the Divine word and grace.**

**VII. In constant reliance on God's covenanted blessing.**

**VIII. To the end of life.**

So as to obtain the crown, &c.

## LXIII

## UNAVAILING PRAYER

"Thou hast covered thyself with a cloud, that our prayer should not pass through."—LAMENTATIONS iii. 44.

THE writer—the occasion—the griefs—patriotism—piety ·—zeal for God. How affecting these lamentations. Some of the thoughts are most tender. What bitter tears—what sad regrets; chap. i. 1-4; ii. 10, 11. So his personal experience; chap. iii. 1-8. Now this verse is akin in spirit to the sentiment of the text. The day dawns; v. 22, 31, &c. But again sadness and wailing come out in our text.

Notice,

**I. The calamity itself.**

A "covered God"—"A thick cloud"—Prayer unable to penetrate. We do not wonder that God is thus,

1. To the *incorrigible sinner*. Case stated; Prov. i. 28. Or to,

2. The *miserable apostate;* Isa. i. 4-15; Jer. xi. 10-11; Ezek. viii. 17. Or to,

3. *Nominal* and *unbelieving prayers*. This people draw, &c. "Ye have not," &c.; James iv. 3. But see it in the case,

4. Of *eminent saints;* Job xxiii. 3-8. Paul; 2 Cor. xii. 8.

**II. The sadness of this calamity.**

1. *Spiritual darkness.* God unrecognized—Heaven, with the sun's total eclipse.

2. *Spiritual discomfort.* No light—way dark—mariner in night tempest. Paul's voyage; Acts xxvii.

3. *Spiritual peril.* Darkness is danger. Wild beasts —bloody men.

4. *Spiritual distressing apprehension.* Storm brooding —lightnings, &c.—forebodings of wrath, &c.

**III. The occasions of this calamity.**

Not Divine eccentricity, pique or changeableness. The occasion is with man. It may arise from,

1. Our *unfitness* for prayer. Worldly, selfish, earthly, angry, petulant, unloving, self-righteous.

2. The *worthlessness* of our prayers. Formal, Pharisaic, cold, heartless, ungrateful.

3. Our *spiritual state* not adapted for prayer. Frivolous, pleasure takers, fashion seekers—fit for anything but devotion. Fit for the tavern—ball room—the fair—or the races.

4. *Unbelieving disobedience.* God has sought, asked, entreated—have we not often disregarded, refused, &c. Notice,

**IV. The remedy for this sad calamity.**

1. *Unfeigned repentance* and *humiliation* before God. Words of confession—heart contrite—smitten breast, prostrate, &c.

2. *Faith* in the Mediator. A day's-man is necessary

—a Mediator—Advocate.   Christ in His person, offices, work, righteousness, blood, &c.

3. The Spirit's *sanctifying power*—"helpeth our infirmities," &c.

4. Importance of *persistent supplication.*   Jacob, Moses Syrophenician woman.

### APPLICATION

1. To the prayerless.   What a sad state.

2. To those experiencing the truth of the text.   How distressing.

3. To all, as to the spirit and mighty power of true prayer.


## LXIV

## LOVE OF THE BROTHER ESSENTIALLY ALLIED WITH LOVE OF GOD

" That he who loveth God loves his brother also."—1 JOHN iv. 21.

LOVE is the essence of all acceptable religion.   But it must embody both tables—love to God and love to man.   Either department only presents one division of heaven-born piety.

Notice,

**I. The love of God must be first and paramount.**

Here religion begins.   Carnal mind renewed.   Rebellious heart changed.   God's love winning back the rebel—the enemy.   The soul subdued, melted, enflamed with God's love—shed abroad in the heart, &c.   The process is by the Gospel, and the power of the gracious Spirit.   This love of God will be conscious, supreme. Delighting in God, and doing His holy will.   It must be first in priority. First in intensity—first in its manifest fruits and evidences.

**II. The love of our brother will ever accompany our love to God.**

"Love his brother also."

Notice, that this love of the brother is,

1. The same affection in its *human direction*.

It does not possess some of those sublime elements that love to God does: as adoring gratefulness—absolute supremacy, &c., but in its nature and essence, it is the one burning, sacred affection of the soul.

2. It will give *undeniable evidences* of its *existence*.

The tongue will speak out this love. The life will exhibit it. All kind help will shew it forth. It will be gracious, tender, self-denying, and self-sacrificing, &c.

3. Its *fruit* will be more *observable*.

Its acts and outgoings will be open to all. So that by this all men shall know, &c.

4. It will *grow* in its *vital power*, as *our love* to God *increases*.

The more we love God, the more we shall love our brother.

1. The subject is a fit test of our real Christianity.

2. Should be assiduously cherished and cultivated.

3. Exhibited to all the brethren. The disciples of Jesus.

4. These are two essential links of the golden chain of salvation.

## LXV

## MINISTERING BEFORE THE ARK

"So he left there before the ark of the covenant of the Lord Asaph and his brethren, to minister before the ark continually, as every day's work required."—1 CHRON. xvi. 37.

THE services of the Tabernacle were most orderly arranged—everything in exact place and time. The ark of God was now in its resting-place, and Asaph and his musical brethren were to minister before it.

Now observe,

### I. The service here referred to.

To "minister." It was the service of holy song; see v. 7. Now this service is,

1. The *loftiest* of all services. Glorifying God—raising the soul—exhibiting the loveliest phase of religion.

2. It must ever be *sustained*—every day. So the Psalmist says—"Every day," &c.

3. It includes other *departments* of *worship*. Narrative of events; v. 16, &c. Exhortation to piety; v. 30. United emulation in holy ascription and adoring sentiments; v. 24-29. Excitement to liberality; v. 31.

Notice, this service,

### II. Must be before the ark of the Lord.

Observe, the ark,

1. Was the *symbol* of God's *presence*. Our praise before Him—to Him—of Him.

2. The ark was the *exhibition* of God's *mercy*. "The mercy-seat," place of reconciliation. "I will meet thee," &c. This is "the Throne of grace." We need mercy —sing of mercy—celebrate, &c.—seek mercy, &c.

3. The ark *contained* the *tables* of the Divine law. So we worship before it in relation to our knowledge of

duty—excitement to obedience—obedience the result of mercy and grace.

4. The ark had the *representation* of the *cherubim* at each end looking into it. So in holy praise we may think of the angels—emulate—be stirred up, &c.

5. But in the ark were the *signs* of *mediation* and *acceptance*. No legalism will do—no merit—no worship as if unfallen. Our praises need Christ's merit and mediation.

But, observe,

### III. The continuity of the service.

" Continually "—" every day."

1. God is *ever* to be praised. In every thing, time, place, circumstance. The seraphim and cherubim continually do cry, &c.

2. The *variety* of the service. "As every day's work required." Some festival days—some commemorative —some days of special labours, of mourning, &c. So the variety was to suit the different occasions. So our hymnology has respect to seasons, times, events. Subjects must be appropriate, significant, in harmony, &c., to meet the requirements.

But notice,

3. The *altered character* of this service under Christianity. We now,

(1.) Enlarge the choir. Not Asaph and his brethren merely, but all Christians—the whole Church.

(2.) We increase the themes. Now Christ and His work and life, &c.—redemption—now the Holy Spirit— Gospel, &c.

(3.) We have additional aid. The gracious Spirit in His fulness to exalt the mind—to fill the heart—to excite the spirit—to open the mouth.

(4.) Prolong the service. Christian praises are for

the whole Christian dispensation to the end of the world, and then they will be taken up by the glorified ones in Heaven. The same theme—subject. They sing the Lamb, &c., in hymns above, &c.

### APPLICATION

1. How blessed this service.
2. How we should cultivate our power of musical service.
3. How sacred it is.
4. How grand the choruses of eternity will be.


## LXIV

## THE LOWLY AND THEIR PRIVILEGES

" He giveth grace unto the lowly."—PROV. iii. 34.

PRIDE is natural to human nature. It has its seat in the heart. It is seen in the look. Heard in vaunting words, and is the plague spot of the character and life. It is hateful to God. A sign of unregeneracy; and utterly unfits for the service of the Lord. The opposite of this is the character in the text,—" The lowly."

Let us,

**I. Survey this character.**

And it is not to the lowly in condition, or the low and mean-spirited; but the lowly in heart. So that,

1. It is *supernatural*. Made so by the operation of the Holy Spirit of God. God in His saving operations brings down, and prostrates the sinner in the dust of abasement, at His feet.

2. It is *manifest*. As clearly seen; as its contrast --pride. The walk and conversation will evidence it.

The whole life exemplify it. Humbly before God, and modestly before men. And self-renunciation in religious things will be visible to all. It will be especially observable,

3. In *religious services*. Self will be crucified, and Jesus exalted. No self exaltation—nor parade—nor religious pretentiousness. It will be the garment of the whole man. In prayer—in praise—in work.

See,

**II. How God treats the lowly.**

"He giveth grace." That is, He gives His favour, and the tokens and evidences of it. He giveth,

1. The grace of *inward peace*. He dwells in the soul —keeps it—comforts and cheers it.

2. He gives the grace of *holy contentment*. They seek not high things, nor expect them. "I have learned," &c.

3. He gives the grace of Divine *vigour* and *growth*. Like trees planted in the rich and fertile vale. They grow and are fruitful.

4. He gives the grace of *religious stability*. To persevere and hold out on the way to Heaven.

5. Of final *victory* over all *enemies*. Sin—Satan— death. Notice,

This grace involves prayer and faith for its attainment. The exercise of the grace given. And grateful joy for the grace possessed.

## LXVII

## OBSCURING CLOUDS

"And now men see not the bright light which is in the clouds; but the wind passeth, and cleanseth them."—Job xxxvii. 21.

THE condition of this world is obscurity. Not gross

darkness—not noon-tide light—but gleams of light, intercepted by darkening clouds. Sometimes we see the text in its literality. It is day—the sun is in the heavens, but we see him not, for clouds obscure him, &c. Now it is just so in the spiritual world where Christ is known. It is day, not night—yet the light is imperfect—not full—not meridian blaze, &c. Let us see how we can use this text profitably.

I. **Look at the spiritual day we have.**

The night is gone—the night of Pagan darkness—the night of the Jewish moon is past. The day-star and the sun, &c., have risen.

Now,

1. We have the *day* of *revealed truth*—a sacred book of Divine light—a day book of facts and histories and principles. Thy word is light, &c. Now this revelation is copious—is often distinct—is sufficient—able to make us wise, &c.—make the man of God perfect, &c.

We have,

2. A *day* of *Gospel joy*—joy and light. Now the Gospel is the shining of gracious light—the light from Christ—of Christ—leading to Christ—glad tidings of great joy.

We have,

3. A *day* of *holy counsel.* The revelation regards conduct, life, acts, words, what to do, and how to do it as servants of God.

4. A *day* of *prospective glory.* The future is revealed —the world to come—life and immortality—the light shining through beyond the grave, opening up the land afar off, &c.

Now, observe,

II. **We have capacity for receiving the light of the day we possess.**

1. The *mind's natural capacity*. Understanding—judgment, &c. Have the power of knowledge—man made for it, &c. The soul to be without knowledge is not good, &c.

2. We have *gracious aids* besides natural capacity. The Holy Spirit opens the eyes—clears the vision—assists us to see and know and understand. This is the anointing by which we know all things. Yet,

3. Our *knowledge* at *best* is but *feeble* and *limited*. We only can see the light we have—don't see the bright light beyond the cloud.

Now let us then notice,

**III. What the clouds obscure to us.**

And here we can only select a few instances.

1. God Himself is *obscured*. With the light we have, canst thou by searching find out God? &c. Does He not to us, in many respects, dwell in thick darkness, or in light too dazzling for our vision? His nature, spirit, we know rather by what it is not. His perfections in the same manner—how He is self-existent, almighty, everywhere present, &c.

2. Then *look* at the *glorious* Saviour. How paradoxical His character. The Eternal and the child—the God and the man—the Infinite and the creature—the Life and yet dying—equal to the Father, yet His servant, &c.—in Heaven, and yet on earth.

3. *Look* at *yourselves*. Mystery surrounds our human constitution, as exhibiting a Tri-unity—body—soul—spirit. The lines of separation of the three, and the lines of union. The influences of each—the end of each. The natural body—the spiritual body. Dying, yet ever living, &c.

4. The *future* of *man* in the *world* to *come*. The what?—the where? How!—the when? The essentials,

and specialities, and generalities of the future existence. Let these suffice—and

**IV. See how these obscurations may be removed.**

" But the wind passeth, and cleanseth them."

We refer,

1. To the *past*. The Divine breath, or wind, has removed much practical darkness. Ye were darkness, &c. The Spirit said " Arise, and Christ will give thee light." Ye were blind, but now, &c. So that past experience helps us to see how the text may be true.

2. In Christian *experience*. Much darkness has been removed. Things you did not understand, now you know. Things imperfectly, now clearly. You have advanced from dawn towards noon. " The path of the just," &c. In chastening providences, how often the Psalmist refers to this. " My feet," &c. See Psalm lxxiii. 2, &c.

3. The *winds* of *mortality* will *clear* the *horizon*. A vessel at sea, near land, and yet invisible. At length, the breeze scatters the mists. The traveller and the fog, close to the landscape, &c., clouds,—then the winds clear it, &c. So beyond is the full-orbed sun—the world of unclouded day. John speaks of this: Revelations xxii. 5. " No night"—" God the sun"—" Now they see as they are seen." Know as they are known. See God, the invisible, in the glory of Jesus. Dwell in the light. No cloud, &c.

### APPLICATION

1. Realize present privileges.

2. Seek personal advancement in grace, and in the knowledge of God, &c.

3. Avoid sinful curiosity. " What thou knowest not," &c. Wait.

4. How attractive the future glory in the cloudless world.

## LXVIII

## THE HAPPY HABITATION

" He blesseth the habitation of the just."—Prov. iii. 33.

The contrast to our text is found in these words—
"The curse of the Lord is in the house of the wicked."
Let us look at,

**I. The home of the pious.**

Here called the "habitation of the just." God's
people are just, as they are justified by faith in the
Lord Jesus Christ. As renewed and righteous persons,
made so by Divine grace. And as practically obeying
the Divine commandments. The habitation in the text,
therefore, will be governed by just principles, and distinguished for the exercise of justice in all the concerns
of life—in all their dealings—in all their household
arrangements; and in the constant recognition of God's
holy authority. Profession of piety will be vain and
valueless without uprightness of heart and life. There
is justice in the family relationships, and in reference to
servants, as well as tradespeople, and those with whom
we deal.

Notice,

**II. The declaration concerning this home of the pious.**

That "God blesseth the habitations of the just."

1. With His Divine providential care.
2. With His gracious smile.
3. With the tokens of His beneficence.
4. With the bestowments of spiritual blessings.
5. With the sunshine of heavenly love and joy.

He does so, because they are His portion—His children —He is in covenant with them; and He has given them exceeding great and precious promises. It has ever been so, and must be so always. So in the habitation of the just,

1. There should be the recognition of the Divine blessing.

2. Praise for its communication.

3. And the exhibition of professed attachment to His name and cause and people.

## LXIX
## ELIJAH UNDER THE JUNIPER TREE

"But he himself went a day's journey into the wilderness, and came and sat down under a juniper tree; and he requested for himself that he might die," &c.—1 KINGS xix. 4.

ELIJAH the Tishbite was one of the most heroic of the prophets. Bold, God-fearing, self-denying, he stands out as one of the bravest of the Lord's servants, and he and the Baptist represent the self-denying and the valiant of the two dispensations, yet we find him now exhibiting opposite traits of character to those we should expect, and his spirit and utterances are of abject cowardice and irreligion.

Let us then see,

**I. The strange course he adopted.**

Observe, the occasion of the whole is briefly given. After his bold attack on the priests ot Baal, and his challenge, and the Divine recognition, and the slaughter of the prophets of Baal; see chap. xviii. 21, 26, &c., 30, &c., 41, &c. Then Jezebel sent a message of vengeance and destruction; v. 2, 3. Then the text. It seems incredible that this threatening should have so told on Elijah. Well, let us see how he acts.

1. As a *coward* he *deserts* his post of honour; v. 3. How great the contrast; v. 18. Moving Heaven— opening the clouds.

2. He *retreats* into *solitude*. Solitude may be good, important, necessary, but not in times of conflict. War waging—the captain should be in the midst of his army. He flees "a day's journey into the wilderness."

3. He *sits* down in *gloomy despondency*. He seems to have lost all heart—paralized—powerless.

4. He utters a *petulant* and *unauthorized prayer*. He wishes to die—he asks God to take away his life. A prayer rash, presumptuous, ungodly—the reason most absurd—"not better." Precedents are not always to be quoted. Noah had no precedent—nor Moses—nor Elijah.

Now see,

II. This strange prayer.

1. The *subject*—*life* and *death*. This is never remitted to us. God is the author of life—He never puts it at our disposal—He only is its arbiter—so it was not a thing to be prayed about.

2. The *peremptory request* was very *irreverent*. "It is enough," and "take," both these points were for God to determine—God knew best, not Elijah. With submission we may seek God's prolongation of life as Hezekiah —or express our willingness to die in God's time as Job did—or state our preference as Paul, who desired to depart, &c. But to dictate to God, and seek God's killing power, was an utter violation of subordination and veneration for God.

3. It *indicated impatience* with his lot. He might be weary—he might be sad—darkness was all around his

soul; but submission, waiting, and patience, surely would not only be right, but best. Now, in every sense, was this prayer unworthy of himself and of God, whose servant he was. But let us notice,

### III. The lessons derivable from it.

1. The *imperfection* of the best of men. There are spots on the disc of the sun. No sinless one, but Jesus. Of some there are no signs of moral infirmity; but, no doubt, they existed. "Not a just man." "I have seen an end of all perfection."

2. The *failings* of the best of men, are generally in connection with the *best* phases of their character. They fail generally in that in which they had excelled. Scarcely any exception to this. Noah, the model, and preacher of righteousness, gets drunk. Abraham, the faithful, prevaricates, and tells lies. Jacob, the open wrestler with God, secretly deceives Esau. Moses, the meekest man, is angry and rash. David, the purest man after God's own heart, is gross and sensual. Solomon, the wisest, becomes a fool with strange women and idols. Peter, the bold, is the miserable poltroon and coward, and denier of Christ. The loving Disciples are those who wish fire &c., to come down. So it ever is.

3. The necessity of *vigilant* prayer. Seek Divine wisdom—help—deliverance. Trusting in God. Looking from ourselves.

4. Sanctified *human nature* is about the same in all ages. Elijah a striking evidence. How frail at best!

5. How needful to be *taught*. How to pray. How to act.

## LXX

### GOD'S COMPLAINT

" I have spread out my hands all the day unto a rebellious people."
ISAIAH lxv. 2.

**I. The intimation of God's gracious regards.**

His hands of mercy—compassion—pity—desire to
save. Outspread hands—waiting to receive and save.

**II. The persistency of God's regards.**

"All the day." Morning—noon—evening. Day of
sinner's life often protracted. So Christ speaks of Jerusalem and its day, &c.

**III. The exhibition of God's mercy to rebels.**

"To a rebellious people." Rebels against God—His
laws—holiness—privileges—blessings—grace. Rebels
against His Son—the Holy Spirit. Open—wicked—
rebellious—having every element of baseness and iniquity. See the account; v. 2, 3, 4.

**IV. A rebellious rejection of mercy must secure judgment
and wrath.**

No alternative. Prov. i. 24; Psa. cvii. 11.

## LXXI

### PRAISE DAY AND NIGHT

" And these are the singers, chief of the fathers of the Levites, who
remaining in the chambers were free; for they were employed in that
work day and night."—1 CHRON. ix. 33.

A GENERAL roll and reckoning of all Israel is given in
this chapter—even to the very porters of the gates—

the various officers and overseers of all the work in the
Divine service; see v. 29-32. Then we come to the
singers, chief of the fathers of the Levites, and their
constant service is stated, day and night.

Observe,

**I. The service itself.**

Service of "praise."

1. It is the service of *universal* nature. By a figure of
speech. Let the heavens and the earth and the sea;
Psalm lxix. 34. "The heavens declare the glory of
God," &c.; Psalm xix. 1. "All Thy works shall praise
Thee;" Psalm cxlv. 10. So one grand universal an-
them; Psalm cxlviii. 2, &c.

2. *Praise* has been the *service* of the Church under all
*dispensations.* The song of Miriam and Moses celebrated
the overthrow of Pharaoh, &c.—The oldest song in the
world; Exodus xv. The song of Deborah—the overthrow of the enemies of Israel. So in connection with
the Tabernacle and its ordinances there is the command
that with all the services, &c., they were to "rejoice
before the Lord seven days;" Leviticus xxiii. 40. Then
the Temple service; 1 Chron. xv. 16—at its dedication;
2 Chron. v. 12, &c. So at the restoration of the
second Temple. The singers of the children of Asaph
were 148; Neh. vii. 44; xii. 40-43. The Christian
dispensation was ushered in by the song of the holy
angels; Luke ii. 13. Christ hallowed the Sacred
Eucharist, the Holy Supper thus; Matt. xxvi. 30. We
have the recognition and counsel of the apostle; Eph.
v. 19, 20; Col. iii. 16.

3. It is the *service* of *Heaven;* Isaiah vi. 1. The
visions of the apocalypse culminate in grand anthems
of celestial choirs and universal choruses. See the
opening of the service perpetuated in Heaven; Rev. iv.

8-11. Then the new song is produced; Rev. v. 8, 9.
Then angels join in the chorus; v. 11. This is repeated;
chap. vii. 9-11. The jubilee of Zion; chap. xiv. 1, &c.;
Rev. xix. 1, 3, 4, 6.

Let us observe,

**II. The essential characteristics of this service of praise.**

It must be,

1. The *service* of the *whole man*. Lip and tongue—
heart and spirit. Not formal—not merely performance
—but the exercise of the whole soul—"all within me,"
&c. Dull praises are a perfect farce—a libel and
burlesque.

2. The *service* of all the *people*. "Young men and
maidens; old men and children;" Psalm cxlviii. 12.
The great and elite to join; v. 11. All His saints; v.
14. So the Psalm concludes—"Let every thing that
hath breath," &c.; Psalm cl. 6.

3. It must be the *service* of all *seasons*. So "day and
night;" the natal day of birth and the night of death.
Simeon; Luke ii. 25, &c. The day of health—night of
sickness; day of salvation—night of trial—"Paul and
Silas;" day of social joy—night of bereavement; day
of mercies—night of judgments—Christ at the Pascal
Supper—and of both worlds.

Observe,

**III. The sublime importance of this service.**

1. It *glorifies* God. "Whoso offereth praise," &c.

2. It *elevates* the soul. It is ascending—rising—lifting
up the heart and soul—soaring upwards and heavenwards.

3. It *cheers* and *felicitates* God's people.

4. It *recommends* religion. It unites Heaven and earth.
"I have been there," &c. But such a service,

**IV. Demands our special attention.**

1. A strong desire that it may be *acceptable* and *please* God. Short of this it is mockery.

2. It demands *preparation*. Order and melody are essential in public praise—so preparation is indispensable.

3. It is worthy of *greatest culture*. In the family—in the school—in the Church of Christ.

4. Must seek the *aid* of the Divine Spirit. "Open Thou my lips," &c. With the "Spirit" God must put the songs into our hearts.

### APPLICATION

1. Devout examination on the subject of praise. Often levity, inattention, self-laudation, ostentation. Must be bathed in the waters of holiness.

2. Labour to excel. God should have the best of voice and heart and soul. Pious singers are God's choir.

3. See to securing its benefits. Present joyousness, edification, life, &c.

## LXXII

## AN IMPORTANT ENQUIRY

" Where is thy God?"—Psalm xlii. 3.

We reply, in answer to this question—

**I. He is in His most holy place.**

Heaven of heavens. Dwelleth on high, &c.; Isa. vi. 1; Ezek. i. 27-8. "Our Father who art in Heaven."

**II. He is in His holy word.**

Revealed in His essence, attributes, will, covenants and promises.

**III. He is in all holy ordinances.**

"Wherever two or three." Wherever His name recorded. With His preached word. Administered services. Baptism. Lord's Supper.

**IV. He is in all places.**

Filleth all things. Heaven and earth. Psalm cxxxix. Not afar off, but at hand.

**V. He is gloriously in the Lord Jesus Christ.**

God in Christ. With us as the Emmanuel. Fully declared in Jesus. Manifested in Jesus. Living—speaking—working by Jesus. In Jesus always. See how it is stated—John xiv. 8-11.

In conclusion—

Faith sees the invisible God.

Love embraces Him by ardent affection.

Hope looks to Him with confidence.

And devotion enjoys fellowship with Him.

## LXXIII

### INTENSITY OF LOVE

"Set me as a seal upon thine heart, as a seal upon thine arm : for love is strong as death. Many waters cannot quench love, neither can the floods drown it."—SONG OF SOLOMON viii. 6, 7.

OF this gorgeous allegory the text is one of the brightest gems. It is the fervid address of the Bride—the Church, to her beloved royal Bridegroom, and the love of God is ever to have the supremacy of all affection. The love of Christ is to have the pre-eminency. Jesus is God's incarnate love—the love of God is pre-eminently manifested in the gift and person of His Son, who became the evidence as well as the fulness of the love of God towards us.

Observe,

**I. The ardent desire of the Church; v. 6.**

" Set me as a seal," &c. It is a request to have,

1. A *deep place* in His *loving heart*. Engraven within —permanently within—and abiding in His heart's love.

2. A *visible place* in His *offices* and *work*. " A seal on His arm "—the heart first and the arm next—a sign to those without. The Church—the world—an interest in His arm's support and defence, &c. " Who is this leaning," &c. In one word, to be identified with His love and work.

**II. The grounds on which this desire is pleaded.**

1. The *intensity* of *love*. "Strong as death." Now this is true,

(1.) Of love to Christ. Highest—deepest—most constraining of all the affections; giving impassioned desire —vehement devotion—ever present realization. But the uttermost consecration of life, labour, toils—death itself. So the apostles lived and died martyrs. But see how still more true,

(2.) Of Christ's love to us. The whole being of the Saviour given for us. Unparalleled condescension—the deepest abasement—the extremest sufferings—the most ignominious death—"even the death of the cross." And this love of the Church and of Christ are mutual. First from Christ to us—second from Christ in us—and then, third, from us to Christ. But we are led,

**III. To contemplate this marvellous love.**

In its extraordinary attributes,

1. It is *inexorable* as the *grave*. Jealous of rivalry—of opposition—to the enemies of the object beloved; and then zealous in prosecuting the designs of the Saviour loved. As the grave insatiable—as the grave knowing no distinction. See it in Paul's utterance—"if any man

love not," &c. No matter whom, enemy or friend—
alien or kindred—let the anathema rest, yea, even on
angels, &c.; Galatians i. 8.

2. In its *vehemency*. "Coals of fire"—a flame of God
—fire of Heaven—sacred, pure, celestial—not cold, cal-
culating, formal.

3. Its *inextinguishableness*. "Many waters," &c. Adversity, trials, afflictions, prisons, Baptists drowned for
Christ.

4. No *price* adequately can be *given* for it. Honours,
offices, treasures, &c.

### APPLICATION

Do we possess it?

Does it absorb us?

Do we evidence it?

Learn its Divine source and its eternal sacred influence,
power and preciousness.

## LXXIV

### SEEKING GREAT THINGS PROHIBITED

" And seekest thou great things for thyself? Seek them not."
JER. xlv. 5.

**I. The great things prohibited.**

Evidently refers to the things of the world. Great
riches — great honours — great positions. Wealth —
power—glory.

**II. Why not seek them.**

Because they are not essentials to life and happiness.
Because they are associated with imminent perils. Because they often become exclusive in their influence

of better things; and, because they are transient and perishing. "The fashion of this world," &c.

**III. God has greater things in store for His children.**

Greater treasures—greater titles—greater privileges and blessing, and even life for evermore.

1. Let us seek the best things first.

2. Leave other things to God's disposal.

## LXXV

## THE SAVING LOOK

"Look unto me, and be ye saved."—Isaiah xlv. 22.

The text is of universal application. Found in the roll of the evangelical prophet—as specific now as then—as precious now as then—as universal now as then. Let us see the great sublime truths the text contains.

**I. The implied truth—our need of salvation.**

The text has no force without this. Men are unsaved —need saving—can be saved. This implied truth arises from,

1. Our *depravity*. Evil nature—evil heart—evil bearings. Holiness absent—God's image effaced, &c.— from, &c.

2. Our *manifold sins*. "All"—innumerable—aggravated.

3. The *Divine penalty*. Sin and woe—sin and punishment—sin and death—sin and wrath—sin and perdition. This condition is universal and individual—true of the whole—and of each man in the world—best and worst.

**II. The announced salvation.**

"Be ye saved." Now, with regard to this salvation, notice,

1. It was *eternally purposed*.

2. It has been *revealed* in all *ages*.  First parents, &c.

3. It is the *express message* of the *Gospel*.  "We bring you," &c.  "This is a faithful saying," &c.  It is the free message of the Gospel—it is the full message of the Gospel—it is the universal message of the Gospel —it is the sincere and express message of the Gospel.

Now this announced salvation,

**III. Is in God alone.**

See chap. xlii. 11.  So text.

Observe, salvation is,

1. In the Father's *originating love* and *grace*.

2. In Christ's *mediatorial person* and *work*.

3. In the Divine Spirit's *conveyance* and *application*. In Jehovah—Father, Son, and Holy Spirit.  In each essentially, but not exclusively.  The Father originating —the Son effectuating—the Spirit applying.  Observe, salvation is in God alone.  Not in angels and their ministration—not in Moses and the law—not in prophets and their mission—not in apostles or evangelists—not in the Church and its institutions—not in worship and ordinances—not in man's own efforts and work—but in God, and God alone.

Observe,

**IV. How it is to be realized.**

"Salvation" is a fact—it exists, but must be experienced—not made, but obtained—received.  How?  The text expresses it—by "looking."  "Look unto Me," &c.

1. A *look* of *perception*.  To know the Gospel truth— to see it as revealed.

2. A *look* of *penitence* and *self-condemnation*.

3. A *look* of *faith* and *trust* in God—our Saviour, Jesus Christ.  See the analogies—Moses said, look to the brazen serpent—so Christ—John the Baptist said, "be-

hold the Lamb !"—So the text, look, &c.—away from all others in Heaven or earth—from self, &c. Look now— look every one. How marvellous—how gratuitous— how universally adapted—how the only way—no other, &c.

In conclusion—

Salvation is in God only.

Salvation is by faith only.

And it is the salvation by faith that produces all the evidences—all the fruits—all the blessings—holiness— and obtains at length,

The eternal life and glory in Christ Jesus.

## LXXVI

### GOD'S MERCIFUL CHASTENING

" The Lord hath chastened me sore; but he hath not given me over unto death."—PSALM cxviii. 19.

MOST extraordinary Psalm. Full of striking, telling truth—especially exhibiting religion in its practical and experimental bearings. The Psalmist had been severely afflicted, and it is obvious his case was considered one of imminent peril; v. 17. Now he piously celebrates the goodness of God shewn to him.

I. His severe chastening.

He refers it,

1. To the *Lord.* "The Lord hath," &c. Afflictions do not spring out of the dust. God always permits them, and not unfrequently sends them. Job—Paul, &c., all recognized God's chastening hand. He speaks of his chastening,

2. As *severe*. "Chastened me sore." Not slight or short, but deep and continued affliction.

3. He describes it as *chastening*. Not wrath, but afflictive discipline. As a father, &c. See Hebrews xii. 5.

Notice,

**II. The limitation of this chastening.**

"Hath not given me over unto death." So that the end was life and not death. Here it is indicated,

1. That *afflictions* and *death* are at God's disposal. He kills or preserves alive. Hezekiah, &c.

2. That *restoration* from chastening is an *act* of God's *goodness*, and should so be recognized.

3. That our *highest praises* are due to God for His *restoring mercies*. See 2 Cor. i. 1-10; Psa. ciii. 4, &c.

4. In the Lord's *hands* all our *highest interests* are *inviolably secure*.


## LXXVII

### CHRIST THE ONLY SAVIOUR

"Neither is there salvation in any other; for there is none other name under Heaven given among men, whereby we must be saved." —ACTS iv. 12.

THE circumstances of the case—miracle had been wrought; chap. iii. 1, &c. The termination of a bold address—full—evangelical—direct. Then the text.

Observe,

**I. The salvation spoken of.**

Not bodily healing or temporal deliverances, but the salvation of the soul. Now,

1. *Salvation supposes peril*. This is the constant

Scripture statement—all men are in a condition of depravity—guilt—condemnation—under wrath, &c.

2. *Salvation* is *deliverance* from all these *conditions* of *danger*. It is illumination—conviction—conversion—regeneration and deliverance from condemnation and the wrath to come.

3. This *salvation culminates* in *eternal life;* John iii. 14-16. Now it will be seen this covers the whole ground of our salvation.

Notice,

**II. The Saviour referred to; v. 10.**

Jesus Christ of Nazareth—crucified—raised—"Head of the corner," &c.    Now Jesus Christ is the Saviour exhibited in the law—described in the Psalms—and predicted by the prophets; Luke xxiv. 44, 46.

1. He did *save* in the *days* of His *ministry.* The woman, the town sinner—Zaccheus, the publican—the thief, &c., all these bad cases.

2. He had *saved* after His *resurrection.* See the crowd —their agony—cry; Acts ii. 37.    The answer; v. 38. The result; v. 41.    They were Jerusalem sinners. Many things might be said of the Saviour as to His Godhead, power and glory, His humanity, compassion, sympathy, &c.    But we hasten to the chief thing in the text.

**III. The limitation of salvation to Jesus Christ and His name.**

"Neither is there salvation in any other," &c.

1. Not in the most *illustrious* of *patriarchs.*

2. Not in the *holiest* of the *priests.*

3. Not in the *greatest* of the *prophets.*

4. Not in the *noblest* of the *apostles.*

5. Not in the *company* of the *beatified martyrs*—Virgin Mary—all saints.

6. Not *among* the *angels* of *Heaven*. They are friends, guides, guardians, deliverers, patterns, but not saviours. In earth or Heaven only one Saviour. Let us see how this is attested by God's word; hear Isaiah xlii. 6, &c. His name and work, Jesus, &c. His office, one Mediator between God, &c.; 1 Timothy ii. 5. His obedience, His teaching, His sufferings and death and resurrection. No other is ever pointed at. He the Lamb slain—the author of eternal salvation. And in the text. So the Word of God refers to no other Saviour, no other possesses oneness with the Father, supreme glory, Divine perfections, omnipotence, omniscience, omnipresence, unchangeableness, eternity!

Observe,

1. The *force* of the *text* as *addressed* to all intelligent responsible persons. It excludes self-salvation and all other.

2. It does not *decide* the *doom* of infants, of idiots, or the heathen. Infants don't require the salvation we laid down—they are not personal sinners, and could not endure the chief horrors of the lost. But infants can attain to purity and blessedness, and this by Christ's work and mediation. Idiots are not responsible. The heathen will be judged by the law they have. But idiots or heathen will be saved, if at all, by the system of infinite love and grace, set up by Christ Jesus.

3. The grand enquiry is, *how* are *men saved* by Christ? See Acts iii. 16. Faith in His name. The Pentecostal multitudes "gladly received the Gospel;" the jailer was told to "believe;" Paul says "whosoever shall call," &c.; the commission runs, "He that believeth shall be saved." So Christ said, "that whosoever believeth," &c. This faith in Christ hears Christ—looks to Christ—comes to Christ—trusts in Christ—receives Christ, and thus realizes the salvation Jesus came to confer.

Notice, the text is,

(1.) A beacon light. None other—no other name—Christ or no Saviour.

(2.) How it should inspire with holy caution and solicitude, &c. Creeds, morality, profession, ordinances will not, cannot. "Christ is able and willing to save all who believe in His name."

> " No other name is found,
> No other name is given,
> By which we can salvation have ;
> But Jesus came the world to save."

## LXXVIII

## DIVINE HELP ENTREATED

" Make haste to help me, O Lord, my salvation."—PSALM xxxviii. 22.

THE text indicates pain and peril, and seeks the Divine interference. In many of our sorrows and difficulties we are utterly unable to help ourselves, and often human help is unavailable,—it is then the text is felt in all its importance, and presented to God with all conceivable earnestness.

Observe,

I. The prayer offered.

"Make haste," &c. Now the blessing sought,

1. Is God's *help* "Help me ! " Syrophenician woman thus prayed—so millions—so we often. It meets all cases of suffering, weakness, and danger. " Peter sinking," &c.

2. God's *help* is sought *immediately*. "Make haste." The danger imminent—enemies rampant—disease deadly—sufferings intense.

3. God's *help* is sought most *directly*. No circumlocution—no waste of words—no preface—no praying about it, but an entreaty most sententious and direct—"Make haste," &c.

Notice,

**II. The special features in this prayer.**

1. It is *offered* to Jehovah. "Lord." One able—near at hand. Having skill, ability, &c., for every emergency. Nothing too hard for Him.

2. It is *offered* to Jehovah as the *soul's salvation*. "My salvation." The Lord had been his Saviour. He was in covenant with Him. Subject of His rich and gracious promises. So his experience. No salvation away from God.

3. All other *helpers* will *fail* if God *does not* save. Vain the help of man, or angels—if the Lord does not incline His ear, and stretch out His hand to save. It will be seen that the text is adapted to every trial and sorrow and peril. It can be moaned on the bed of suffering. It can be ejaculated in deep distress. Jesu's person, merit and work form a most satisfactory plea in connection with this and every prayer.

## LXXIX

## ANGELIC JOY OVER ONE REPENTING SINNER

"Likewise, I say unto you, there is joy in the presence of the angels of God over one sinner that repenteth."—LUKE xv. 10.

ALL the discourses of the Saviour were beautiful, many exquisitely sweet and tender, but some were pre-eminently so. All His discourses like radiant stars, but some were more bright and glorious. In connection

with the text, we have a galaxy—a milky way, &c.
Within the same compass, I doubt if all the world of
literature contains so much refreshing moral loveliness
and beauty—yet how simple. Here is the anxious
shepherd seeking his wandering sheep. Here is the
housewife &c. looking for the lost piece of silver. And
then there is the sublime application in the irrepressible
overflowing joy of the angels in heaven. The gladness
of the good on earth, and then the delight of angels.
We rise from the bliss of earth to the anthems in glory.

Here are three things for our contemplation.

I. The interesting change described.

"A sinner repenting." Now to repent really and
essentially signifies to change, to alter the course
pursued. It is both inward and outward, and affects
the heart and life. And keeping this simple definition
in view, we cannot be misled. Hence it is,

1. A *change* of *mind*. A sinner who has rejected
Christ and the Gospel, changes his mind both as to God
and sin and of himself. "Repent ye"—see differently
—alter your views, and think differently.

2. It is a *change* of *emotions*. Hating and loving
are now directed to opposite objects. God loved—
sin hated, &c. So desire and abhorrence. Now holiness desired and sin abhorred—includes sorrow and
regret for sin.

3. It is a *change* of *spirit*. The proud, rebellious,
selfish, become abased, contrite and docile.

4. It is a *change* of *purposes*. The sinner only purposes
to please himself, and acts as he likes. Follows his own
devices and will and passions. Now he seeks to hear
and do God's bidding.

5. It is a *change* of *action*. A repenting person acts
differently, if not, his repentance is not genuine. The

prodigal repented, and returned home. The Jews repented, and were baptised. And as unbelief is the
natural state of the heart, repentance always involves believing God. Repent ye, and believe the gospel. The
two are never separate. Well, now, notice in the text,

II. **The effect produced.**

1. There is a blessed effect *produced* on the *sinner*
himself. Now a child—now accepted—now is blessed,
clothed, &c.

2. An effect is *produced* in reference *to* God. Now
the Divine displeasure is exchanged for love and delight.
"O Lord, I will praise thee; for though thou wast
angry," &c. But the text refers to the effect produced
on angels. These were the first-born sons of God—
present at the creation of the world—described in
Scripture as holy ones—wise—powerful—obedient—loving. Often employed to do God's will, &c. To minister
to His saints, &c. Officers both of wrath and mercy.
Now here they are joyously affected by the repentance
of even one sinner.

Observe,

1. There is *always joy* among them. World of joy—
holy, therefore joyful. But then their joy is capable
of addition. Always water in the river, but it may
swell and flow over, &c. So, therefore, there is extra
overflowing joy among the angels—spring-tide of rap-
ture. Now, if so, then they must be conversant with
the affairs of our world. Jacob's ladder is the true
explanation of this. The angels always ascending and
descending between the two worlds—so that the events
of the earth are ever known to them. Here then is the
grand result on the minds of angels, rejoicing even
when one sinner repenteth.

Now, let us see,

III. **The grounds on which it may be accounted for.**

One word expresses it—"sympathy." Without this they would not—could not thus rejoice.

1. They have *sympathy* with God—His purposes and plans. They are one with God. Now the repentance of a sinner is an object in which God delights. It is the result of His grace and covenant and means, therefore angels rejoice.

2. They have *sympathy* with *holiness*. They are holy angels, hate evil—hate rebellion. Well, here there is the restoration of the rebel to loyalty, in the repentance of the sinner. Hence there is the bursting forth of holy emotions, &c.

3. They have *sympathy* with *men*. Their spiritual nature is, doubtless, adapted to have fellowship with man's spiritual and moral character—and this repentance is the happiness and safety of man—his escape from exposedness to hell, to the hope of Heaven; therefore they rejoice. But,

4. They have *special sympathy* with Jesus. How often they evinced it. Announced His birth—sang at His Advent—were present at His temptation, sufferings, cross, resurrection, ascension, &c. They are Christ's servants. Now, in the repentance of the sinner, Christ rejoices as the Good Shepherd, and therefore they rejoice too.

5. They have *sympathy* with the *Church*. They are the Church's servants—all ministering spirits—take a deep concern in it—present in her assemblies—often have comforted and delivered the saints—as Peter in prison—Paul during the shipwreck—John in Patmos, &c. Now the repentance of the sinner is one gathered to the fold—the Church's increase, &c.—One saved—one added to the Lord and His people.

6. They have *sympathy* with the *progress* of the *Divine kingdom*. They saw the entrance of sin, have seen the whole course of redemption as it has been unfolded, and they know that Satan must be cast out—Christ must reign, and therefore here they see one trophy—one victory—one spirit rescued—hell so far confounded.

7. They have *sympathy* with *Heaven*. Above there are being collected the jewels of the earth, the saints of God, and these are to be their co-associates and fellow-worshippers for ever. Here are additional companions —new friends—real kindred—and thus there is joy, &c.

### APPLICATION

1. Have you afforded this joy to angels?

2. If angels thus rejoice, why not the holy spirits of the departed? May not your sainted parents, your departed mother, sister, friend, pastor? No reason why they should not.

3. Urge immediate repentance on every sinner.

4. Note the deep interest all real Christians should take in it. Labour, watch, pray and rejoice.


## LXXX

## CHRISTIAN STABILITY

" Be ye stedfast. "—1 Cor. xv. 58.

THE text relates to believers, to God's children. Those having by faith entered the kingdom of God.

Observe,

**I. What the text implies.**

Possible instability—probable wavering, or turning aside. With some,

1. This is *constitutional*. Naturally unstable as water. Lacking persistency, &c.

2. This is *ever possible*. How many cease to walk with Christ. Demas, &c. " Will ye also go away?"

3. This is a course *most perilous*. " If any man draw back," &c. To withdraw the hand from the plough. To forsake Christ and hope and heaven.

**II. Some of the occasions of instability.**

A dead faith — formality in devotion — neglect of means — worldly conformity — ungodly associations — neglected vigilance and prayer.

**III. Why Christian stability should be maintained.**

Our Christian honour. Christian comfort. Christian usefulness. Christian safety.

Then, notice,

**IV. How it may be secured.**

By holding fast the truth.

By studying the examples of Scripture. Noah, Joseph, Moses, &c.

By looking especially to Jesus.

By asking for the gracious aids of the Holy Spirit.

By instant attention to Christian duties and obligations. Stedfastness is most essential, and should be devoutly sought and realized.

Be stedfast then in faith, in works, in prayer, in conflict, until the Crown is given.


## LXXXI

### HOW TO OVERCOME EVIL

"Be not overcome of evil, but overcome evil with good."—Rom. xii. 21.

THIS chapter contains the ethics of Christianity. It

stands in relation to Christianity, as the Sermon on the Mount, and is a sort of supplement to it. It is a perfect code of Christian requirements, and the higher elements of saintly conduct. If it could be transferred in its brightness and power to Christian professors, it would fill the world with its light and glory. I have never known but one perfect living embodiment of it, yet it is the mark at which we should aim—the life we should labour to live. The concluding paragraph is most sublime—the enemy is to be killed—the man saved. Now the text contains a great general principle, one of supreme importance.

Observe in the text.

**I. Two principles.**

"Evil and good." Now the existence of these requires no argument.

Observe,

1. *Sin* is *evil—holiness good*. All sin—thought, imagination, desire, purpose, deed. Holiness includes all good—graces, virtues, purposes and acts.

2. *Ignorance* is *evil—knowledge* is *good*. Symbols—ignorance is darkness, night—knowledge is light, day.

3. *Error* is *evil—truth* is *good*. Error is false, crooked, perversion, &c.

4. *Selfishness* is *evil—benevolence good*. Selfishness, violation of the great law—the second commandment. Benevolence, its exhibition and exemplification.

5. *Malevolence* is *evil—generosity* and *love good*. Malevolence is to hate, despise, curse. Love, to pity, sympathize and help.

Observe,

**II. These principles are in direct antagonism.**

No likeness—the opposites—night and day—evil and good—Satan and God—hell and Heaven: they are in absolute antagonism—in eternal antagonism.  The conflict between the two is,

1.  *Ancient.*  In Heaven—in Eden.

2.  *Persistent.*  Ever since.

3.  *Universal.*  In all persons and places.

4.  Still *rampant.*  We see it daily.  The two elements are most visibly in conflict.

5.  *Evil* is often in the *ascendant.*  " World lieth," &c. In our hearts, &c.  Paganism—barbarism.  All the curses socially the result, &c.

But observe,

**III. Evil may be overcome.**

Evil is not irresistible or invincible.

1.  Jesus in His *own* life *overcame* it.  All His actions —temptation of Satan, revilings, &c.

2.  It is *overcome* in the *sinner's conversion.*  Evil spirit exorcised—evil nature renewed—and evil dominion overthrown.

3.  It has been *overcome* by God's *people.*  Stephen, Paul, martyrs, &c.

4.  It *shall* be *totally overcome.*  Light, truth, love, &c., in the ascendent.  Evil must retire as chaos, &c.

But observe,

**IV. Evil is to be overcome by good.**

This, observe, is the only way—the certain way. Not devil against devil—not sin against sin—not passion against passion—not vengeance against vengeance— but the evil must be overcome by good.

1.  See it in *redemption.*  Satan the prince—sin the curse—woe the doom.  Jesus the good—incarnate love —His grace the power—He conquers by truth and love, by tears and His own precious blood, &c.

2.  See it in the *conversion* of the *soul.*  The good truth—the good spirit—the good grace.

3. See it in the *sanctified life.* All malice and hatred and envy extirpated. The good and renewed nature rising in love and goodness.

4. See it in the *conversion* of the *world.* It must be converted—absolutely certain; but by what—the sword, magistracy, fines, sufferings, vengeance—no, by love, by goodness, the world's darkness by light, enmity by messages of reconciliation—by the loving influences of the loving Christ in the loving Gospel, and by the loving Spirit. So we see that God's own method is to overcome evil with good.

### APPLICATION

1. Here is a grand Christian lesson. In lesser forms of evil—bigotry, exclusiveness, sectarianism—how to be overcome by good—not by evil—not one bigoted spirit casting out another—no, but by the exhibition of love —Divine goodness.

In the text we have,

2. A model for Christian families in their education of children—parental discipline, &c.

3. The great exercise of self-discipline. How hard to bless the curser—feed the enemy, &c. Yet this is possible by prayer—by the good Spirit of God—and by thorough self-discipline.

4. We must proclaim this to mankind. What say infidels? Professed Christianity fights, kills, puts to death, excommunicates. Alas! it is so. But such Christianity is spurious, earthly. The words of Jesus on the cross—"Father, forgive them," &c., and the text, are in principle and spirit one. True religion is the only power by which we can overcome evil with good.

## LXXXII

## CHRISTIAN HOSPITALITY

" Use hospitality one to another without grudging."—1 PETER iv. 9.

HOSPITALITY is constantly enforced in Scripture. The patriarchs and early nations were distinguished for it. High civilization and the provisions of hotel accommodation stand in the way of hospitality. But there are abundant opportunities for its exercise, and its true and hearty exhibition is well-pleasing to God, and honourable to religion. Let us look,

I. At the rites of hospitality.

It is evidenced in giving welcome to the stranger. In supplying the wants of the poor; and in making our dwellings refreshing places to the unfortunate and needy. Hospitality is often demanded from the servants of Christ in their toils and journeys, and necessities. Jesus and His apostles required it. The disciples and evangelists. The first itinerants and missionaries. So the labourers in all the great epochs of Church revival and reformation. Now such hospitality is to be "used" not refused—used as occasion demands, and as we have opportunity, and ability to exercise it.

II. The spirit in which it is to be exercised.

" Without grudging." Not niggardly—not reluctantly —not murmuringly, but with,

(1.) A willing heart.

(2.) Cheerful spirit.

(3.) A generous and hearty manner.

(4.) From love to mankind.

(5.) From a desire to please God.

(6.) It must be exercised with all Christian sympathy, without parade or show, or ostentation.

(7.) As done to Christ himself.

(8.) Thus it will be a feast to our own souls.

(9.) We may entertain angels unawares.

(10.) It will honour religion, and

(11.) Secure the high approbation of the Lord Jesus.

## LXXXIII
## KEEPING GOD'S WORD

" That I may live, and keep thy word."—PSALM cxix. 17.

EVERY verse in this golden Psalm is a gem—the one theme is the Holy Scriptures, under the terms—law, precepts, commandments, judgments, testimonies, word, &c. The Psalmist speaks of it in an experimental and practical manner, not as a theoretical task, or mental exercise merely, but as having God's word in the heart and keeping it there, and so bringing forth the fruits of a holy life.

Notice in the text,

**I. A reference to the Divine word.**

That spoken by the Lord, or revealed to the prophets, &c. All the utterances of Jehovah. Now the subject supposes the Psalmist had it in possession, fully accepted it, and highly valued it, and he now seeks to retain or keep it. Now of this word it may be said,

(1.) It is true.

(2.) Infallible.

(3.) Adapted to man's condition.

(4.) Designed for his illumination, holiness and salvation.

(5.) Perfectly sufficient ; and,

(6.) Given for man's present comfort and final blessedness.

Notice,

**II. The Psalmist's great aim and desire.**

"To keep it."

1. For constant *reading* and *meditation*.

2. For *daily application*. As food, medicine, armoury.

3. To keep it in its *original purity*. Unalloyed, undiluted, unperverted.

4. To keep it in *grateful memory*.

5. To keep *all* the Divine word.

6. To keep it *always*, and not to let it slip.

7. To keep it in a *loving heart* and with a *teachable spirit*. See,

**III. What the Psalmist states for the retention of the Divine word.**

Soul—life, &c. "Let my soul live."

1. A living soul only can *know* or *value* it.

2. A living soul only can *use* it.

3. A living soul only can *enjoy*, and *profit* by it.

4. And this life God must *bestow* and *sustain*.

5. This life must be sought by *earnest prayer*. God the Fountain, the Father, the Source and Spirit of life. He quickens the soul into life—He resuscitates, blesses, sanctifies, and ennobles the life He gives. So we see the appropriateness of the text, and its importance to all God's people.


PRACTICAL QUESTIONS

1. Is God's Word precious to us?

2. Do we seek its indwelling in our hearts?

3. Do we see the connection of this with soul life?

4. And do we devoutly pray for it?

## LXXXIV

## DIVINE OPERATIONS IN THE SOUL

"He hath torn, and he will heal us; he hath smitten, and will bind us up."—HOSEA vi. 1.

THE text, independently of its original application, exhibits the processes of the Spirit of God in the souls of His people. There are the two experiences, of being torn and smitten, and being healed and bound up. Let us look at the subject in this light of inward experience.

Observe,

I. The antecedent state supposed.

A state of self-righteousness, or unconsciousness of evil, self-satisfaction, self-sufficiency, contentment with the natural, the carnal. No convictions, no anxieties, no fears, no desires after God or godliness. A state of insensibility, and therefore unconcern. See,

II. The representation of Divine conviction.

"He hath torn." "He hath smitten."

1. There is the *tearing* away of the *films* from the eyes. Flashes of light into the soul. Opening the blind eyes. Tearing away the veil from the infatuated heart.

2. The *tearing* away the *garment* of *self-righteousness*. By the exhibition of its folly and filthiness.

3. The *tearing* away of *vain delusions*. About other means of access to God, &c.

4. The *tearing* open the *wounds* of the *conscience*, which have been falsely healed, or covered over as though healed. Then,

5. There is the *smiting* of conscience by the word and spirit of God. We see this smiting in the multi-

tude; Acts ii. 37. Of Saul; Acts ix. 1-6. This smiting
may come in connection with severe chastenings, personal afflictions, or public judgments.

**III. We have exhibited the Divine healing and binding.**

1. See the *order* described. Tearing and smiting
preceding the healing, &c. A knowledge of sin—a
conviction—a feeling sense—and remorse, &c. Notice,

2. The *author* is the *same* in *both*. God convicts and
converts—arouses and delivers—tears and binds—breaks
down and builds up—all by the same Divine spirit of
God.

3. The *agencies* are *often* the *same*. Providence and
humiliation—the word and the ordinances. Now the
declaration of the text is,

1. One of *certainty*. He will do both. He does this
most really and truly. He does not fail in doing it.
The subject is,

2. One of *great comfort*. God does not tear to destroy
—but to heal. He does not smite to kill—but to save.

3. This is in *harmony* with the Divine *nature* and *perfections*. It is the result of His essential goodness,
mercy, grace, and compassion. It is His delight to do
so, it is paternal love, Divine clemency.

### APPLICATION

1. The subject should lead to personal examination.
2. To deep submission before God.
3. To entire faith and confidence. And should,
4. Produce real and abounding gratefulness and love.

## LXXXV

## THE HAND OF THE LORD

" Behold, the Lord's hand is not shortened, that it cannot save ;
neither His ear heavy, that it cannot hear."—ISAIAH lix. 1.

GOD is a spirit.  He hath, therefore, no parts ; no material organs, as face, as eyes, ears, feet, or hands.
These indicate to us that God observes, beholds, knows,
hears, goeth forth, or exercises His knowledge and wisdom and skill, and then His hands are used symbolically.  Now let us see how the hand of the Lord is
spoken of.  We are directed—

**I.—To His creating hand.**

So " the Heavens," &c., are the works of God's hand.
So man, thy hands have fashioned me as the potter ;
Jer. xviii. 1, &c.  He laid the foundations of the earth.
He formed the dry land, and the sea is His, &c.  Now this
hand of God is glorious in power.  Strong is thy hand,
high thy right hand ; Psalm cii. 25 ; xcv. 3, &c.

**II.—There is His sustaining hand.**

Psalm xcv. 4, &c.  Job xii. 10.  Psalm xxx. 24.  " So
he keepeth all his bones."  Then,

**III.—There is the delivering hand of God.**

Exod. xii. 3, and in contrast none can deliver out of
His hand ; Acts vii. 25.  In reference to Moses and
Israel,

**IV.—There is the governing hand of God.**

Isaiah xl. 10, &c.  " My times," &c.

**V.—There is the supplying hand of the Lord.**

Psalm civ. 28.  " These all wait," &c.  " Thou openest
Thine hand."  They are filled with good ; Psalm cxlv.
15.  Satisfiest,

**VI.**—There is the prospering hand of the Lord.

Nehemiah and his co-workers felt the importance, &c. of this; Ezra vii. 9; Nehemiah, ii. 18. So Ezekiel xxxiii. 22. So in reference to the Lord's work; Acts xi. 21. So the Psalmist prayed that God would prosper the work of their hands, &c.

**VII.**—There is the renewing hand of the Lord.

2 Chron. xxx. 11. "God worketh in you," &c.; Philip. ii. 13.

**VIII.**—There is the leading and guiding hand of the Lord.

"Thou shalt guide me, &c.; Psalm lxxiii. 24; xliv. 3.

**IX.**—The chastening hand of the Lord.

Job entreats the pity of his friends. For the hand of God hath touch me; xix. 21.

So Peter exhorts—humble yourselves under the mighty hand of God, that He may exalt you in due time; 1 Peter v. 6.

APPLICATION

The subject demands the acknowledgement and adoration of God.

Trust and confidence in His wisdom, goodness, and power.

Recognition of the Lord by constant prayer.

Praise and rejoicing.

For his good hand. Entire dependence.

The all-sufficiency of God's hand.

For every good we need.

## LXXXV

## HAND OF JESUS

" Behold, the hand of the Lord is upon thee."—ACTS xiii. 11.

WE referred in a former discourse to the hand of the Lord. The declaration put by the prophet is a most important one, "Not shortened that it cannot save." Now the saving hand of God is put forth in His Son, the Lord Jesus Christ. A reference to His hand during His wondrous life, will be most suggestive to us. Now, in looking at the hand of Jesus, behold,

**I. His healing hand.**

1. In restoring the leper; Matt. viii. 3; Luke v. 13.

2. In curing the fever of Peter's wife's mother; Matt. viii. 14.

3. A group of the afflicted; Luke iv. 40.

**II. Behold His life-giving hand.**

1. Ruler's daughter; Matt. ix. 25.

2. Widow's son; Luke vii. 14.

**III. Behold His kindly hand and the little children.**

"He laid His hands on them," &c.; Matt. xix. 13.

**IV. Behold the delivering hand of Jesus.**

Peter on the sea. The storm. Began to sink—and immediately Jesus stretched forth His hand, &c.; Matt. xiv. 26-30.

**V. Behold the ministering hand of Jesus.**

Christ came to minister. To wait upon—to serve. Striking instances with His disciples. John xiii. 4, &c. As our model; v. 15.

**VI. Behold His supplying hand.**

Two striking forms. The loaves and fishes, &c. Multiplied, &c. The sacrament. The bread and the wine. Blessed—gave—sanctified. The symbols of His body and blood.

**VII. Behold the preserving hand of Christ.**

How are His people kept, holden safely, &c. His servants—the pastors—the stars are in His right hand; Rev. i. 16. But likewise all His people—My sheep; John x. 27.

**VIII. Behold the blessing hand of Jesus.**

He has died, &c., risen—going away to His kingdom and glory. He stands on Olivet, &c.—His disciples gaze, &c.—"And He lifted up His hands and blessed them;" Luke xxiv. 50, 51.

Then, last of all,

**IX. Behold His crowning hand.**

His mediatorial reign is over—He comes to receive His saints. Now is realized the hopes of untold myriads. Paul alludes to it; 2 Tim. iv. 7, &c. So the promise; Rev. ii. 10.

### APPLICATION

1. Faith connects us with Christ's hand in all its operations. Healing, helping, &c.

2. Our best interests are secure, for they are in Christ's hand.

3. The great hope will be attained—"the crown."

4. What confidence, love and praise are due to Jesus.

## LXXXVI

## LOVELINESS OF CHRIST

" Yea, he is altogether lovely."—Song of Solomon v. 16.

THERE is only one being to whom the words of the text are fully applicable, and that is " Jesus." It is the design of Holy Scripture to set this forth. The Gospel is the mirror exhibiting all the loveliness of the Saviour —reveals Him as full of grace and truth. So ministers must labour thus to make it known—"we preach Christ." Ordinances also symbolize it.

Observe,

### I. In what the loveliness of Christ consists.

1. In His *essential* glory. We beheld His glory,—the glory of the only-begotten of the Father; John i. 14. A glory Divine, as one with the Father—higher than that of angels, &c.—Burst forth at His transfiguration; Matt. xvii. 2.

2. In His *absolute* purity. The holy child—the holy Son—the holy High Priest. No sin in His nature, attributes, life. "Which of you convinceth me of sin?" No guile, &c.

3. In the *perfection* of His goodness. Love was the essence of Christ—His life—His mission—His words— thoughts—His nature and His name, &c. So bright, changeless, universal, infinite—"To know the love of Christ," &c.

4. In the *symmetry* and *perfection* of His graces. Not distinguished for one, but all—meekness, patience, gentleness, pity—all in harmony and perfection.

5. In all the *actions* of His life. Not one flaw—not one weakness—never erred—all goodness, and always. Came into the world with an anthem which expressed it—left it with prayers for the world's salvation.

Observe,

### II. The universal declaration of Christ's loveliness.

"Altogether." Look at this,

1. As *compared* with the *best* of *men*. Adam was lovely—the first created in the image of God—but he betrayed his trust—wrecked the vessel of humanity.

Noah—how elevated, &c. The one great living preacher of the old world, &c.—but his frailties, &c. Abraham —the great and illustrious father; but he succumbed— spots on the disc of that great sun. Moses—the learned, magnanimous, meek, devout; but he erred, &c. So all the *élite*, David, Solomon. All their excellencies are in an infinite degree in Christ, without their defects, &c.

2. Nothing *unlovely* in Christ. Examine, test, take the moral microscope and apply it—not one element of the unlovely.

3. No *loveliness wanting* in Christ. Not only no evil, but no want of the lovely. Try to find out one defect, any thing that would have added lustre, grace, virtue, &c. All the beauties of the universe were in Him, and in "perfection."

4. All *loveliness* in Christ was in an *infinite degree*. No limited excellencies—no small features—all grand and glorious.

5. He was *always lovely*. No change—the sun is not always full-orbed—the seasons alter, but Jesus was ever lovely. As the holy infant—as the holy youth—as the teacher—as the example in all His life, even when bathed in bloody sweat. As persecuted, when tried, condemned, dying, rising, ascending, &c. Now at the right hand, &c.

6. He is, to all His people, *altogether lovely*. Abraham desired to see His day. David sang and played on his harp in sweet prophecy—"Thou art fairer," &c.; Psalm xlv. 2. Isaiah soared and predicted, &c. To Him all the prophets gave witness, &c. So John the Baptist; so the disciples; so in all ages. Ye confessors, martyrs, holy reformers, living saints, dying disciples, &c. No exception—not "one," each, all, every one.

7. He is *altogether lovely* to the holy angels. How

they are mixed up with His coming, working, suffering, resurrection, ascension. "They sing the wonders of the Lamb," &c.

8. He is *altogether lovely* to His heavenly Father. At His baptism and transfiguration; "This is My beloved," &c.; see John xii. 27, 28; xvii. 25, 26.

9. He will be *transcendantly lovely* at His second coming. As conqueror, as prince, as judge, as the resurrection, &c. His own glory, His Father's, the holy angels, &c.

10. He will be *altogether lovely* in His heavenly kingdom for evermore. The one visible object of worship—the one sun—the one tree of life—the one subject of eternal praise; Rev. v. 9-14.

### APPLICATION

1. Is Christ lovely to us—to the eye of faith?

2. Can we adopt the language connected with the text—"This is My beloved?" &c.

3. To all, Christ desires to reveal His love and grace

4. At His table we renew our impression of His Divine loveliness.

## LXXXVII

## THE WORLD'S SAVIOUR

"The Saviour of the world."—1 John iv. 14.

Jesus, the Son of God, is the illustrious person spoken of in the text. He was with the Father and dwelt in His bosom, and the Father in due time, sent Him forth to be the Saviour of the world.

**I. What Christ is.**

"Saviour." So His name signifies—so prediction pronounces—types and sacrifices had all declared or foreshadowed His name, offices, work, life, death, resurrection, ascension, intercession, are all connected with His designs as Saviour. His incarnation, temptation, sufferings, and crucifixion, were essential to His great work as Saviour. He is Saviour from guilt, condemnation, pollution and the wrath to come. In one word, He is Saviour from sin and all its influences and results. He is the Divine Saviour—the great Saviour—the only Saviour; and He is able and willing to save the chief of sinners.

II. The extent of Christ's influence as the Saviour.

"The world." Kosmos. Not one section, or nation, but the world, including every man.

1. In His *assumption* of *humanity*. He is the Brother —Redeemer of all humanity.

2. In His *offices*. They are for the benefit of all men. Prophet and Teacher for all—Priest and Sacrifice for all —King and Ruler over all.

3. In His *death* and *resurrection*. He died and rose again for all. Ransom, propitiation, &c., for all.

4. His *Gospel* is for the *whole world* and *every creature*.

5. He can *save* to the uttermost every *class* of *sinners.*

6. He will finally *subdue* the *world* to Himself, and *destroy* the *works* of the *devil*. Such then, is the Lord Jesus Christ as "The Saviour of the world."

1. We see what we are to *preach*. To limit Christ and to circumscribe His saving work is to dishonour Him, rob Him of His glory, and is the direst cruelty to souls.

2. To *receive* Christ is *essential* to the realization of His saving grace.

3. *Rejection* of Christ is black *unbelief* and terrible soul *suicide*. For there is no other Saviour.

## LXXXVIII

### FILTHY LUCRE

"For filthy lucre's sake."—Titus i. 11.

Money in itself is a good, a great good, a necessary good, so good that it answereth all things. But perverted, idolized, it becomes the curse of the soul and the root of all evil. The text refers to false teachers, Mammonites, who teach things they ought not, and they do it for filthy lucre's sake.

**I. When is lucre filthy?**

Not in itself, but,

(1.) When basely obtained, as in the text.

(2.) When basely estimated as the chief good.

(3.) When basely used for purposes of evil.

**II. The evils connected with filthy lucre.**

It defiles all it touches, the hands that handle it, the mouth that speaks of it, the heart that loves it. It casts down God, and becomes the idol of the soul, carnalizes the mind, encrusts the spirit with the earthly. It is the source of untold vices and crimes and woes.

Then we ask,

**III. How we shall be saved from it?**

(1.) By having the heart filled with heavenly treasure.

(2.) By possessing the true spirit of faith in God—as Moses, &c.

(3.) By imitating our Divine self-denying Lord.

(4.) By ever seeking the things that are above.

(5.) By remembering the temporary evanescent character of all worldly good. In Christians, how odious is the spirit of love to filthy lucre—in ministers and pastors how indescribably degrading.

## LXXXIX

## THE INIQUITOUS BABYLON

" MYSTERY, BABYLON THE GREAT, THE MOTHER OF HARLOTS AND ABOMINATIONS OF THE EARTH."—REV. xvii. 5.

WHAT a true and graphic picture of anti-christian Rome and its mysteries and abominations, fitly represented,

**I. As Babylon—Babylon the great.**

With earthly pomp, grandeur, wealth and historic glory, known and recognized by the kingdoms of the earth—with its gross, sensuous idolatry. But it is,

**II. Mystery.**

Full of marvels and lying wonders—human mysteries exalted as Divine. Prostrating reason—exalting carnal institutions, &c.—Purgatory—papal power and glory—transubstantiation. Priestly domination, angelic, saintly, and Maryolic idolatry. One vast, dark, delusive, servile mystery.

**III. The mother of harlots.**

False doctrines and dogmas are spiritual fornication—worship of saints, &c.; every species of spiritual whoredom defiles this Babylon.

**IV. The source of the abomination of the earth.**

Abominable theological dogmas—modes of worship—superstition and mental debasement, teaching all sorts of venial trickery and lies and blasphemy and persecution—darkness and bloodshed—oppression and destruction—crushing out human intellects, individualism and self-respect, and blasting the aspirations and hopes of mankind. Every abomination that ever defied God or cursed man is to be found in "this Babylon the Great."

1. Rejoice that her doom of destruction must be near at hand; see chap. xviii.

2. The cross is the antidote to the crucifix, and Christ the one high priest, is in antagonism to the pope and all the high pompous ecclesiastics of mystical Babylon. So the living word of God shall smite and destroy it.

3. Her overthrow shall be the jubilee of the world; see chap. xviii. 20, &c.


## XC

## THE OPENED EAR

" He openeth also their ear to discipline," &c.—JOB xxxvi. 10.

SPIRITUAL deafness as well as blindness, is one of the diseases of the soul. Men will not hearken to the Divine voice within, or to the voice of God's glorious works, or to the voice of revealed truth, but by stubborn unbelief reject the counsel of God against themselves, so that, in order to the conversion of men, the ear must be opened, and attention given to the things of the soul.

Notice,

I. Scripture reference to this deafness of the soul.

Like all inward moral evil it is traceable to our apostacy and corruptness and unwillingness to hearken to God. The subject is one of constant notice in the Divine Word. Pharaoh would not hear Moses and Aaron; Exodus vii. 16. So Israel would not hear Moses, but acted with sinful presumption again and again; Deut. i. 43; see 2 Kings xvii. 14; xviii. 12; so Neh. ix. 29; Isaiah xxviii. 12. Unrenewed sinners and prostrated backsliders, alike refuse to hear, even when God speaks. Hence the appeals made—" O earth, earth, earth, hear the word of the Lord"—"hear and your

souls shall live," &c.—"If any man hath ears to hear,"
&c. These representations abound in Scripture, showing the deafness of men with regard to holy things. See,

**II. How the ear that has been deaf is opened.**

Sometimes this is done,

1. By *extraordinary means.* An instance is given;
chap. xxxiii. 16., in reference to the dream and vision of
the night, &c.

2. By *disciplinary means.* As in the text, where discipline is stated as the agency employed—often by the
discipline of poverty, afflictions, bereavements, judgments, &c. A home calamity—a storm at sea—direful
visitations. Hence the rod of discipline breaks through
the deafness of the soul.

3. By the *proclamation* of the *truth.* The voice of the
prophet, the Baptist, the Saviour, the apostle, the
evangelist—even the dead dry bones in the valley of
visions heard the prophesying of the prophet Ezekiel.

4. By *spiritual operations* in the soul. In this way the
mind is aroused, quickened, and a way of access opened
for the truth, and the ear effectually opened for its
reception.

Then notice,

**III. The results arising from the opening of the deaf ear.**

1. *Attention* to *Divine things.* Now recognized—pondered—heed given to them, &c.

2. *Submission* to the *Divine authority.* God acknowledged—soul contrite—bowed down, &c.

3. *Obedience* to the *Divine demands.* This involves
faith, repentance, and turning to the Lord to do His
gracious will.

4. *Rejoicing* in the *Divine ways.* As the baptized
Eunuch—as the people of Samaria, who heard and received the Gospel.

In conclusion, observe,

1. Moral deafness is a crime as well as a calamity. Men can close their eyes and ears against God and His truth.

2. Opening the ear is God's gracious work.

3. He seeks to do this to all who place themselves in an attitude of attention.

## XCI
## THE OPENED EYES

"I send thee, to open their eyes," &c.—ACTS xxvi. 17, 18.

THE analogy between the bodily senses and the mental and moral faculties is most striking. The soul has its organs of vision as well as the body—there are spiritual eyes as well as natural, and to these our subject refers. Let us then consider, in reference to the text,

I. **The condition supposed.**

Eyes closed—blind—in moral and spiritual darkness. Now this blindness,

1. Is *natural*. Man's normal condition—he is so from his birth—the result of his fallen and depraved condition. Like the young man in the Gospel—blind from birth.

2. This *darkness* relates to all *spiritual things*. To God and His attributes—to the Divine law and its claims—to man's carnal and evil nature—to the Gospel and the claims of Christ. In one word, to all things connected with the spiritual and Divine. See it fully stated; 1 Cor. ii. 11, &c.

3. This *blindness* is *obvious* in the character and life. The thoughts and words and conduct evidence this blindness, this want of holy, saving light.

4. This *blindness* is a *condition* of *wretchedness* and *peril*.

How pitiable natural blindness, how much more the darkness of the soul. The fruit is bitter—the end death.

5. It is *incurable* by *human agency*. Learning of any kind, philosophy, science, art, have all failed—the world with all its wisdom knew not God, nor the way of peace, nor of the world to come—that is clearly and distinctly true.

Now see,

**II. The Divine instrumentality for opening blind eyes.**

1. There is the *living agent*. " I send thee." Paul the apostle—the preacher—he raises up the ministry of the Gospel for this end—for this work.

2. There is the *word* of *light* and *power*. The Gospel, God's word is the omnific fiat, commanding light to be, and removing the darkness of the soul. See how expressly it is stated; 2 Cor. iv. 4, 6. " The entrance of the Divine word giveth light," &c.

3. The *enlightening influence* is of the *Spirit* of God. The Holy Spirit takes away the films, gives to the sightless eye-balls power to see, and then floods the soul with the saving knowledge of the Lord Jesus Christ. He takes of the things of Christ, and makes them evident and saving to the soul. We have this threefold agency in all spiritual work; the Gospel, the preacher and the essential power of the Holy Spirit—or the Holy Spirit doing this gracious enlightening work by the ministry of the Gospel.

APPLICATION

Let the subject lead,

1. To an appeal to all present as to their condition of blindness or sight.

2. To the preacher as to his obvious work, to open blind eyes.

3. As to the progress of the Church for this preaching of the Gospel, being crowned with the presence and power of the Holy Ghost.

## XCII

### THE UNDERSTANDING OPENED

"Then opened He their understanding," &c.—LUKE xxiv. 45.

OUR subject is connected with one of the most interesting narratives of the New Testament. The journey of the Disciples to Emmaus. Christ joining them by the way—their communication on the journey, &c. Then following this narrative is the record of Jesus again appearing to His Disciples, and His affecting address; and teaching as to the future work of His Disciples in preaching His Gospel to mankind; v. 47, &c. To enable them to do so fully and scripturally He referred to the testimony given of Him in the law and in the prophets and in the Psalms; and that they might clearly see this, and be able to learn it—"Then He opened their understanding," &c. The subject refers,

**I. To the understanding.**

That faculty of the soul by which we apprehend and clearly perceive the things presented to us. So that it is by this we have certified knowledge of truth revealed, and a perception of its nature and bearings and importance. Thus we understand God's teaching in His holy word—know it as presented—and comprehend it in its various bearings and importance. Notice, the text assumes,

**II. That good men do not always understand Divine things.**

The apostles often did not, even to the end of

Christ's life.  They did not perceive the meaning and bearing of what their prophets had written.  Were slow of heart, and dull of apprehension.  Did not know what Christ had taught about His kingdom, death, resurrection, &c.  So we see that the Eunuch did not understand what the prophet Isaiah meant in the passage he was reading.  So Apollos did not know the will and word so clearly, till taught by Aquilla and Priscilla.

**III.  That to have the understanding opened is most necessary and important.**

To save from ignorance, error, and superstition.  To comprehend the meaning of Scripture, and the way of salvation.  Our peace and comfort, as well as our spiritual safety, are here involved.

**IV. The Lord Jesus can open the understanding.**

It is His prerogative and work.  As in the text He did so often for His disciples.  He made man.  Knows him fully and perfectly, and therefore can restore to saving light, impart the saving power to the mind, and enable us to comprehend the blessed truth of His holy word.  As He gave sight to the blind in the days of His flesh, so now He is the source of spiritual light to the understanding of all His people.  So Saul's sight was given to him, &c.

Notice,

**V. The blessedness of an opened understanding.**

Without this we are in darkness, ignorant of God and the way of peace.  But with it we,

1. *Receive* the *true knowledge* of God and His Son Jesus Christ.  " We know both the Father and the Son."

2. We *perceive distinctly* the *way* of *salvation*.  This is a solace to the soul.  Hope to the spirit.  Satisfaction and joy in the Holy Ghost.

3. With this we have *access* to all the *treasures* of

*knowledge* and *wisdom*. All truths are ours. All brought from above. All Scripture is for our edification.

4. This is both our *security* and *well-being*. To have the light, walk in and by its cheering rays. This is the basis of all religious progress, &c.

This subject,

1. Should lead to enquiry—has our understanding been opened?

2. Are we conscious of its influence in our minds and character?

3. Are we increasing in all holy knowledge and wisdom?

4. The glory of this belongs to the Saviour—"He opened," &c.


## XCIII

## THE HEART OPENED

"Whose heart the Lord opened."—ACTS xvi. 14.

LYDIA was a pious Jewess, but ignorant of Christ and the Gospel; and so the Lord disposed, and gave her grace to receive the message of mercy, and thus she became a disciple of Jesus.

I. See the processes by which this change was effected.

1. Her providential visit to Philippi at this important juncture.

2. Her religious habit of life. Worshipped God—was disposed to Divine things and evidenced it.

3. She heard the apostle Paul on the subject of the Gospel.

4. She attended unto the things spoken. And thus,

5. The Lord, by His gracious Spirit, opened her heart for the reception of the love of Christ.

Notice,

**II. The evidences of this great change.**

1. Open profession of Christ by baptism; v. 15.

2. Her influence over her family; v. 15.

3. Her loving hospitality to the apostles. "Constrained us."

4. Her open house to the Lord's people; v. 40.

LEARN.

1. Lydia's character is most lovely, devoted and earnest.

2. All real religion begins with the heart, naturally closed against God and Divine things.

3. The Lord only, by His Spirit and grace, can open and then possess the heart.

4. The opened heart is full of love both of God and His people.

XCIV

## CHRIST'S MANY CROWNS

" And on His head were many crowns."—REV. xix. 12.

THE text is a brilliant star in a galaxy of celestial glory. The historical condition of the Church is being completed. Anti-christ hurled, &c.; chap. xviii. Jesus reverenced; v. 1, 2. Now the glory of Christ acknowledged and celebrated; v. 1. Anthem of universal praise; v. 5, 6. The beauty of the Church—the royal bride. Now heavenly splendours burst forth; v. 11. Now the majesty of the Saviour. Text.

Notice,

**I. The royal majesty of Jesus.**

This had been,

1. *Typified* under the *ancient economies*. Melchisedeck —David—Solomon.

2. Ministry *predicted*. Psalms and prophets. "I have set," &c. "Thy throne, O God," &c., and rule thou. Psa. cx. "Higher," &c. A righteous king shall reign, &c. "O Zion, thy king cometh," &c.

3. His *mediatorial work* is included in this. Set up a kingdom. Pilate. Born for this—Title on the Cross.

4. Look at the *apostolic testimony*. Peter says, "killed the Prince of Life," &c. Exalted to be "Prince and Saviour—Lord of all." Paul. 1 Tim. vi. 14. "See Jesus crowned with glory and honour," &c. Jude 15.

5. Apocalyptic *visions*. "The Prince of the kings of the earth." So on the white horse. "A crown" given. So on His vesture, &c. Then the climax of the text. Notice,

## II. The many crowns encircling His royal head.

His eyes omniscient—His mystical name, &c. One diadem with brilliant crowns around it. See the legitimate crowns which belong to Him.

1. The crown of *creation*. He once dwelt in the solitudes of eternity. John i. 3; Col. i. 16; Rev. iv. 11.

2. The crown of *universal dominion*. King of kings. All creatures—all kingdoms—all orders, &c. Eph. i. 20. All power, &c.—all dominion—all in His hands.

3. The *crown* of human redemption. World apostate. He came to restore—His great work. Most difficult of accomplishment. To dissipate darkness—roll away the curse—honour the law—bear the penalty—seek and save the lost. His incarnation. His life and toils, tears, agonies, cross, curse, resurrection, ascension.

4. The crown of *multitudinous* salvations. Foundation —message. Souls saved. Churches of the saved. Every nation. Exalted. A countless throng. At length His triumphs complete—Alleluia! "The kingdoms of this world," &c. Now the "many crowns." And,

5. The crown of *eternal* glory. Never dims, nor fades. His kingdom universal. His enemies His footstool. His glory filleth the earth and the heavens. "His name shall endure for ever," &c. Psa. lxxii. 17. Such the many crowns of the blessed Saviour. Learn the many weighty lessons the subject suggests. Observe, therefore,

(1.) The high and lofty sentiments we should cherish. Exaggerations—Hyperbolies impossible. The highest place of Name and glory are His. "All men honour the Son, even," &c.

(2.) Our personal interest in the Saviour's glory. Are we gems in His crown? Our Saviour—our Lord. Bow the knee. His glorious subjects.

(3.) Our sympathy with His progress and triumphs. Admiration—grateful joy—personal union and effort. Do we go forth with Him? &c. Our life-work for His glory.

(4.) What place shall we have at His final coronation? Be present with exceeding joy. Join in the glorious services. Sing the celestial songs. Unite in the loud ascriptions of praise.

## XCV

### "ALMOST"

" Then Agrippa said unto Paul, Almost thou persuadest me to be a Christian."—Acts xxvi. 28.

OUR text is connected with one of the finest narratives ever written. Look at the persons. The illustrious Paul—the royal Agrippa. The momentous occasion. The unfolding processes of the case. The earnest appeal, and then the candid admission—" almost," &c. The text is often misunderstood. It is not "almost a Christian"—but "almost persuaded."

Notice,

### I. To what the "almost" refers.

Almost persuaded to be a Christian. You must look,

1. At a *Christian* as it was *then understood*.

(1.) There were Pagans of various kinds and schools. Believers in many gods, &c.

(2.) There were Atheists. Non-believers in a personal deity, &c.

(3.) There were Jews of great variety. And now had recently sprung up,

(4.) Christians. The origin of the name is given. They had been called disciples, brethren, Nazarenes, &c. But at Antioch they were first called Christians.

Notice,

2. What the name *implied*.

(1.) Believers in Christ. (2.) Disciples of Christ. (3.) Worshippers of Christ. (4.) Followers of Christ. (5.) Lovers of Christ. (6.) Servants of Christ. (7.) Confessors of Christ. Now such were the "Christians;" and they had been converted from Judaism and Paganism. Nothing less than these seven points made the Christian. Every one necessary—essential, &c.

Now the text intimates,

### II. How men became Christians—"persuaded."

Notice,

1. None become Christians by *natural descent* or by *birthright*. It is not by a lineal process.

2. Nor by *compulsory* processes. Neither parental—educational, nor magisterial. Legal force must fail.

3. But men become Christians by *moral suasion.* Now moral suasion includes,

(1.) Knowing their errors. Acts xxviii. 23. Enlightenment. The removal of ignorance—darkness, &c.

(2.) Conviction of our evil—misery—peril.

(3.) Acceptance of the message and blessings of Christianity. Faith.

(4.) Consecration, &c. This suasion is that of knowledge, truth, and love.

Then see,

**III. The reasons of men being only "almost" persuaded.**

It may result from,

(1.) Misunderstanding. Not clearly apprehending Christian truth. False views, &c.

(2.) Prejudice as to Christianity. Its origin — its members—its institutions, &c.; or,

(3.) It may be from a rejection of its terms. The young man—the ruler—worldliness—pleasure—associations.

(4.) Latent indifference to real piety.

(5.) Or the spirit of procrastination.

(6.) Or substitution of something in its place. These are the general common reasons why suasion fails. So in Agrippa, &c.

APPLICATION

Learn,

1. How fatal this "almost" is. As where the "door" is just closed. The old adage is, "a miss is as good as a mile." A ship almost sound, and having only a leak, foundering. Only a vein ruptured, &c.—death.

2. How from this moral state, by all means, persons should emerge. Violently seize the kingdom of God.

3. That they should do so now.

4. Seek God's effectual grace for this end.

## XCVI

### "ALTOGETHER"

"And Paul said, I would to God, that not only thou, but also all that hear me this day, were both almost, and altogether such as I am, except these bonds."—ACTS xxvi. 29.

WE exhibited to you the "almost" persuaded Christian. The reply of Paul to King Agrippa was most pertinent and powerful; listen—"I would to God,"—how solemn and yet how benevolent—as I am, "except these bonds." A Christian in its dignities, privileges and blessings, without the degradation and suffering of bonds and affliction. Now Paul puts himself before Agrippa, both almost and altogether, "as I am, except," &c. No egotism in this—no vain-glory—no self-righteousness—it was clear, noble, manly, Christ-like. Paul was a model Christian, of the highest type—of the most exalted character. Let us see then, what special elements of "altogether" the Christian is composed.

It involves,

**I. Entireness of evangelical knowledge.**

To know God and Jesus Christ is essential; but clearness of knowledge—fulness of knowledge—completeness of knowledge—bright and unclouded, serene, distinct—of the excellency of knowledge of Christ Jesus.

**II. Invincible faith in the Lord Jesus.**

We know and believe. Faith, with its two hands laying hold,

1. On Christ's ability.

2. Christ's willinghood, or on power and grace. The eye of faith fixed on Christ—the foot of faith firm on the rock.

**III. A public and noble confession and profession of Christ.**

Not Nicodemus-like, but Paul-like; Acts ix. 20. So when Christ appealed to Peter—"Thou art the Christ," &c.—so the young blind man—"one thing I know." Now see how this confession is presented as the result of faith—if thou shalt believe; Rom. x. 9. So Christ—whoso shall confess Me before men. A personal, free, full confession of Christ—baptism was the symbol of confession—the mouth speaking, &c. This is all necessary to the altogether Christian.

#### IV. Supreme love to the Lord Jesus.

Peter had been presumptuous, had fallen, but repented and restored—and now what is the question—Simon, son of Jonas, "lovest," &c. How Paul loved Jesus—how it wrought in forsaking all for Christ—living, labouring, suffering, dying for Christ. So Jesus said—if any man love father, or mother, or wife, children, &c.

#### V. Full consecratedness to His service.

Rom. xii. 1. Altogether the Lord's—no part must be kept back—head, heart, hands, &c., body, soul and spirit. Now Paul was altogether—how entire—how wholly—fully, from the day of his conversion to the day he lay down his neck. "I have fought," &c.—ready to be offered up, &c. Now this altogether,

1. Is our safety.

2. Our joy.

3. Our usefulness.

4. Our glory. The Church needs this—the world—the Master.

#### APPLICATION

Observe,

1. This is sterling Christianity—genuine coin—current of Heaven.

2. No substitute for this.

3. Should be our high aim.

4. Grace provided—to attain to it, Christ must be altogether our sufficiency, &c.

## XCVII

### " OVERMUCH "

" Be not righteous overmuch."—ECCLESIASTES vii. 16.

THE text sounds strange, overmuch righteous—is it not impossible? Is it irony? Is it the language of an enemy, or of a formalist? Or what? We think it is to be considered literally, but with careful safeguards.

Let us see,

**I. What it cannot signify.**

1. It does not refer to our *justification* or *pardon*. These are entire, full, complete—no defect—addition— no *via media* between being justified and condemned— pardoned or being in guilt.

2. It cannot refer to the *righteousness* of *regeneration*. Regeneration is entire—begotten and born of God—the whole man—old man dead, new man complete—old things, &c., all become new.

3. It cannot refer to *sanctification* or *holiness*. Sanctification in body, &c.—holy in imitation and resemblance of God—no excess possible.

4. It cannot refer to *practical righteousness*. Honesty, justice, truth, &c.

5. It cannot refer to any part of the *Christian character*. The tongue, the heart, the spirit—see what God is to have—"thou shalt love," &c.—nor to man, "love thy neighbour," &c.

See then,

## II. What the text signifies.

1. It may signify the *attempt* at an *absolute perfection* here. Mystics, pietists, Methodists, have believed this —professed this—absolutely holy, so as to have no sin or sinful infirmity—nothing to lose or to gain—the goal of perfection reached—the end gained. See how different this to Paul; Philip. iii. 12, &c., two years before his martyrdom. Two classes of this kind—the Antinomian clothed with Christ's imputed righteousness—the evangelical Arminian concluding he has wrought it out.

2. It may signify extreme *scrupulosity* in doubtful *things*. In Sabbath observances—a day of gloom— weariness, &c.—In asceticism, meats and drinks, fasting, &c.

3. In *excess* with regard to *right* things. Services in the closet prolonged—as monks, nuns, &c.—in the family, tedious and extended worship—in the House of God—neglect of home and its duties—attaching grave importance to the times and length.

4. In *adding* to the Divine *claims*. As a Pharisee— mint, anise, &c.—exalting titles and non-essentials—in the penances of Romanism, &c.

5. In exalting certain parts of *religion* against *others*. Ordinances, creeds, modes of worship, &c., magnifying these as essentials.

6. In yielding *service* in a Pharisaic *spirit*. Measuring it, &c., with others, more righteous, &c.—boasting of attainments—liberality with ostentation—so alms-giving, &c.

### APPLICATION

Observe,

1. True religion is clearly defined.
2. The spiritual and real cannot be exceeded.

3. Humility, self-renunciation, &c., are the highest evidences of a healthy state.

4. Seek the real righteousness.


# XCVIII

## JESUS THE UNFAILING SAVIOUR

"He shall not fail."—ISAIAH xlii. 4.

THERE is no doubt as to the person of whom the text speaks; v. 1-4. See Matthew xii. 17, &c. The idea is, that he should not faint and give up his purpose and work, either through exhaustion or the power of his enemies. Now some say Christianity is a failure—others that it will never convert the world. We take the text as replying to both.—"He shall not fail." Now we take two standpoints to view the text.

**I. That occupied by the prophet himself.**

He lived and wrote some 700 years before Christ's time. So his predictions had to cover that space as well as all that was written concerning Him. From Isaiah's standpoint,

1. He shall not *fail*. To appear as the promised and predicted Messiah. From the fall He had been promised. Renewed to Abraham—Isaac—Jacob—Moses—David— Solomon. Law—Psalms—prophets. Well, all had to be fulfilled. He did not fail as to time—place—. manner.

2. In the great *offices* and *work* He would *fulfil*. Teacher—prophet—priest and Lord, all exhibited in Him.

3. In the *opposition* and *sorrows* of His life. In reference to His poverty—abasement—rejection. Nazareth

malignant—calumny—hatred—blood, &c., thirsted for.
Then the culmination of the whole—desertion—betrayal
—arrest—trial—death. Not fail,

4. To *survive* and *set up* His kingdom. Hence His
resurrection. Preached in Jerusalem. Reign in the
midst of His enemies. Triumphs of His grace.

5. First Church not *fail*. To extend His victories
among the Gentiles. The commission. Judaism—
Samaria—all the Roman empire. Success everywhere
—in Rome, &c. One event of interest, Julian the
apostate. His death—exclamation. Three hundred
years have run their round. Now Christianity is more
widely spread—more converts than ever.

Now let us take our stand,

**II. In our own age, and see some reasons for reiterating the
declaration of the prophet—" He shall not fail."**

1. He shall not *fail* to *overcome* all the *opposition* of
His enemies. None more bitter than the past, or more
formidable. The whole Roman empire against 120
feeble Christians. Recent victories. Fiji—South Sea
Islands—Madagascar.

But He shall not fail,

2. To attain to *universal* dominion. All men bless
Him, and be blessed in Him. Have all dominion. All
know Him. The kingdoms of this world, &c. Now
the grounds of this are manifold. Take a few—

1. The Divine covenant. Seems exhibited; Isa. liii.
10 and 11 : and in connection with this, Philippians ii. 6.

2. The Divinely renewed prophecies and declarations
—to Moses—to David. Psalm ii. 6 ; lxxii. 17 ; Habak.
ii. 14.

3. To the *efficacy* and *sufficiency* of the Divine Gospel.
Power of the Spirit. To look,

4. At the *impossiblity* of Christ's *failure*.

1. As the Divine.　The Divine cannot.
2. As the true, &c.
3. The omnific.　The Almighty cannot.
4. The unchanging, &c., cannot.
5. The Divine purpose and glory.

See the converse of all these—

1. Failure of Christ would be the triumph of ignorance.
2. Of superstition.
3. Of malevolence and evil.
4. Of satan and hell, over Jesus and heaven.

### APPLICATION

1. The world has been full of failures.　Philosophers —founders of religion, &c.
2. Christ never fails to be all that sinners need.
3. Labourers have reason to work, &c., in hope.
4. How futile all opposition.
5. Emmanuel's victories will be sung for ever.

## XCIX

## JESUS EXCLUDED

"There was no room for them in the inn."—LUKE ii. 7.

THE incident mentioned by the Evangelist, in the text, is both striking and instructive.　Divine providence secured the birth of the Saviour in the place the prophets had foretold.　The bread of life must be found in Bethlehem—the House of Bread.　David's son, as well as root and Lord, must be identified with David's city. But Joseph and Mary reside at Nazareth, and hence the poll tax, which required all to be enrolled in their own city, renders it indispensable that they journey to Bethlehem, where Christ is to be born; v. 1-3.

Now let us look,

**I. At the illustrious travellers.**

Joseph and Mary. Their record is brief; chap. i. 27. Matt. i. 18. The account given of Joseph is short but significant—"a just man." A man of religious integrity. The discovery. Mary's condition is stated; chap. i. 18. His anxiety to preserve her reputation; v. 19; and then the mission of the angel to him; v. 20. This testimony he accepted, and hence the marriage union was completed; Matt. i. 24. Mary the honoured mother of Jesus—the most exalted of women. Like Joseph, was of the royal line of Judah; and now was near the time of her delivery.

Notice,

**II. The journey they took.**

From Nazareth to Bethlehem. In the circumstances of Mary's cirtical condition, it was a journey of considerable risk and difficulty. The distance would be probably about seventy miles. How accomplished is not stated. Most likely with the family ass. Mary riding and Joseph walking by her side. In this journey they would pass by places of deep interest to the pious Jew. In sight of Tabor, Nain, Shunam, Sychar, Shiloh, Bethel, and would most probably pass through Jerusalem, and then on to Bethlehem. At length they reach the end of their journey. Probably great numbers might be arriving for the same purpose, and, therefore, this may account for,

**III. No place of suitable reception.**

"No room for them in the inn," or caravansery, a large building, without furniture, open to all travellers, where they were sheltered from the open air, and where they ate and slept, having their food and cooking utensils with them. This place was pre-occupied, and, therefore, they had to retire to the outer buildings, erected for the horses and mules, &c. Here Mary was delivered—Jesus born—and his first cradle the manger. Now it will be seen Christ's exclusion from the inn was purely accidental, and not designed, though it contains important lessons for us.

Now let us see these various lessons,

**IV. The subject supplies.**

1. The *miraculous condescension* of the Son of God.

Think of his dwelling in the bosom of the Father—on the throne of glory, with the acclaim of angels, and the infinite honours of Divine majesty, and then his descent into our world, and becoming the reputed son of a carpenter, and the real child of Mary. The journey of his parents, how significant of the great design of Christ's advent, to seek and to save the wanderers and the lost.

2. Christ's *exclusion* from the inn exhibits the *moral condition* of *men* in *general*.

The world makes room for its own. For trade and merchandize—for worldly pursuits—for mammon and pleasure—for dignity and honours, and for the service of sin. Heroes, philosophers, scientists, warriors, are all welcomed and to the chief places; but Jesus is excluded, crushed out, to take a place with the inferior creatures, in the stable.

3. Here, however, we gather *hope* for the *lowest condition* of our race.

Few of the rich or *élite*, ever come near Christ; but He went to the poor, and the common people welcomed Him gladly. The self-righteous Pharisees only just bore with Him, and treated Him with proud contumely and bitter persecution; but publicans and harlots wept, repented, and accepted Him joyfully. Jesus came to the lowest stratum of society—to the outcasts; and He did eat with them, and showed the deepest sympathy and mercy.

4. Exclusion of Jesus *must* be *followed* by *lamentable results*.

When this is wilfully done, how heinous the sin, and how inevitable the doom. Men can reject Christ, but how fearful the consequence,—let Capernaum sunk down to hades, testify,—let desolated Jerusalem bear witness. Surely our Brother, Friend, Saviour, Curse-bearer, Lord, and Master, should have the best and warmest reception into our hearts and homes; or we may be excluded from His presence and glory at His second coming.

5. How Christ's humiliation and griefs should reconcile us to the *trials* and *sorrows* of this *earthly life*.

Like Him, sojourners. Often in poverty—persecution —neglected—despised—cast out. But if we suffer with Him, we shall also reign with Him, and be glorified together. We must bear His Cross, if we would wear His Crown.


## C

## CHRIST THE EVANGELICAL MINISTER

" Jesus came into Galilee, preaching the Gospel of the kingdom of God."—MARK i. 14.

CHRIST came to fill a variety of offices. He came to be a sympathizing Priest. To be the Friend of the outcasts, &c. To be the Teacher of the people. To be an example of purity. To reveal God His Father. To do good to the poor. But He came also to be the great evangelical preacher of the Gospel. So the text. Let us look,

## I. At the preacher—"Jesus."

Saviour. God had sent various preachers—Noah, Moses, Aaron and the priests, Samuel and prophets, Ezra and the Scribes, John the Baptist. But Jesus differed from all others in several respects.

1. He was *Divine.* From God, of God, one with God, the Divine Son of God. Higher than the children of men, than angels—others are merely human, He was both human and Divine, a Teacher and Preacher sent from God. So He was omniscient, saw into the heart, &c.

2. He was *infallible.* As Divine, this follows. He knew all things—did not, could not err. All He taught was pure, solid truth.

3. He was *most sympathetic.* Could read the griefs and agonies of His hearers, &c. Felt their anguish, as the nerves and brain the afflictions of the body. So Christ, with all poverty, sickness and sorrows of men. "Jesus wept" at the grave of Lazarus.

4. He was most *clear* and *simple.* "Common people heard Him gladly." The officers sent to take Him said, never man spake, &c.

5. He was most *interesting.* People hung on His lips. He was parabolical and pictorial in most of His discourses. Just look at the "woman seeking the piece," &c.—good shepherd looking for the wandering sheep—net and fisherman—leaven and meal.

6. Most *faithful* and *earnest.* His Sermon on the Mount—His often discourses to the Pharisees; Matt. xxiii.

7. He preached most *affectionately* and *tenderly.* One of His very last appeals—"O Jerusalem," &c. He wept over it, &c.

Observe in the text,

## II. His theme.

The Gospel—"Glad tidings" of the Messiah—the Saviour—the Shiloh.

1. He was the *subject* of His own *ministry*. His name Jesus—Himself the Saviour. We preach Christ, not ourselves. Christ did refer to Himself—prophets and priests did not, nor apostles, &c.; see John viii. 12. To the woman of Samaria—"I am He." He also,

2. *Proclaimed* the *kingdom* of God. The spiritual reign of God in Christ His Son. Not earthly nor secular —not temporal—but everlasting. The kingdom of righteousness, peace and joy, &c.

3. The near *approach* of this *kingdom*. He announced, saying, the time is fulfilled—the patriarchial time—the Mosaic—the prophetical; see Dan. iii. 44. The harbinger had come and was in prison, &c.; v. 14.

4. The *sphere* of His *ministry* at this time was Galilee. Palestine, divided into Judea, Samaria and Galilee— Galilee including Nazareth, Cana, Tiberias, Capernaum, Sea of Galilee—Christ chiefly here. Now the world is the field of the Gospel. "Go ye into all the world," &c.

Notice,

**III. The special appeal He made.**

Two things—

1. He *urged repentance*. Change of mind—think otherwise and feel otherwise—resolve otherwise—act otherwise. Turning from sin and towards God.

2. He *demanded faith*. "And believe the Gospel." The Gospel news must be heard and received as true— embraced as true. The heart opening to it—the soul accepting and resting and trusting and hoping for the realization of its blessings. Hear, see and accept, &c.

LEARN

1. We have the same Saviour.

2. The same Gospel—now complete by His resurrection and gift of the Holy Spirit.

3. Its blessings are ours on the same terms—repentance and faith. Go ye, &c. He that believeth.

4. Men perish by not believing the Gospel of Christ.

## CI

## THE HEALING TOUCH

"And Jesus said, Who touched me?" &c.—LUKE viii. 45.

THE whole scene around the text is graphic. An afflicted woman—fearfully diseased—hopelessly incurable—miserably helpless—absolutely insolvent—"spent all." But now providentially near to the all-sufficient Saviour. Now look at the crowd of people—waiting; v. 40. The rulers; v. 41. The throng, v. 42. Crowd pressing, &c. Now the poor diseased woman came behind, &c.; Matt. ix. 21. How she felt—what she said to herself. Now the question, "Who touched me?" &c. Observe,

I. The answer to the question.

"Christ knew." As in Peter's case. "Who?" &c. The question itself was not one of ignorance. He knew, &c., but it was to develope the woman's condition, and present her to His disciples and the people. "Who?" &c.

1. It was *darkness* coming to the *realm* of *light*. She had been in the cloudy region of science, &c. Now she rises to a higher plane of the spiritual, and the sun, &c.

2. It was *disease* in the *region* of *health*. Her disease is sad—disgusting—long. Now there has come the health-giver. The great physician. The infallible.

3. It was *weakness* recognizing the Divine *power*.

How weak—how abased—how helpless! But there is the incarnate power in Christ. The mighty Saviour.

4. It was *extremity* coming to the *fountain* of infinite *resources.* Powerless—moneyless—almost hopeless; but in her extremity she comes to the great fountain of riches. Ability—means, &c.

5. It was *self-abasedness* hiding itself *behind* the *Redeemer.* Does not rush—does not intrude—is not bold —does not clamour, but shrinks behind Christ—came trembling behind Christ, &c.

6. It was *extraordinary* faith realizing Christ's *graciousness* and *power.*

(1.) She did not think virtue was confined to His person.

(2.) Nor to His voice.

(3.) Or direct volition; but His vestment was permeated with it, even to the fringe, &c.

(4.) That the voltaic battery of mercy had only to be touched, and healing be received.

And now see,

7. *Humility* and *lowliness* obtaining their *reward.* Blessed are the poor, &c. Immediately she was healed —not slightly improved—but healed. Entirely—instantly, &c.

8. And then the *question elicits* the healer's *confirming testimony.* She explains and tells all; v. 47. And then Christ proclaims her touch, and bestows His peace; v. 48.

Now see,

**II. The lessons it suggests.**

1. We may *crowd* around Christ and *not* be the *better.* The multitude did this—do this now around ministers, ordinances, &c., and even mentally see and hear Christ, and yet no blessing.

2. *Individual contact* with the living Christ is *essential.*

Touch, preceded by a sense of misery, with longing desire, faith, &c. For ourselves—no one can do it for us.

3. The *spiritual vitality* of *true religion.* Not forms, ceremonies, creeds, but life.

4. The *true* and *full power* of *sympathy.* Christ came down full of it—surcharged with it—full of grace and truth. Touched with the feelings, &c. The connection of Christ and healing and salvation.

5. *Never* any *cause* for *despairing.* "*Nil desperandum.*" Look at this woman—all look and learn—all look and come—all look and touch. Let it be the touch of faith —not cold formalism—not superstitious ceremonials. "Faith, mighty faith," &c.

6. The *responsibility* of *men* to *come* to Christ and *touch* the Saviour. She came,

7. *Simplicity* of the *way* of *salvation.* Not prudence or self-righteous preparation, but with trust in Christ, and believing in His power and grace.

## CIII

### CHRIST'S EXCELLENT DOINGS

"He hath done all things well."—MARK vii. 37.

THE text explains itself—but the truth of it is of vastly wider scope.

I. It has a grand significancy in the creative works of Christ.

II. In His Divine government of this and all worlds.

III. Its climactaral glory belongs to redemption.

He undertook the world's redemption, and effected it, by

1. Obedience to the law.

2. Suffering the penalty for sin.

3. Conquering the powers of darkness.

4. Bringing life and immortality to light.

5. Obtaining the Holy Spirit.

**IV. In the salvation He obtained and bestows.**

An entire salvation of the whole man—a free salvation of sovereign grace—a salvation for the whole race—and a salvation to eternal glory. "He does all things well,"

**V. In the experience of His people.**

He sought and found them—He forgave and healed them—He renews and sanctifies them—He keeps and upholds them—and He glorifies them for ever. Ask the penitent believer—ask the tried Christian—ask the dying saint—ask the beatified in glory. All, all—no exception—exclaim "He hath done all things well." Therefore love Christ—trust in Christ—praise Christ—commend Christ to all—glorify Him with body, soul and spirit, which are His.

We see how heinous the sin that rejects Christ.

And how extreme the folly of any preference, to the exclusion of Him.

We see also Christ's glorious supremacy, above all creatures on earth or in Heaven.


## CIV

## THE DEVIL'S PALACE

"When a strong man armed keepeth his palace, his goods are in peace."—LUKE xi. 21.

IF the Gospels are true narratives and not myths, then they present to us the existence and influence of a foul, wicked and malignant devil. His kingdom, for he is a monarch, is described as one of darkness—his subjects as the wicked and unbelieving of mankind—his power as great and most destructive—his allies, the flesh and the world—and his palace as the human heart.

Let us have,

### I. A few words concerning his real personal being.

His personal being is stated again and again in both the Old and New Testaments. He is the murderer from the beginning—the father of lies—the deceiver of our first parents—the tempter of the Lord Jesus—the enemy of mankind—the god of this world—and the prince of the power of the air, &c. Now, if devil only signifies a personification of evil, it would not apply to,

1. Our *first parents*. They were holy, unfallen—Nor,

2. To *Christ*. For He had no sin. But he is represented as assailing Christ—quoting Scripture—being repulsed, &c. Against him we are warned. The provided armour described.

3. The *overthrow* of his *kingdom* is distinctly *predicted*, &c. Now as a fallen monarch—Christ speaks, and says, I saw Satan as lightning fall from Heaven. And John describes his final destiny; Rev. xx. 1, 2.

As a king,

### II. Satan has his palaces.

In all parts of his dominion. Satan's palace is the human heart. He dwells and reigns in the hearts of the disobedient. The rooms of this palace he suitably furnishes and occupies.

1. Look at the *room* of the *understanding*. This he darkens, keeps out the sun.

2. Of the *judgment*. This he perverts and shrouds with error.

3. The *room* of the *imagination*. He pollutes and fills with filthy monstrous forms.

4. The *room* of the *affections*. He occupies with carnal passions, &c.

5. The *room* of the *conscience*. He bolts and bars against the truth and knowledge.

6. The *room* of the *will*. He fills with weapons against God and goodness, and to alienate and carry on war against Heaven and holiness.

### III. The devil fortifies his palace by mighty power.

Strong "one" armed, &c. His mighty arms are,

1. *Ignorance.* Gross darkness of God, sin, &c.

2. *Prejudice.* Prejudging and preventing wise judgment.

3. *Superstition.* Making the earth a pantheon of false gods—Paganism, &c.

4. *Malignity.* Evil loving, hating, wrath, cruelty, destruction. So he is Apollyon the destroyer.

5. *Unbelief.* As he began with Adam and Eve—refusing the truth—rejecting the truth, &c. By the potency of these he keeps his palace and goods in peace.

See,

### IV. How he is dispossessed.

He is dispossessed,

1. By a *stronger* than himself. He potent, mighty. The stronger than he is Christ the Son of God—"for this purpose," &c. He is omnipotent, almighty—all power in Heaven and earth—power of God—the mighty God, &c.

2. Jesus did *cast him* out in the *extirpation* of the demons. Deaf, dumb, mad, legions, &c.

3. Jesus *does cast* him out *still*. Men are delivered—brought out of the kingdom of darkness, &c.

4. Christ *does this* by the *counter weapons* of his *kingdom*. Knowledge, truth, faith, goodness.

5. Christ *alone casts* out Satan. This is His special

work, committed to Him, and only by Him to be accomplished.

1. The degradation of the sinner—the palace of the devil.

2. The misery and woe of the sinner—he inherits to defile and destroy.

3. The hope of the sinner; see Matt. iv. 23. The true hope—the only hope.

4. The blessedness of the believer. Christ in the soul —the temple of Jesus—" Whom we preach," &c.


# CV
## GRAND OBJECT OF CHRIST'S MISSION

" For the Son of man is not come to destroy men's lives, but to save them."—LUKE ix. 56.

OUR text is part of a very affecting narrative—the bigotry of the Samaritans; v. 51, 2. The vengeance of the disciples; v. 54. The goodness and mercy of Jesus; v. 55. The great purpose of Christ's mission; v. 56. Now we take the text away from its connection. It is a subject complete in itself.

Observe,

I. The negative declaration of the text.

Christ came not to " destroy lives" of men. Two kinds. Natural and spiritual.

1. *Life* of the *body*. Precious in itself. Precious in its privileges—responsibilities. The seed time of the soul. Period of consideration—repentance—faith—salvation.

2. *Life* of the *soul*. Its spiritual existence. Its blessed

existence. Glorious existence for ever. Now the negative declaration of the text is, Christ came not to kill the body, nor destroy the soul. He never did so. Not one instance. He exhibited compassion—goodness—love—mercy. All His teaching—acts—miracles proved this, &c. Now there is,

**II. The positive declaration of the text.**

He did come expressly to save men's lives. Look at five announcements of this.

(1.) The angel of the Lord to Joseph; Matt. i. 21. "Call his name," &c. "He shall save," &c.

(2.) Christ himself. "God so loved," &c. Not sent to condemn. So the text.

(3.) Paul. "This is a faithful saying," &c.

(4.) Peter. "God having raised up Jesus, sent Him to bless you," &c.

(5.) John. "This we know and testify that the Father sent the Son," &c. Now observe,

1. How Christ came to save *men's lives*. By teaching the way of life. By being Himself the way, the truth, and the life. By offering them life. By dying that they might have life. By rising, and bringing life and immortality to light. By the specimens of His life-giving power and grace. He restored natural life in three instances. Maiden—widow's son—Lazarus. He gave spiritual life to many. To all His sheep—to all believers—to the dying thief. But see,

2. The *principle* which *regulates* Christ in *saving men's lives*.

(1.) Not partiality as to men's outward condition, or station, or learning.

(2.) Not to the morally excellent. "He came not to call the righteous."

(3.) Not to any nationality. Syrophenecian, woman

of Samaria. But to all believers. Looking to Him. Trusting in Him. Accepting Him. No other conditions.

Observe,

1. Christ and His mission the same.

2. The principles the same.

3. The power and willingness the same.

4. The ruin of men the same. "Ye will not come unto Me," &c.

## CVI

### THE CRUEL PURPOSE

" And destroy Jesus."—MATTHEW xxvii. 20.

IT would be concluded generally that moral beauty would be admired—excellency praised—goodness extolled. With the wise and good and holy, this would be so; but the evil hate the good, &c., and would crush it out. No one more lovely than " Jesus," and yet he was envied, hated, persecuted and crucified.

Observe,

### I. The efforts to destroy Jesus.

The first attempt was made by Herod; Matt. ii. 1; ii. 17. By the Nazarenes; Luke iv. 28. In the final conspiracy, hired Judas. Suborned and bribed false witnesses. Sent the soldiery to Gethsemane. Led Him to Caiaphas; v. 26; chap. xxxvii. Charged Him before Pilate; v. 27-1, &c. So the text. They so succeeded as to have Jesus tried—condemned—put to death. But Jesus revived—rose—and liveth evermore. So that He was not destroyed. His victorious exclamation—"I was dead, and am alive!" &c. Since then Jews, Pagans, Mohammedans, sceptics, have laboured to destroy Jesus. Some His very existence—others

His divinity—others His miracles, &c. All anti-believ-ers labour to destroy Jesus.

**II. Why have they sought to destroy Jesus ?**

1. Not on account of the *viciousness* of His life.
2. Nor His *opposition* to law and order.
3. Nor the *evil tendency* of His doctrines.
4. Nor the *injury* He did by His influence.

Hear the testimony of his betrayer; Matt. xxvii. 4. Hear Pilate; Luke xxiii. 14. Hear Pilate's wife; Matt. xxvii. 19. No, it was,

(1.) Enmity to truth.
(2.) Envy of His goodness.
(3.) Hatred of His person.
(4.) Love of wickedness.

So they tried to destroy Jesus.

Notice now,

**III. How they have failed to destroy Jesus.**

Herod failed. The Jews and Pilate, though they killed Him. But He verified His own teaching—"Fear not them that can kill the body," &c. He rose. He could not be holden, &c. He died a victim—He rose a conqueror. The haters and persecutors of all ages failed. He lived on, in His body the Church. Julian the apostate. French infidels abrogated the Sabbath—deified a harlot, &c. But Jesus was not destroyed. So the German infidels. English, &c. Shaftesbur y, Boling broke, down to Paine and Carlile and Strauss and Renan—but they could not destroy Jesus.

Jesus is the Divine, and cannot be destroyed. Jesus is the immortal light. Jesus is the eternal truth. Jesus is the unchanging good, &c. Jesus is the pure, immacu-late. Predictions say—"He shall live," &c. Psalm lxxii. 15-18. His titles—He is the Alpha and Omega, &c. "Same yesterday," &c. "King immortal." Keys

of death and hell He holds in His hand. But observe—
The enemies of Jesus shall be destroyed. Herod—
Pilate—the bitter priests—Julian—enemies lick the
dust, &c. So the future. The nation that will not
serve Him. Disbelievers, unbelievers—shall all perish.

## LEARN

1. The baseness of the human heart to try to destroy
Jesus.

2. Our obvious duty and interest to accept and honour Christ. He should have,

3. Our devoted and consecrated hearts and lives.


## CVII

## WITHOUT GOD

" Without God."—Ephesians ii. 12.

The text is true,

**I. Of the Atheist.**

Who says "No God." I know no God. I acknowledge no God. I worship no God.

**II. Of the Pantheist.**

He denies a personal God. He poetises, and by a
process of fiction, he makes the universe a Pantheon of
imaginary gods.

**III. The Deist admits a personal God.**

But is uncertified as to His nature, attributes and will.
So he is truly without God.

**IV. The Unbeliever.**

However he may concede a God, is personally without God. He neither worships, nor obeys, nor consults
Jehovah—so that to him, he is no God. Practically
without God.

**V. The mere Nominalist.**

May admit any or every creed; but in his understanding and affections he is without God. Such a state is deplorably wretched, and fearfully perilous.

# CVIII

## A CHRISTLESS CONDITION

"Without Christ."—EPH. ii. 12.

THE unbelieving Jews, equally with the idolatrous Gentiles, were in this condition. All disbelievers—all unrepentant sinners—all unbelieving rejectors of the Gospel, are in this fearful and wretched state. God has provided and sent forth a Christ, the Saviour of the world. But untold myriads are without Him.

**I. All ignorant of the Gospel.**

For Christ is revealed and brought nigh to us in the Gospel. But if we don't know the Gospel, we must be "without Christ."

**II. All in a state of impenitent sin.**

Christ is not felt as a necessity by such. A conscious feeling sense of sin is indispensable to our welcome of Christ.

**III. All self-righteous persons.**

Christ did not come to call the righteous, &c. Such are whole, and need not a physician.

They are rich—satisfied—building on their unvarying acceptance—obedience. Pharisaism is in direct collision with Christ and His work.

**IV. All who have not fled to Christ and accepted Him.**

Such are necessarily away from Christ and without Him. To be without Christ,

1. Is to be without light, and is a condition of darkness.

2. A state of condemnation, both by the law, and by conscience.

3. A state of imminent peril. No deliverance—no pardon—no peace—no salvation without Christ.

4. Such are to be exhorted and pressed to come to Christ, and to believe in His name.

## CIX

### HOPELESSNESS

"Having no hope."—EPH. ii. 12.

GODLESSNESS, and being without Christ, must result in "having no hope:" Without God there can be no hope. Without Christ there is for the sinner no hope.

To what,

**I. Does the text refer—"Having no hope."**

No well-grounded expectation of the Divine favour, or of life in the world to come. All the future a dark impenetrable mist—No foreshadowing of future glory.

**II. What are the signs of this condition.**

1. Darkness of mind.

2. Unbelief.

3. The servitude of sin.

4. Ungodliness of heart and spirit.

**III. The inevitable results of this state.**

1. Wretchedness of life.

2. Inward want and dissatisfaction.

3. Gloomy apprehensions of the future.

1. Then let the Gospel be faithfully presented to them.

2. Let them be urged to look to God in Christ, and thus receive the light of joy and hope into the soul.

3. A hopeless condition is a most foreshadowing of the despair and horrors of the second death.

## CX

## THE END OF FAITH

"Receiving the end of your faith, even the salvation of your souls."
—1 PETER i. 9.

WITHOUT faith it is impossible to please God. Faith is essential to pardon, holiness, eternal life.

Notice,

**I. The faith of the text—"Your faith."**

So it is clear that this faith,

1. Is evangelical. Faith in the Lord Jesus Christ, and in the Gospel of salvation.

2. It is saving. The end, the salvation of your souls. Much that is called faith is simply an acceptance of Scripture inspiration and authority, but recognizes no personal sinfulness, penalty or peril. Saving faith realizes guilt, deplores it, confesses it, and finds salvation in the person and work of the Lord Jesus Christ.

3. It is personal—"your faith." Not the creed of a sect, or the belief of a multitude, but the faith wrought in your heart, and exercised consciously in the Son of God.

Now, notice,

**II. The receptivity of this faith.**

"The salvation of your souls." This "receptivity" includes,

1. Justification and the remission of sins.

2. Acceptance with God.

3. Peace and joy in the Holy Ghost.

4. A renewed heart.

5. A good hope of immortality and eternal life. Now salvation includes these, all these, and nothing less.

Observe,

1. This salvation is God's free gift.

2. The result of Christ's offices and work.

3. Imparted by the Holy Spirit—and only,

4. Realizable by faith. Unbelief shuts the eye—closes the ear—hardens the heart—and refuses the mercy of Heaven. Faith looks to the Saviour, and in Him finds the salvation.

## CXI

### GOSPEL CHARIOT

" King Solomon made himself a chariot of the wood of Lebanon," &c.—Song of Solomon iii. 9, 10.

THE whole book allegorical. Many of its similies are most applicable to Christ—the Church, and the Gospel, &c. In this sense it has ever been precious to the Church. In any other sense, it would be simply an oriental love poem.

Now the text will give us some important views of the glorious Gospel, and its design as a magnificent chariot, to bring souls to the heavenly palace. In this application of the text,

I. **For Solomon we have the more glorious Saviour.**

"The Lord Jesus Christ." The typical element is seen realized in Christ,

1. As the *offspring* of David.

2. As the *monarch* of peace.

3. As *amazingly* rich. " Unsearchable riches of Christ."

4. For His *extraordinary* knowledge and wisdom.

5. For the *glory* of His kingdom.

6. For His *world-wide* celebrity and fame.

Unlike Solomon—

(1.) He possessed supreme divinity.

(2.) Universal royal dominion.

(3.) Was the root of David and his Lord.

(4.) His kingdom everlasting.

Observe,

**II. His royal chariot.**

A royal chariot is for the conveyance of persons in state, and Christ's chariot is the glorious Gospel.

Observe how Solomon prefigured it,

1. It is the *Gospel* of the son of man. "Wood of Lebanon." Fragrant—precious—incorruptible. Christ's humanity holy—precious—immortal.

2. It is the *gospel* of the divine Christ, the Son of God. "Bottom of gold." A divine Saviour essential. Look &c. "I am God"—"God manifest," &c.

3. It is the *Gospel* of *sacrifice*. "Covering of purple." "Without shedding of blood," &c. "Redemption," &c. Atoning blood is the covering—by it justified, sanctified, &c. As the Passover; Exodus xii. 21.

4. It is the *Gospel* of infinite *love*. "Pavement of love." The basis—the source, &c., love. "God so loved the world," &c.; and

5. It is the *Gospel* of *glad tidings*. Pillars of silver. To enrich—to bless, &c. Gospel silver trumpets.

Now see,

**III. The Divine use of the Gospel of Christ.**

Solomon's was—"For the daughters of Jerusalem." The types of believers—the Church of the Lord Jesus Christ. None else are benefitted by the Gospel—the Gospel chariot,

1. Only brings *believers* into the Church. Unbelief rejects the message—refuses.

2. The Gospel chariot brings *all* believers into the Church. All the children of God by faith.

3. The *Church* is the palace of the Lord Jesus Christ.

His court—audience. He is in and with His Church always.

4. The Gospel chariot conveys *believers* to the palace of glory. Heb. ii. 10. So Christ promised. "If I go away," &c.

**IV. Look at some particulars concerning this Gospel chariot.**

1. Its *gratuitousness*. No price, no merit, no righteousness—only believe.

2. Its *certainty* and *safety*. All believers are safely brought into the spiritual Church of Christ and to eternal glory. "My sheep," &c. Abiding in Christ—no perishing—salvation absolute.

3. *One* Gospel *chariot only*. One God—one Mediator —one atonement—one spirit—one way—one life, &c. So one Gospel.

4. One *chariot* for all *classes* and *conditions* of mankind. No party division—no pauper department—no slave pen—monarch and beggar must go together, &c. The once profligate and moral, &c.

We ask,

1. How many of you are in it?

2. Who will enter it to-night? Plenty of room— millions are in it, &c.—yet room for all. We ask the young—parents—the aged—the poor—the rich. We ask all.

3. Then some counsels to those in it. There must be exhibited a suitable spirit—suitable conversation—constant praise and rejoicing,—abiding in it.

4. Some cautions. Beware.

1. Of the devil's chariot—gaudy, exciting, attractive.

2. Beware of the pope's chariot. It is all anti, against. Anti-Christ, anti-faith, crucifixes, priests, penances, confession, purgatory. Then there is the imitative chariots in the Church of England.

3. Beware of the self-righteous chariot. Now behold
—believe—enter the chariot of the Saviour, looking for
the mercy of God to eternal life.


## CXII

## CHRIST OUR LIFE

" I live ; yet not I, but Christ liveth in me."—GALATIANS ii. 20.

CHRIST our life is an apostolical expression. So first is
our natural life and spiritual death. Then our death
unto sin and life in Christ—as Christ died and then lived.

Observe,

**I. The spiritual resurrection.**

Once dead, now I live—dead in trespasses and sins—
dead to God—in the grave of pollution. Now quickened, raised, &c.

Now this is,

1. An entire change.

2. Evident change. Holy pulse, heart, breath, action.

3. Essential change. Dry bones, and army of God, &c.

Observe,

**II. This new life-living in us.**

The negative is given. Not I—not myself—not by
my power—no corpse can raise itself—not my work,
but God the Father's—the Holy Spirit's—Christ's.

1. Christ is the *author* and *source*. He is the "life,"
fountain, resurrection and life—giveth life.

2. Christ is the *inward life*. Christ in you—I in you
—He the life in the soul. Now this is spiritual, not
sacramental or corporeal—but by His Spirit, the spirit
of Christ. See,

3. Christ is the *life sustainer*. He keeps, preserves.

I am the vine, ye the branches. He the head, we the members. He the bread, the living water, &c.

4. Christ is our *life modeller*. He shapes, gives direction, form, power, distinction, &c.

5. He is our *entire life*. Life of justification, regeneration, sanctification, perfection. He is the life of our graces, faith, hope, love, &c. Life of our holiness—life of our obedience and services—prayer, praise, goodness, knowledge, wisdom, &c.

6. He is our *eternal life*. He the giver of the title, the object, the fulness, the glory, and the everlasting, abiding. The crown, the robe, the praise and the felicity. Be like Him, &c. And,

7. He is our *only life*. I live by the faith of the Son of God. Life in no other—life nowhere else.

### APPLICATION

Importance of the Gospel proclamation of the text to all. All dead—Christ died for all that all may live, &c.

The one life to, for, and in all believers. All saints have the same experience and testimony—"I live," &c.

This life of Christ in us has its responsive duties. To hear Christ—to follow Christ—to live as Christ did—to trust in Christ—to hold Christ fast—to believe to life eternal.

So hope and wait for its glorious consummation at His second coming, when Christ shall appear, &c.


## CXIII

## AFFECTION FOR THE BROTHERHOOD

" Love the brotherhood."—1 PETER ii. 17.

THE brotherhood and the love we are to cherish towards them, will bring out the teaching of the text.

**I. The brotherhood.**

Comprises all the children of God, male and female, for there is no sex in religion.

The brotherhood includes,

1. The spiritual children of our Heavenly Father. All of them—without distinction or exception.

2. The partakers of the Divine nature. All believers have the same new regenerated nature, and therefore are essentially related to each other.

3. Possessors of the Holy Spirit. He dwells in them, and they can cry, Abba, &c.; see Romans viii. 14-16.

Now observe,

**II. The spirit we are to cherish towards them.**

It is the spirit of love. "Love the brotherhood."

(1.) Feel kindly towards them.

(2.) Speak kindly of them.

(3.) Minister kindly to them. Here will be the heart and mouth, and life, evincing this true and real affection.

And this love of the brotherhood,

(1.) Will be real and true.

(2.) Generous and beneficent.

(3.) Sympathetic and tender.

(4.) Firm and persistent.

(5.) Open and avowed.

(6.) Self-denying and devoted. "Laying down the life," &c.

Notice the results,

**III. Of obedience to this injunction.**

(1.) It will be promotive of our own piety and happiness.

(2.) It will be honourable to religion.

(3.) It will glorify Christ.

(4.) It will silence gainsayers. "See how those Christians love one another."

(5.) It will pre-eminently please God and secure His blessing.

Then,

1. How it should be cherished.

2. Manifested.

3. Never be neglected nor abandoned; 1 John ii. 9, 10; iii. 23; iv. 7, 20; v. 1.

# CXIV
## DEITY OF CHRIST

" Christ came, who is over all, God blessed for ever."—Rom. ix. 5.

IT is impossible for words to be more explicit, clear and direct than those of the text. Either Christ is supreme God, or the words are most misleading. We assume their distinct and satisfactory declaration of the Divine Majesty of Jesus.

It is obvious,

**I. That Christ is over all humanity.**

A name and authority above the most exalted of mankind. Over the patriarchs, over Moses and the prophets, over the priests and rabbis, over the princes and kings of the earth. These are but as planets revolving around the great sun of righteousness. Equally is the text true of the Baptist, evangelists and apostles.

**II. Christ is over all angels.**

Explicitly stated; Heb. i. 3-6; Col. i. 15, 16; Eph. i. 20, &c.

**III. Christ is over all dispensations.**

He is the subject of patriarchal faith and hope. He is over Moses and the legal economy. He is over the law, the Psalms and the Prophets. All dispensations end in Him.

**IV. Christ is over all worlds.**

The moral world, and the world to come. Over hades—over Heaven; Rom. xi. 36; Rom. xiv. 9.

As such,

**V. Christ is God blessed for ever.**

He has been ever blessed, praised, exalted. He is now blessed and glorified in His people. He shall be blessed and glorified for ever; Psalm lxxii. 5-9, xv. 19.

Observe,

1. Christ is thus represented by prophets and apostles, and by God Himself.

2. Christ claimed this glory, even absolute equality with the Father; Heb. i. 6, 12.

3. The ascription of saints and angels in the Apocalypse established it. So,

4. We may give all glory and honour to Jesus, even as we do to the Father. "For He and the Father are one."

5. Saints and angels, seraphim and cherubim, adore the Lamb for evermore.

## CXV

## LOVE, GIFTS AND TEACHING

"Follow after charity, and desire spiritual gifts, but rather that ye may prophesy."—1 Cor. xiv. 1.

THE Church had to be qualified for its great mission. This qualification was of God—from Heaven—by the gift of the Holy Ghost. Christ promised the "Holy Spirit" should supply His place, and carry on His work. The first-fruits of this was given on the resurrection evening, when Jesus breathed on them, and said, "receive ye the Holy Ghost." But let us look at the intimation given by Christ; Luke xxiv. 49; Acts i. 4-8; Acts ii. 1-4. Now here came down, in accordance with Christ's promise, the Holy Spirit, to give every necessary qualification for building up the kingdom of God. Now the early Churches possessed these gifts, and in Corinth these were abused and made the occasion of ostentation and display. Paul had been showing the infinite superiority of love in chapter 13, and then, in the text, gives this strong practical advice,

**I. What is to be first pursued.**

That is charity or "love." The love of the thirteenth chapter. Now this is,

1. *Put first.* It is so in itself, the greatest of these. It is of the Divine nature, celestial, from Heaven. The love of God—the mind of Christ—the fruit of the Spirit. It is the atmosphere of life—the evidence of our trans-formation—we know that we have passed, &c. Christ's special commandment—the beginning, centre and end of religion.

2. It is the *gold around* and *within* the *altar* of the *heart.* Adapted to the heart's affections, must be treasured there—the grand essence and beauty of the Christian character.

3. This *love* may be *driven away.* Coldness, selfish-ness, pride, envy, bigotry, all are set against it, to expel it from the Church of God. This is Satan's main business—to divide. See third chapter.

4. The *absence* of *love* is the *Ichabod* of the Church. Glory departed—no substitute for it. It is indispensable or spiritual life ceases—God's spirit vexed. Now,

5. To *retain* or *bring* it *back* we must *pursue* it. "Follow after"—be eager—be earnest—be devout—be self-sacrificing. It is the pearl, so we must go to the depths of the sea to get it. It is the gold, and so we

must dig, &c. It is the precious balm, and we sicken without it. Now this is to be done first of all.

Then see,

**II. What is to be fervently desired.**

"Spiritual gifts;" chap. xii. 31. Divine gifts are ot various kinds and orders and degrees of worth. Clay, iron, silver, gold.

Observe,

1. The *distinctive character* of the *gifts.* Spiritual. Not natural parts—not secular acquirements—not learning nor philosophy—all have their place and use and value, but spiritual gifts are to have the precedence.

2. The *source* of these *gifts.* "To be desired"— sought of God. "Every good gift and every perfect gift; James i. 17. Knowledge is one of these. Virtue or courage. Zeal or fervour of spirit. Self-government, &c.; 2 Peter i. 5, &c.

3. These *gifts* are to have our *fervent solicitude.* "Desire," inwrought, intense. Stir up the gift that is within thee. These gifts are our spiritual adornments —qualifications for usefulness. The Church and the world need them. They are the external glory of Christianity—so to be ever and ever more desired, valued, sought, &c. They grow by use. Brighten by polish. Multiply by diffusion, &c.

Observe,

**II. What is to be practically attended to.**

But rather that ye may "prophesy." Graces and gifts are for use, and one of the great uses is that of prophesy or teaching.

Now see,

1. The *necessity* for this. Men are ignorant and must be taught. Ignorant of themselves—of God—of Jesus

Christ—of the way of life, and we are bound to teach them.

2. *Converts* in the Church are only *partially instructed*, and they must be *taught*. The new convert is like a babe, &c.

3. The *children* of the *pious* must be *taught*. How explicit under the law; Deut. vi., &c.; Psalm lxxviii. 4. Equally under the Gospel; Eph. vi. 4. Now the fruit of love and the end of gifts is to be made practical. But a few questions may be necessary.

1. Who are to prophesy or teach? All who have the gift. Parents at home—teachers in the school—Christians in the means of grace—preachers and pastors.

2. May Christian women teach. Surely mothers. See the whole of the last chapter of Proverbs. Surely other Christian women. Priscilla taught the great Apollos. But may they teach in public? Let Paul decide; 1. Cor. xi. 4, &c. He never disputes that they may, but decides the "how," in what manner. The possession of a gift involves the Divine purpose that it is to be employed. As poetical composition and music in Miriam. As ruling authority in Deborah. As queenly influence in Esther. As in kindly ministrations, as the holy women. As in helping the ministers and pastors in the Church as evident; Rom. xvi. 1-3; Philip. iv. 3.

In conclusion, observe,

1. The Divine order. First love, second gifts, third labour. The heart—the head—the tongue.

2. The Church needs all.

3. God gives all.

4. Unemployed gifts will be the hidden talent.

5. Let the spirit of the text be earnestly cherished by one and all.

# CXVI

## REMEMBERING AND MEDITATING ON GOD'S WORKS

"I remember the days of old; I meditate on all Thy works; I muse on the work of Thy hands."—PSALM cxliii. 5.

THE Psalmist had been in great trouble. His consciousness of his sins; v. 2. His bitter experience of persecution; v. 3. His deep depression; v. 4. And now his holy resolve as in the text.

Now observe in the text,

**I. What he would remember—"the days of old."**

It might be,

1. The *days recorded* in Holy Scripture. Psalmist celebrates these; Psalm cvii. God's doings, &c. with His people—days of intervention and deliverance, and days of distinguished favour, &c.; see Psalm lxxv. 5.

2. Or the *days* of his own *experience*. Remember all the ways, &c. Retrospect is the prerogative of man—an important duty—a profitable exercise.

**II. On what he would meditate—all God's works.**

1. His *creative* works. The heavens and the earth; Psalm viii., &c. How great—how marvellous—how comprehensive—how instructive! Matter for day and night, and all the seasons.

2. His *governmental* works. The Divine government—sublime, mysterious, grand, often dark, and,

3. His *gracious* works. Remembrance of Israel. His loving-kindness, &c. His covenanted mercies. His constant care and fidelity.

Observe,

**III. On what he would muse—"the works of God's hands."**

This seems like repetition. Meditation looks abroad and views and compares. To muse is the inward thoughts carried out. Extended thought. Deep and silent reflection. One is general, the other particular and minute. A landscape—a general view, and then a minute examination.

1. There is God's *delivering hand*. Israel, Daniel, &c.

2. God's *upraising hand*. Joseph, David.

3. God's *supplying hand*. Widow, Elisha, &c.

4. God's *guiding hand*. Israel in the wilderness.

5. God's *keeping hand*. Jacob and Esau. Kept David from Saul, &c.

6. God's *fashioning hand*. In our being—in our renewal, &c.

7. God's *chastening hand*. Loving heart and deep concern for our best interests; Heb. xii. Now these may be matter for general musing, secret thought and reflection.

### APPLICATION

1. We all need to imitate the Psalmist.

2. Seek grace to do it profitably.

3. Often stir up ourselves to do it.

4. Especially in times of sadness and sorrow.


## CXVII

## A CAUTION AGAINST SCEPTICAL BABBLINGS

"Avoiding profane and vain babblings, and oppositions of science falsely so-called."—1 TIMOTHY vi. 20.

THERE are three modes of treating religion and the Holy Scriptures.

1. The *credulous*—who simply take the Bible and religion for granted. They have never examined it, nor sought for evidence of the truth. Would have been

Buddhists in China, Mahommedans in Turkey, or Jews in Palestine.

2. There are the *sceptical*—two or three classes. Some of these are sincere seekers after truth, and should be treated with kindness, candour, and respect. Some who, through pride and self-will, ignore all religious teaching and boast of their disbelief; and still a third class of sceptics who, by pretentiousness and noise, are ever opposing the truth, and trying by philosophy and science, falsely so-called, to attack the citadel of the Christian religion. These are the persons noted in the text "vain babblers." It is worthy of remark that infidelity is constantly repeating itself. Many of the grounds of scepticism are as old as the first and second centuries, and are the reiterated babblings of Celsus, Porphyry, and Julian. So Darwin's scheme of evolution is only the reproduction of English and French infidels of the last century. No marvel after men have ignored a God, they should degrade and abase themselves to a kind of level with apes, &c.

Now Christian men and women must so study the evidences of Christianity as to be able and ready to avail themselves of the apostle's advice—"O Timothy," &c. To help you in this is the design of our subject this morning.

**I. Don't imagine that all men of learning, science, and Philosophy are sceptically disposed.**

We have a galaxy of the illustrious and the *élite* in favour of the religion of Holy Scripture—a glorious phalanx.

1. I take the *greatest dramatist* the world ever *produced*, Shakespeare, a volume of distinct Bible quotations, &c.

2. The *sublimest poet* of any *age*, Milton.

3. The *wisest philosopher* of modern *times*, Lord Bacon.

4. The *most learned astronomer* and *mathematician*, Sir Isaac Newton; and nearer still to our times, John Dalton, Cuvier, Farraday, and Sir David Brewster—all alike giants and ornaments both of science and religion.

**II. Look at sceptical babblers in their varied and opposite phases.**

There are grand principles and land marks banding all Christian religions together, well, do sceptical babblers thus agree? Let us see,

1. There is the *dry hard-shelled Deists*, the devotees of nature, inward light and conscience. No Providence—no Bible—a God of fixed laws and destiny. Man may or may not be immortal. There may or may not be retribution.

2. The *stern Materialist*. All is material—no spiritual existencies—soul refined brain,—death—decomposition—electrical change and blackness without one ray of hope of future being.

3. The *bold Atheist*. No God—no personal intelligent Creator or Ruler—no presiding moral Governor.

4. The *fanciful Pantheist*. All, he says, is God. God is light, air, fire, water, the planets, the sun, the stars, man. Nature is God, and there is no other. So Atheism and Pantheism sing the dolorous dirge over the exclusion and destruction of a personal deity. We ask that these babblers should meet, confer, and agree before they go on their crusade against God and Bible religion.

**III. Ought we not to ask these babblers for a book of their sceptical principles in place of the Bible?**

We have nature as well as they, and reason; we find these insufficient, so we appeal to the Holy Scriptures. If they reject our book, let us have theirs. It might begin thus—Nature, reason, fate, which at sundry times and in divers manners spake in ages past by Celsus,

Porphyry, Bolingbroke, Paine, Renan, Holyoake, and Darwin. Now such a book should contain an account of the creation of the world—origin of man—rise of moral evil and history of the world. The source of Jewish fables and the myths of the patriarchal ages. It should expose Israelitish juggleries and prophetical rhapsodies. It should explain all about the Galilean fanatic or impostor, or both. It should disrobe the evangelists and apostles, and should disentangle the skein of what millions have called their personal religion, Christian experience, and hopes of a future immortality.

**IV. They must give us also a code of morals.**

First, the Ten Commandments repealed, revised, or superseded, if so—what? Shall we read them backwards, &c., or make them permissive, or positive, or negative, as it may be convenient? Will they reverse the domestic system, change the social compacts, and national institutions?

**V. They must supply the materials for real happiness.**

All will admit, men are not so, they want it. Where? How is it to be had? In sickness—death—at the grave. Shall it read thus—Be happy and rejoice, the Bible is a fiction! No God! No spiritual nature! No future! No assembly of the just! Can you conceive of greater folly than to expect happiness from scepticism—happiness from negations? It would be as reasonable to expect to be handsome and strong from breathing the east wind. The blessings of Christianity, they say, are mere imagination, delusion, &c., but they answer the purpose of reality.

1. The Christian says, my *knowledge* of God is *real* and *true* to me, and to know God, &c.

2. My *knowledge* and *faith* in Jesus is a *reality* to me, for though I see Him not, &c.

3. My *conversion* is to me a *reality.* "For old things,"
&c.—"Once I was blind," &c.

4. My *hope* of *glory* is to me a *reality*, for it *supplies* me
with *joy unspeakable* and *full* of *blessedness.*

5. My *consolation* at the *grave* of Christian friends is
*full* of *solace*, and surely with the heathen Socrates, I
may hope to meet them in the elysium of the *élite* and
good.

In conclusion we ask,

1. The doubter to be candid and diligent in searching
for the good the soul needs. "Who will shew," &c.

2. We call on the Christian to rejoice in the Lord
Jesus, and to have "no confidence in the flesh."

3. We say to all saints, "Avoid vain babblings," &c.

## CXVIII

### GOD A GENERAL AND SPECIAL SAVIOUR

"Who is the Saviour of all men, specially of those that believe."—
1 TIMOTHY iv. 10.

THE text contains a most glorious and important truth,
and yet exhibits a most necessary. distinction. The
truth is this, that God is the Saviour of all men. A
broad affirmation of God's universal love and mercy—a
truth full of interest and moment to every child of man.
But this truth might be misunderstood or perverted.
It might be supposed that God eventually would save
all men—that none would finally perish—and hence the
most careless might reckon that at last they would be
safe. Now the text guards against this by the most
important addition of the latter clause of the verse
—"specially of those who believe."

The text refers,

### I. To a universal Saviour.

"The living God." God the essence and the source of life—the fountain of being. Or it may apply to Jesus, who has demonstrated His divinity by His resurrection, and who is emphatically "The living God." But applying the text to the Father, observe, He is the Saviour of all men,

1. As He *exercises* His *sparing mercy* to all. All sinned —all deserve to die—all have some measure of life and probation given them. He is patient and long-suffering to all—not willing that any should perish, &c.

2. As He has *provided* an *atonement* for all. Here the Divine Word puts forth this truth in several varied forms.

(1.) Jesus the brother or kinsman of all. Our own nature, &c.

(2.) He was sent for the salvation of all. "God so loved the world," &c. His birth was to be "good news to all men," &c.

(3.) He actually died for all. "All we like sheep," &c. "Behold the Lamb of God." "One God and one Mediator," &c. "He is the propitiation," &c. He died, evidently for those who perish. "Destroy not Him," &c. Words cannot express any doctrine more clearly or fully.

3. *Salvation* is *offered* to all. "Go ye into all the world," &c. "Every creature." Observe how particular —not to miss one—then there is a Gospel for all. "For thus it was written," &c. "I saw another angel;" Rev. xiv. 6, &c. Then is it not clear that, as to the Divine mercy, Divine provision, Divine offer and intention, God is the Saviour of all men. Here then the glorious truth of the text stands out, and it cannot possibly be gainsayed without trifling and perverting the Word of God.

But the text directs us,

**II. To a limited salvation.**

"Specially of those who believe." Now momentous truths are here clearly involved.

1. That *believing* is *necessary* to salvation. This is universally taught us. Christ even insisted and demanded it. So the apostles. It is part of the great commission—"He that believeth," &c. And so John iii. 15, 16, &c. Now this believing is receiving the Gospel testimony as true, and trusting in it. See the case of the Ethiopian Eunuch; Acts viii. 37; see v. 12.

More, this believing was,

(1.) Something the people could do.

(2.) Something that they were always required to do.

(3.) And condemned if they did not do it. So it is still—faith is the tenure on which salvation is offered.

(1.) Not merit.

(2.) Not works.

(3.) Not ordinances—but simple faith.

2. That only those who *believe* are *saved*. Salvation is illumination—faith only admits the light. It is the eye beholding the Lamb of God. Salvation is pardon—faith only accepts it as God's gracious act. Salvation is God's gift—faith opens the hand and receives it. Salvation is the announcement of God's favour—faith hears and lives, &c. Unbelief, or the opposite of faith, refuses the message of Christ—despises the offer of salvation—rejects Christ, &c. "He came unto His own, and His own received Him not." Unbelief exclaims, we will not have this man to reign over us—"away with Him," &c. How then can such be saved, they will not accept the remedy of mercy, and therefore die. They will not take the waters of life, and therefore perish. They reject pardon, and therefore continue

condemned. Will not walk in the opened way of peace, and therefore go down to the pit.

Now learn,

1. Salvation is of God. No salvation elsewhere, &c. "Look unto me and be ye saved, for I am God," &c.

We see,

2. None need despair—"God is the Saviour of all men." Every class, rank, or condition. "All" includes each and every one, and excludes none.

3. Yet faith is essential, as looking to enjoy light—as eating to sustain life—as accepting and using the medicine is to restoration to health. Unbelief is perverseness, rebellion, and therefore ruin.

4. No excuse for any who perish—no terms so gracious or so adapted to man's condition. "But ye will not come," &c. Christ with tears says, "I would have gathered you, &c., but ye would not."

## CXIX

## PLEASING MEN FOR THEIR PROFIT, THAT THEY MAY BE SAVED

"Even as I please all men in all things, not seeking mine own profit, but the profit of many, that they may be saved."—1 Cor. x. 33.

THE text contains certain forms of speech, called hyperboles, that must be explained, and a certain paradox requiring definition. He does not mean when He says all men, absolutely all mankind, but those with whom he came in contact, whether Jews or Gentiles, illiterate or learned, religious or profane. He does not mean that he sought thus to please these men in all things literally, for no man was more faithful to conscience or truth than he. Hence how he suffered persecution for his fidelity as a servant of the Lord Jesus, and how he severely censures the perverted saints in Galatia, and withstood Peter to his face for his time-serving conduct; Gal. i. ii. But he means that he exercised all care and prudence, so as not to come in collision with the prejudices of people, and thus render his ministry a failure; see 1 Cor. ix. 19, 22. And he did this that his chief object might be secured in their salvation.

Now, notice then,

## I. The apostle's self-denying spirit.

"Not seeking mine own profit." In how many respects did Paul make this strikingly manifest.

He did not seek,

1. *Worldly* or *ecclesiastical honours*. Was willing to be reckoned a fool for Christ and the Gospel's sake.

2. Nor *pecuniary recompense*. Labouring with his hands, that he might present the Gospel free of charge.

3. Nor *human applause*. Reckoning himself less than the least of all saints, and "as nothing."

4. Nor *apostolical distinction*. Willing to be abased and be the servant of all. Ready for Christ's work in any place, and among any class of sinners, Jews or Gentiles, &c.

Nor did he seek,

5. His *ease* or *personal comfort*. His whole life one of trials, sorrows, adversities and afflictions. Read 2 Cor. xi. 23, 33.

Notice,

## II. His true benevolent designs.

Not seeking his own profit, "but the profit of (the) many." That is of the masses among whom he laboured as an apostle of Jesus Christ.

Their profit,

1. In *presenting* to them Gospel truth for their *accept-ance*. To illumine their minds—burst their bonds, and bring them into the liberty and blessedness of the children of God.

2. In *publishing* Gospel blessing for their *joyous recep-tion*. Pardon, peace, adoption, sanctification, heirship with the Lord Jesus, &c.

3. In *labouring* to *secure* their *personal devotion* to the *cause* of Christ. Thus ensuring their personal conformity to the Saviour, and the joyous hope of the rewards of faithful labour, even eternal life in the world to come. And inclusive of all these that they might,

4. Be *saved*. Now delivered from all the guilt and penalty of sin, and consequently from the wrath to come. Salvation, with eternal glory, by Christ Jesus.

Observe,

**III. The spirit by which the apostle was thus influenced.**

1. It was the *constraining love* of Christ in his own *soul*. See it clearly stated, 2 Cor. v. 13, 14.

2. It was the *spirit* of *deep sympathy* and *love* for *souls*.

3. It was the *spirit* of *holy zeal* for the *cause* of Christ and His Church.

4. It was the *spirit* of *conscious fidelity*, that he might not lose his reward. All these thoughts will be comprehended in the paragraph; 1 Cor. ix. 16, to end.

### APPLICATION

1. What a test of principles and character.
2. What an example for imitation.
3. What an incentive to entire devotedness.

## CXX

## A PRAYER SUITED TO ALL

" O remember not against us former iniquities; let thy tender mercies speedily prevent us; for we are brought very low."—Psalm lxxix. 8.

WE may all use this prayer, and on some occasions it may be more than ordinarily appropriate. Its admissions—its earnest entreaties—and its appeal, may most profitably be copied.

Notice,

### I. What is deprecated.

"God's remembrance of former iniquities." Now three thoughts are here suggested. We are conscious,

1. Of our *iniquities*. Crooked, perverse, evil ways and doings—a foul blot on our life's record—an evil stain on our consciences—and heinously wicked before God.

Observe,

2. The *continuity* of our *iniquities*. We might divide them into many kinds and degrees, but the word "former" reminds us of those in earlier life—iniquities of youth and of early manhood, or of past days. There are later and more recent iniquities, and they are all to be confessed before God. "I will acknowledge mine iniquity," &c.

3. He *seeks* that God will *not remember* these "*iniquities.*" God's perfect and infinite knowledge renders it impossible for Him to forget anything, but while this is so, He has said, in reference to His true repentant people, He will remember their iniquities no more, that is, in the sense of charging them with them, or punishing them on account of them. So this is what is sought in the text. God might both remember and punish

them.  His holiness and justice would seem to demand it.

Notice,

## II. The plea he presents on this account.

God's tender mercies.  "Let thy tender mercies speedily prevent us."  See this plea in its various parts.

1. God's *mercies*.  Not mercy, but mercies—adapted to all sorts of iniquities.  These mercies are the overflowing of goodness, love, compassion, pity, &c.  They are even of old—flow in varied forms—are everlasting —universal—over all God's works.

2. *Tender mercies*.  As the father's towards his children—as the soft gushings forth of the loving mother.  In themselves tender, in their manifestation tender, &c.  Father and prodigal—Jesus and woman sinner.  He asks that these iniquities may be prevented by His "tender mercies."

3. *Go before*, or *prevent* us.  Prevent our arrestment, trial, penalty, misery and ruin.

4. *Speedily*.  For our anxiety is extreme—our conviction deep—anguish great—forebodings terrible.  We are perishing, therefore "speedily," &c.

See,

## III. The humble admission.

"For we are brought very low."  Low,

1. In our *sinful degradation*.  As the prodigal.  Low,

2. In our *moral weakness*.  Moral vigour gone— righteous strength exhausted.  As wasted by disease helpless, &c.  But low also,

3. In our *sense* of *wretchedness*.  Without joy or peace or comfort.  As in the mire and clay—as in a gloomy prison—as close to the yawning gulf—yet not too low to cry for help and implore mercy.

APPLICATION

Our subject is one,

1. Of personal importance. That we should all individually realize it.

2. How often applicable to families and households. Jacob's, Eli's, David's, &c.

3. It may be appropriate to Churches. See Rev. ii. iii.

4. Or to nations. How clear, direct and simple is the spirit of the text. Let all labour to feel and then express the prayer.


## CXXI

## THE MOMENTOUS ENQUIRY

" Will ye also be His disciples? "—JOHN ix. 27.

HOW interesting the chapter. Bitterness—prejudice. Religious intolerance the worst of all the various classes. The Jewish officials. Young man. The parents. The cross to be taken up. Excommunication; and then see the searching question of the text.

I. To what the question related.

"Discipleship," pupils, scholars, followers. Philosophers had their disciples; religious teachers theirs— Moses, John the Baptist, sects, &c. Disciples, in all cases, were supposed,

1. To *learn*. Christ said, " Learn of Me."

2. To *profess*—by their confession of His name.

3. To *obey*.—" Ye are My friends if ye do," &c.

Notice,

II. To whom the text referred—to Christ.

1. He was a *teacher*, the greatest, divine, from Heaven.

2. He had *disciples*—reference to seventy—many others.

3. He *sought persons* to become His disciples. Preaching, invitation.

4. He *offered special blessings* to His disciples. Kingdom of God, pardon, rest, peace, life, the eternal kingdom of glory.

Observe,

**III. How important the text is still.**

Christ still seeks, &c., and his ministers still ask, Will ye also be, &c.

1. We *ask all*, for He is the Saviour of all.

2. We *especially ask* the *young*, for we may suppose,

(1.) They are not absolutely fixed as yet.

(2.) Early discipleship is more easy.

(3.) More honourable.

(4.) More safe.

(5.) More acceptable to Christ.

(6.) More useful.

The question of the text, observe,

**IV. Is worthy of an answer.**

1. It *can* be *answered*. " Will you also ? " you may, you ought.

2. It *should* be *answered* by each and all.

3. It *should* be *answered now*. Will ye now? &c. If you will, then a few words of advice. Be earnest. Look to Christ only. Seek His grace, enter His school bear His yoke, and learn and follow Him.

## CXXII

## GOLIATH AND DAVID

" Then said David to the Philistine, thou camest to me with a sword, and with a spear, and with a shield ; but I come unto thee in the name of the Lord of hosts, the God of the armies of Israel, whom thou hast defied."—1 SAMUEL xvii. 45.

THERE are few more memorable events in sacred history

than the deadly combat between Goliath and David. Points of extraordinary contrast stand out in every part of the narrative. In observing these we shall involve all the valuable truths and principles the subject suggests.

Notice,

### I. Goliath was the representative of idolatry.

An alien and enemy of Jehovah. Ignorance, unbelief, superstition, were the essentials of his anti-religious character. He and his people hated the true God and His people Israel, and were in bitter antagonism towards them. David was a son of Israel, and the representative of the religion of Jehovah. His lineage was that of pre-eminent piety—he was the offspring of saintly parentage—he was a personal servant of the living God, and the subject of special and Divine mercies.

### II. Goliath was the champion of his nation.

As such he was of extraordinary size, at least nine feet or more in height, and then see the nature of his personal armour; v. 5-7. Then he was a bold boaster, and, withal, his presence struck terror in the eyes of all beholders; v. 8, &c. David at most was a man of ordinary stature, and he lived a shepherd's life, and had no signal weapons, either for personal defence, or wherewith to attack an enemy.

### III. Goliath dared all Israel to find a man to single combat.

His pride, arrogant, vaunting self-sufficiency, were daringly exhibited; v. 8-11. So fierce and terrible did he appear, that Saul and all Israel were dismayed and greatly afraid; v. 11. David came forth as the champion to meet this daring foe of God and Israel. As such he pleaded his past evidences of courage in slaying the lion and the bear; v. 34, 35. He expressed his entire faith and trust in God; v. 37. He felt assured that Goliath the uncircumcised Philistine, who had defied the armies of God, should fall in like manner; v. 36.

**IV. Goliath scorned and contemned the youth.**

"Come to me, said he, and I will give thy flesh unto the fowls," &c.; v. 44. David prepares for the combat with weapons apparently ill-fitted for so dreadful a conflict. He puts away the armour of Saul the king; v. 38, 39, and then he took his staff in his hand, with five stones from the brook, and his sling in his hand, and drew near to the Philistine; v. 40-42. Then David utters the words of the text, and avers, "This day will the Lord deliver thee into mine hand: and I will smite thee, and take thine head from thee, and I will give the carcases of the host of the Philistines this day unto the fowls of the air," &c.; v. 46, 47.

Now then comes,

**V. The actual battle between Goliath and David.**

David took his sling and a stone, and ran and smote the Philistine, and slew him, stood upon him, and took Goliath's sword, and drew it out of the sheath, and cut off his head, &c.; v. 50, 51. And so panic stricken were the armies of the Philistines that they fled, pursued by the men of Israel and Judah; v. 52.

The lessons the subject suggests are,

1. *Personal might* and *power* are *not invincible*, or Goliath would not have fallen.

2. *Weapons* of *war*, however *mighty*, do not inevitably *secure success*, or Goliath would have been an easy conqueror.

3. Boasting *before* the *battle* is no *indication* of *victory*. For Goliath did this abundantly, and yet was slain.

4. God alone can *ensure* such *results* as He *pleases*, and

with *any weapons* that may be used.   Hence the effec-
tiveness of the sling and the stone.

5. The *enemy* may *supply* the *very means* for their
*abased overthrow.*   For Goliath's own sword decapitates
its vaunting owner.

6. Here is *symbolized* the *certain victories* of every
Christian *warrior* in the *moral conflict.*

7. And finally, here is *foreshadowed* the *eventual
triumphs* of Jesus and of *truth* over *Satan* and the *powers*
of *darkness.*

8. And here is *material* for *hope* and *courage* under the
most apparently *untoward circumstances.*   How appropriate the text in the mouth of every good soldier
of the Lord Jesus Christ.   "Yea, we are more than
conquerors," &c.


# CXXIII

## THE BRAZEN SERPENT

"And as Moses lifted up the serpent in the wilderness, even so
must the Son of Man be lifted up."—JOHN iii. 14.   (See also NUM.
xxi. 5.)

THE exact method of salvation is here beautifully
specified by Christ.   An Old Testament incident illustrates the great New Testament doctrine of redeeming
grace.   Now the analogy holds in the following particulars,

**I. In their sins.**

Numbers xxi. 5.   It was rebellion against God, heart,
lip, life.   So was the first and all sin.

**II. In their punishment.**

"Fiery serpents," bite, disease.   Sin thus introduced

by the old serpent, the devil. The results, moral corruption, death. Observe between the bite and death a
certain connection, an incurable complaint, a fatal
conclusion. Death is the penalty of sin.

Notice,

**III. The utter helplessness and misery of the Israelites.**

Could not help themselves or each other, nor Moses.
Misery and ruin inevitable, so is man's fallen condition.

Now notice,

**IV. The Divine interposition.**

Their deliverance and remedy were of God, of His
sovereign rich mercy. So our salvation. "God so
loved," &c., "Not by works," &c., grace is the origin and
source.

Then observe,

**V. The remedy God appointed; v. 8.**

1. It was *like* the *cause* of *their disease*, &c. Fiery
serpents and serpent of brass. By man sin and death,
by man redemption. Two serpents and two Adams.
First Adam God's Son, so the second. First had no
human father, so the second. Both perfect men, but
observe—the first depraved and ruined, so the fiery
serpents destructive. The second of brass, no venom
—so the second Adam, holy, &c. no sin.

**VI. The serpent of brass was an effectual, full remedy.**

1. Nothing else.

2. Nothing more.

3. Infallible, &c. So Christ is the Saviour, His
mediation perfect.

But observe,

**VII. The uplifting of both.**

"Set it up on a pole." So Christ was to be lifted up.
Intimated Gal. iii. 13, John viii. 28, and xii. 32. Here
was the death and the manner of it.

**VIII. There was the publishing of both remedies.**

Now the Divine remedy had to be announced, proclaimed, and no doubt urged. The priests, &c., would do it in the camp. So the apostles, &c., the Gospel, "Go ye into all the world," &c.

**IX. One thing is demanded of both in order to a cure.**

Looking, believing. Both would involve,

1. A *sense* of *misery* and *peril* as the *result* of *guilt*.

2. A *belief* in the *proclamation*.

3. A *trusting* to it. This is doubtless the experience of every restored believer.

**X. In both cases, looking or believing is sufficient.**

Nothing more, nothing less—he that looked was healed and lived. "He that believeth," &c., and,

**XI. The extent and efficacy of the remedies.**

Same "whosoever"—"every one." Of every grade—every age—every degree of disease—just expiring—no exception—no partiality.

**XII. The duty of the healed alike.**

Gratitude—devotion to God—holy life. Here then is the complete type in every particular. Now the position of all the unconverted is like that of the Israelites. To them we publish God'sgrace, scheme of mercy. We ask all to look, and to look now, to believe, &c. We give Christ's assurance that "whosoever," &c. This is the "one" and only remedy. No one rejected, &c., but "he that believeth not shall be damned."

# CXXIV

## THE GREAT FEAST, AND WHAT CAME OF IT

"Belshazzar the king made a great feast to a thousand of his lords, and drank wine before the thousand," &c.—DANIEL v. 1.

OUR text contains one of the most extraordinary

accounts of one of the grandest banquets ever held. Indeed every thing contributed to its magnificence. It was one gorgeous whole, and yet it was followed by one of the most fearful catastrophes on record. We invite you to come and gaze on its two-sided pictures, and contrast could not go further than in the scenes presented. But we must look at the various striking phases in which it is given to us:

Notice,

### I. The city where it was held—"Babylon."

One of the greatest cities of the ancient world. Situated in Chaldea, built on both sides the Euphrates, so that celebrated river flowed through its midst. It included a circuit of 56 miles—the entire area 200 square miles. It was surrounded by a double wall, 350 feet high, wide enough for four horse chariots abreast, and had on it 250 towers. There were 100 brass gates by which the city could be entered. In the city were 676 elegant squares. There were also a very high mound, garden, terraces, and here grew some of the finest trees; so that it seemed like an earthly paradise. Here was the great Temple of Belus enriched with gold, silver and precious stones—the great image or idol, which cost probably 10,000,000 of pounds. Nebuchadnezzar employed 10,000 men for many years in constructing its defences, and fabulous sums in promoting its magnificence and glory. Well, this was a city for a feast, and such was the place where it was held.

Now let us see,

### II. The giver of the feast—"Belshazzar."

He was probably joint king with his father, Nabonedus, and he might be grandson of Nebuchadnezzar; see v. 2. He was obviously a heathen idolator, though he could not be ignorant of Nebuchadnezzar's confession of the glory of God; chap. iv. 34.

Now observe,

### III. The guests and splendour of the feast; v. 1.

"A thousand of his lords." The guests are further described; v. 2, 3. Now this feast was of course in the king's palace. Few, if anything like this, had ever been seen. Some striking particulars are given. Wine bibbing—the praises of the gods; v. 4. This was in keeping with the king and his religion and guests.

But now look,

### IV. At the impiety of this feast.

Not content with praising idols, &c., but they wickedly and basely desecrated the sacred vessels of the Temple of the Lord; v. 2. Here was open insult to the God of Israel; v. 3. Here was profane revelry and open devilry, and this last act filled up to the brim the cup of Belshazzar's impiety and wickedness. And now gaze on the thousand guests—look at their costumes—hear their songs and bacchanalian rioting!

When lo!

### V. The scene suddenly changes.

Read the occasion; v. 5. "In the same hour," &c., a supernatural hand. The hand writes upon the wall opposite to where the king sat. The king saw the moving fingers, and the inscription abides on the wall. Observe the king's terror; v. 6. The king's proclamation; v. 7. The king's disappointment; v. 8. Now comes God's interpretation; v. 11, &c. The solemn preacher—the sermon about his grandfather; v. 18-21. Application to himself; v. 22, and the interpretation and the solemn sentence; v. 25, &c. And then the tragic supplement; v. 30. The enemy had been surrounding the city. They deemed it invulnerable, but while the whole city was given up to revelry, the enemy turned the stream of the river, and marched up through the dry bed, took the city, and slew the king.

1. See the peril of voluptuous revelry.

2. See the close connection between the banquet and the slaughter.

3. See the heinousness of impiety.

4. The peril of the most exalted transgressors.

## CXXV

## THE CHURCH'S INCREASE

" And believers were the more added to the Lord, multitudes both of men and women."—ACTS v. 14.

GOD effects His purposes both by terrors and mercies— judgments and goodness—by the outpouring of the Spirit on the Day of Pentecost; Acts ii. 47. And now by the death of Ananias and Sapphira, &c.

Now let us,

**I. Explain the text.**

1. *Believers* were *those* who had *heard*, *felt* and *accepted* the Gospel *testimony*. These would be easily distinguished from disbelievers, the careless and unbelieving. Now,

2. They were *added* to the Lord.

(1.) Brought into saving acceptance with the Lord.

(2.) Professed their faith in the Lord.

(3.) United to the Lord's people.

3. A *great number* were thus *added* to the Lord. There was excitement, interest, general acceptance. "Men and women." No sex in religion. Neither male nor female, &c. "Only believers" were or can be.

**II. The importance of such a general interest in the Gospel.**

1. To the *people* themselves.

2. To the *labourers* in the *vineyard*.

3. To the *Church* itself.

4. To the *glory* and *joy* of Christ.

**III. How we should labour to secure such a general interest in religion.**

1. By faithfully *setting forth* the *truths* of the Gospel.

2. By *exhibiting* the *efficacy* of Divine grace in our own souls.

3. By *affectionately inviting* those around us.

4. By *earnest prayer* for the Divine spirit and blessing. The Holy Ghost descends and works in answer to prayer. What need to feel the importance of the subject in our day. How Romanists, Ritualists and Infidels, &c., are labouring. This is to be the burden of the whole Church—every one—in harmony with God's will.

# CXXVI

## THE DISCIPLES IN THE CLOUD

"While he thus spake, there came a cloud, and overshadowed them; and they feared as they entered into the cloud."—LUKE ix. 34

IT is almost impossible to exhaust the wondrous lessons of the transfiguration. The place, the scene, the persons, their emotions, the lessons, the conversation! Here Heaven and earth—God and man—the Law, the Prophets and the Gospel—Moses and John, &c. And yet on earth every thing is imperfect. Light and darkness—good and evil—joy and sorrow—life and death. The mount is above the earth, and yet not Heaven. The scene glorious, not abiding—the meeting transient —the conversation momentous—and then life's duties crowding. Our text relates to one incident. While Peter was speaking—suggesting the Tabernacles, &c.—

"a cloud," &c. And then its influence on them—"they feared," &c.

Now notice,

**I. The antecedents of the cloud.**

Christ transfigured; v. 29. Overwhelming sleep— the sight of Christ and Moses and Elias. These were too much for men in the body—could not bear it. It had already thrown them into sleep. The vision overpowering—so the cloud came in mercy to break the overwhelming blaze of brightness. Thus the cloud was one of mercy to their frailty.

**II. The lessons of the cloud.**

1. *Expressive* of the Divine *presence*. As on Sinai; Exodus xix. 18. So on the consecration of the Tabernacle; Exodus xl. 34. The Temple; 2 Chron. vi. 13.

2. *Expressive* of *human frailty* and *imperfection*. No cloud in the celestial Temple—God the sun—light efficient. But then the worshippers are spiritual, holy, perfect.

Observe, our imperfection,

(1.) Relates to our gross material bodies. Of the earth, earthy—bind us to the earth—dim our spiritual sight—our spiritual hearing, communion. Now all this tells on the experience of the soul. When unclothed or covered with the spiritual body, how different, &c.

(2.) Of our limited knowledge. On the Mount they saw much, and heard much, but not all—and now the cloud shuts out much, &c. How Moses and Elias went back. The opened doors of glory—the holy angels. So it is with us. The loftiest intellect has the cloud over it—most expansive mind. We know in part at best, but only the alphabet or elements of Divine knowledge.

3. *Imperfect holiness.* We see frailty cleaving to the

best. Moses and Elias perfect saints—Jesus absolutely holy—the disciples still only labouring to the higher life.

4. The *cloud* would *intimate* our *interrupted joys*. Joys on earth must be interrupted by secular concerns—earthly encrustations—daily temptations—encroaching trials, &c. Sunshine and shade—day and night—bliss and tears,—so now for awhile.

5. The *cloud* was as the *veil* of the *holiest* of *all*. It separated the holy and the holiest—it was thick, &c. None saw the great high priest ministering within, or the glory there. So the cloud divides the worlds—divides the dispensations—divides the Churches triumphant and militant.

Then observe,

III. **The influence of the cloud on the minds of the disciples.**

"They feared"—were filled with "awe"—as Moses feared.

1. From a *sense* of the *present majesty* of God. Presence of angels have inspired this—much more God.

2. A *consciousness* of *unworthiness*. "Who am I?" &c. Isaiah and the vision—"Woe is me," &c. So Peter—"Depart from me, O Lord," &c.

3. From the *awful uncertainty* that *impressed* them. What next—what other prodigies of wonder—how could they tell or even infer how it would end, &c. How becoming this fear, in all worship—in all spiritual duties—in all seasons of solicitude.

But observe,

IV. **The re-assuring voice.**

Observe,

1. The *voice* was *out of* the *cloud*. Where the fear was produced came the antidote.

2. It was *God's voice*. They had not seen God, nor

could they, but He utters His voice, and they heard it. The God of Israel—the Jehovah.

3. It *recalls* their *attention* to their Divine *Master*. It speaks of Jesus—it passes by Moses and Elias and every thing—"This is My beloved Son!" &c.

4. It *demands* for Jesus their *obedient regard.* "Hear ye Him"—He is your Lord and Master—He is God's Son and representative—"Hear ye Him." Now, when ye leave the mount—when He is in the depths. of humility—in the hands of His enemies—in His agony— "Hear ye Him."

LEARN

1. This is a world of clouds.
2. Our experience is one of clouds.
3. But God speaks to us out of the clouds.
4. Jesus will direct if we hearken to Him.

CXXVII

THE WEEPING BABE

" And when she had opened it, she saw the child; and, behold, the babe wept."—EXODUS ii. 6.

OUR world has been fitly styled a "valley of tears." The great and the best of men have been the subjects of tears. Hezekiah, the king, wept. The daughters of Jerusalem wept. The Lord Jesus Christ wept. An ancient commander, who surveyed his immense army, wept. The tears of the text, were the tears of a babe. Let us look at,

**I. The babe referred too.**

1. His *parentage*. They were the slaves of Pharoah; v. 1; chap. vi. 20.

2. The *circumstances* of his birth; chap. i. 22. These
circumstances were peril—extreme peril—peril of life.

3. His *name*. "Moses." "Drawn out," of the water.
A name suitable. One of great and perpetual renown.

4. The *situation* in which he is presented to us. Had
been concealed three months;—concealment no longer
possible. The maternal course adopted; v. 3. Little
ark of bull-rushes. Conveyed to the edge of the Nile.
Watched by his illustrious sister. Notice,

5. The *Providential interposition*. Daughter of Pharoah;
v. 5. What she saw; v. 5. What she did—"sent her
maid;" and then comes the text—"The babe wept."
Notice,

**II. The tears of the babe, and what they indicated.**

1. Tears of *helplessness*. Nothing so helpless as a
babe. See the lamb. Helplessness is the true indication
of childhood. It needs everything, and can do nothing.

2. They were tears of *felt sorrow*. Born to it. The
mother's knee. The mother's bosom. The mother's
home. Not a cold ark. Not a river's edge, &c.

3. They were tears of *peril*. The ark fragile. The
dangers great. Left exposed, and death certain. How
countless the perils of childhood!

4. Tears of *pitiful appeal*. It could not speak. It
had no resource but tears. All it could do was to weep.
So with childhood's sorrows always and everywhere.

Observe,

**III. How effectual these tears of the babe were.**

1. They *elicited* the *compassion* of Pharoah's daughter;
v. 6. "She had compassion." They went to her
womanly heart. They softened—affected—moved her.

2. They obtained her *timely interference;* v. 6. "This
is one of the Hebrews' children," &c.

3. They were *overruled* by Divine providence for *good*.

Now the sister comes forth; v. 7. How wise the question! How eloquent the appeal! So she said "go"—a word of two letters; v. 8. And so the sister fetched her mother; v. 8. How marvellous the working of Providence!

4. It led to the *careful preservation* of Moses; v. 9. Now the child is safe. Its real mother the nurse. A princess its foster mother.

5. It ended in the *advancement* and *education* of Moses; v. 9, 10. And now he has a palace for his home. All the learning of the Egyptians as his portion. Worldly glory before him. Such is the subject. The lessons are many.

1. Children are dependant on others.

2. The many perils of children. Physical, mental, moral.

3. Children appeal to others for sympathy. Surely they should have it.

4. Children of lowly estate may become great and illustrious. So with Moses.

5. A greater than Moses appeals to us—Jesus. To-day we respond, &c.

# CXXVIII

## GRACIOUS STABILITY

" The true grace of God, wherein ye stand."—1 PETER v. 12.

OBSERVE—

### I. The position of God's saints.

" They stand!"—were prostrate—in the horrible pit, or going on the downward plane of sin and darkness. But they have been arrested, restored, and now they stand as the upright disciples of the Saviour. Psalm xl. 1, 2.

(1.) They stand on the one Divine foundation. 1 Cor. iii. 11.

(2.) They stand accepted in Christ, the beloved.

(3.) They stand as the open witnesses for Jesus.

(4.) They stand in believing confidence on the rock of ages.

(5.) They stand as monuments of Divine and saving mercy.

(6.) They stand as the professors and confessors of faith in Christ. Fast, firm, unyielding. But the text refers,

**II. To the source of their stability.**

Not apostatizing, but standing fast, &c. "It is the true grace of God, wherein they stand."

1. Their *saintship* is *derived* from this grace. Grace sought them—called them—justified them—renewed and sanctified them.

2. Their *standing ability* is *derived* from this. In themselves weak, frail, erring; but in this grace strong, stable, magnanimous and unfailing.

3. They *stand* in the *principles* of this grace. Not in their own views and notions, but Christ's gracious truths. Not in self-righteousness, but in Christ's. Not by their own merit and worthiness, but the mediation and sanctifying power of Jesus.

4. They *stand* to the *glory* of this grace. All the believer's glory is from Christ and to Christ. He glories not in himself, nor in men, nor even apostles; but they glory only in the Lord, and magnify the marvels of His grace. But see,

**III. The special features of the grace, as given in the text.**

1. It is *Divine*. "Grace of God." Of the Father—of

the Son—of the Holy Spirit. And, therefore, it is the outgoing of unbounded, illimitable, everlasting grace of God.

2. It is *genuine.* " The *true* grace of God." Not fictitious—not grace separate from purity—not grace, that is opposed to holiness, or that pleads that sin may abound—not grace without spiritual life and power and fruit; but the true—the wheat, not the chaff—the coin of gold, not the counterfeit—the substance, not the shadow. The true grace of the true God, of the true Mediator, of the true Divine Spirit of the true covenant, of the true promise, of the true word as it is in Jesus.

Questions arising out of the subject:—

1. Are we the Lord's saints—manifest, open?

2. Are we standing—erect and open and firm for Christ and truth?

3. Do we realize the true grace, as the source and security of our stability?

4. Do we extol the grace thus supplied?

## CXXIX

## THE MANIFESTATION OF THE GLORY OF THE LORD

" Blessed be the glory of the Lord from his place."—EZEKIEL iii. 12.

THE call and work of Ezekiel were distinguished by a series of extraordinary events, favoured with the most magnificent visions. He was a prophetical eagle—to him was unveiled the cycles of the seraphim and cherubim—he beheld the living vitalities, &c.—witnessed the accompanying fiery concentrated wheels—saw the operations of the Divine Spirit impelling and controlling their motions—then at last he saw the

symbol of the Divine glory in connection with humanity
—the whole encircled with the green radiant bow of
hope. The voice of the invisible spake to Ezekiel, and
inaugurated him in his sublime mission—revealed his
work—demanded fidelity. Then the Spirit took him
up, and he heard behind a voice, &c., "Blessed be the
glory of the Lord," &c.

**I. Of whom the text speaks—"the Lord."**

1. The *essential attributes.* "Jehovah." All names
inferior to this. God, self-existent, "I am," eternal,
independent, infinite, almighty, omniscient, ubiquitous,
unchangeable.

2. But *look* at Him in His *moral perfections.* Justice
absolute, righteousness inflexible, holiness immaculate,
goodness unbounded, mercy illimitable, grace unspeakable, pity most tender, long-suffering, patient, &c.

3. But it is *Jehovah* in *connection* with *humanity.*
Light and fire the symbols of the Godhead. But see
God in humanity; chap. i. 26; then read John i. 18;
Heb. i. 3; John xiv. 8. Such then is the glorious being
of whom the text speaks.

**II. Notice the glory to which the text refers.**

Glory belongs especially to God. In the highest
degree—above the Heavens—His glory is infinite.
Name, throne, dominion, works, word, all glorious! But
to specify some features,

1. The *glory* of His *nature.* Exalted, pure, spirituality
most high—most blessed. See the graduated scale—
living beings—God the most exalted and glorious.

2. *Glory* of *absolute perfection.*

3. *Glory* of *unbounded dominion.*

4. *Glory* of *illimitable blessedness.* The blessed God—
His essential blessedness—His communicativeness in
creation—in providence—in redemption.

See,

**III. The blessedness and the place of its manifestation.**

"His place."

1. The *throne* of the *universe* is His *place*; Isaiah vi. 1, &c.; so Daniel vii. 9.

He made,

2. Sinai His *place*; Exodus xix. 16.

3. He *chose* the *Tabernacle* and the *Temple* as His *place*; 2 Chron. v. 14.

4. He *makes* the *revealed oracles* His *place*. Magnified His Word.

> " A glory gilds the sacred page,
>     Majestic like the sun ;
> It gives a light to every age,
>     It gives, and borrows none."

Especially the " Gospel," full of His glory.

5. *Pre-eminently*, " Jesus is His *place*." " We beheld His glory," &c.; John i. 14. He filled it—it burst through on Tabor, &c.

6. *Every house* of *spiritual worship* is His *place*. Now, not the Tabernacle nor the Temple. " Wherever two or three are met together," &c.—by His spirit in all places—" in all the ordinances "—services, &c.

#### APPLICATION

Observe,

1. The holy grandeur of the theme.

2. Do you, like Moses, seek to behold it.

3. Faith is the only medium. " Seeing Him who is invisible," &c.

4. Praise should celebrate it. " Blessed be the glory," &c.

## CXXX
## EZRA'S ADDRESS

" And now for a little space grace hath been showed from the Lord
our God," &c.—EZRA ix. 8.

ISRAEL had often suffered for their sins, especially for
idolatry. Worsted by enemies—latterly carried into
captivity. Now after seventy years, restored. Now
Ezra relates his experience. Deep sorrow and shame
for their sins; v. 2, &c. His distress, prayer and confession, &c. In the midst of this comes our text, full
of instructive counsel, &c. The subject shows,

**I. The grace they had experienced.**

Observe,

1. In *bondage*. Not desert, but grace—undeserved
favour.

2. Grace *from* Jehovah, their covenant God.

3. Grace to *preserve*. "A remnant." Seventy years'
captivity. Not all extinguished. Some kept, sustained
—and a remnant only.

4. To be *restored* to their land—nation—city, &c.,—
worship—inheritances and home.

Notice,

**II. The exalted position to which they had been raised.**

1. A "nail," or "pin"—these were inserted in the
building of the place. Designed,

(1.) For ornament.

(2.) For usefulness.

(3.) For permanence. So Christ the Messiah. Isa.
xxii. 23. Levites were nails, pins. The priests—the
High Priest—an exalted place. The musicians.

2. In the *holy place* of God. Tabernacle—Church of
the old covenant. Not in palaces—schools of learning
—halls of science—academies of philosophy; but in the

far higher, holier Church of the living God.  Observe
this is expressive,

(1.) Of their honour—true dignity.

(2.) Of their security.

(3.) Of their privileges and favours.

Then, observe, we are taught,

**III. The blessings connected with these privileges.**

And here there is reference,

1. To *spiritual* illumination.  " God may enlighten,"
&c.  Psa. xiii. 3; xxxiv. 5.

(1.) Eyes to see their own unworthiness.

(2.) Their own helplessness.

(3.) The Lord's goodness.

(4.) The Lord's will and ways.

2. Spiritual *reviving*.  Re-kindling of the fire—stirring
up—re-inspiring—re-strengthening—reviving.  Faith—
hope—zeal—love—obedience.

3. *Gratefulness*, &c., for deliverances.  In our bondage
—that God should shew grace.  Deliverance from it,
&c.  And now gratefully reviewed it, &c.

4. The *brevity* of these *signal* mercies—"a little space."
For working—fighting—building up ourselves.  Also
the Church—" little space."  We are reminded of this,

(1.) By those who have passed away.  The fathers,
&c.  Those we have known—succeeded.

(2.) By the advance we have made in life.  Look
back to childhood—youth, &c., how changed!

(3.) By the uncertain, fragmentary remains, we can
only possess.  " Time is short," &c.  " We spend our
years as a tale that is told."  The Judge at the door.
" I must work while it is called day," &c.  " Whatever
thine hand findeth to do," &c.  Let the subject be,

1. A test of character.  Are we of the remnant?
Called—the chosen—the faithful !

2. An appeal as to our position. In the Church, a nail or pin—somewhere. A question as to our desires,

3. Are we seeking the reviving? An exhortation,

4. Appeal to those outside the Church to come with us, &c.


# CXXXI

## SELF-CONSTRUCTION

" But ye, beloved, building up yourselves on your most holy faith, praying in the Holy Ghost."—Jude i. 20.

CHRISTIAN co-operation with the Divine Spirit, and with the influence of the Saviour's grace, everywhere recognized. Not alone—not in the spirit of self-righteousness, but in reliance on the Divine Spirit—working with God, and acted upon, and re-acting.

Observe,

**I. The designation.**

" Beloved " of God—of Jesus, the Mediator—of the apostles—of one another. Term indicates relationship —endearment—complacency. Notice,

**II. The assumption.**

"That they were on the right foundation." Every building must have a base, or foundation. Coming to Christ and building on Him. He is the one foundation. Sure—tried—precious—everlasting.

**III. The duty—" Building," &c.**

1. Here is Christian *individualism*. " Ye "—everyone —all, &c.

2. Here is religious *personalism*. " Building up yourselves." May assist others—but here is the primary, the first work.

3. This personal religion is *progressive* and *heavenward*.

" Building up "—rising—ascending—structure growing heavenwards—living above—seeking the things, &c.

4. The great *starting point.*   On your faith—most holy faith—faith justifies—faith sanctifies.   All real faith is holy.   Now there is,

1. The Gospel of our holy faith.
2. The Word of faith.
3. The Ordinances of faith.
4. The Grace of faith.
5. The Profession of faith.
6. The Work of faith.
7. The Source of faith.

Observe,

**IV. How we are thus to build up ourselves.**

(1.) By the Spirit's gracious aid.
(2.) By sanctified perseverance.
(3.) By devout reliance on Jesus.
(4.) By fidelity to instituted means.
(5.) By a simple Christ-living experience.   " I live, yet not I, but Christ liveth in me."

**V. The importance of realizing the condition indicated.**

1. To our Christian *establishment.*   Thus we become settled—grounded—fixed.

2. *Growing conformity* to Christ.   Thus we rise to be assimilated to Christ.   Become like Christ.   Changed into His image, from glory to glory, by the Spirit of the Lord.

3. The *increase* of all our graces.   Hope—love, &c.

4. Our *abiding* consolation.   Thus we obtain assurance and peace—both growing, &c.

5. Our *salvation.*   Avoiding apostacy—shipwreck—cast-aways, &c.   Fulness of grace, and meetness for glory.

The subject should lead—

1. To examination, full and repeated.
2. Earnest supplication for efficient grace.
3. A close imitation of the Saviour's life.
4. Nonconformity to the world.
5. Some have not come to the foundation. Come now; and then act on the teaching of the text.


## CXXXII
## WITHOUT CHARITY NOTHING

"And though I have the gift of prophesy, and understand all mysteries, and all knowledge; and though I have all faith, so that I could remove mountains, and have not charity, I am nothing."—1 Cor. xiii. 2.

MISTAKES about the word—"love" is the term; the original word, "agapee," is a pure Christian word, and it is said is not found in any heathen writer whatever. Now this magnificent chapter, or grand poem, stands alone.

Now let us,

**I. Look at the word in its comprehensive significancy.**

And here it stands out in various forms and phases.

Look at it,

1. As an *animal instinct*. All creatures have it—the bear—the hen, &c. So it is the basis of all human relationship—parental, filial, conjugal, fraternal, &c.

2. In its *social elements*. Binding society together—distinct relationships—social circle.

3. In its *patriotic sphere*. Country—nation.

4. In its *extended philanthropy*. Love of species—the balm of humanity—God made of one blood—all brethren—anatomical form the same—physical characteristics and emotional nature, &c. All the sons of one father. Then we see the special idea in the text.

5. Divine *love*. Heaven-born charity—Divine love implanted—fire from the celestial altar. The love of God shed abroad in the heart by the Divine Spirit. Essentially of the Divine nature.

Now this love,

(1.) Ascends to its Divine source — loving God supremely.

(2.) Extends to His Divine family.

(3.) Comprehends all mankind. Such is the nature of this love.

**II. Look at its attributes.**

How it is to be known. It is,

(1.) Long-suffering; v. 4.

(2.) Kind and benignant.

(3.) Unenvious.

(4.) Modest and humble.

(5.) Well-behaved; v. 5.

(6.) Unselfish.

(7.) Pure in its delights; v. 6.

(8.) Candid and hopeful; v. 7. How God-like and loveable it is—the image of the Father—the mind of Christ—the very spirit of the Holy Ghost. Such are its essential perfections—such the leaves and fruit of this tree of life.

**III. Its essential necessity.**

"Without charity we are nothing." How striking, express, absolute, the term "nothing." Nothing, a cypher—a nonentity.

1. See this in its *lower forms*. A father, mother, brother, sister, friend, patriot. See this,

2. In its *religious character*. This is the Divine image, without it we are nothing. The great commandment, &c. Evidence of our union and oneness with Christ, without it nothing. We are temples of the Holy Spirit, but without the spirit of love, nothing.

3. In *religious services*. Without it nothing—Christian duties—prayer, praise, worship, hearing, preaching, baptism, Lord's Supper, suffering, dying; v. 1, 2. I am nothing in myself—nothing for Christ, or the Church, or mankind. I could not be a true man without it, nor a good Pagan, or Mahommedan, nor Jew, much less a good Christian.

Now see, in application,

1. For this there is no substitute. Learning, knowledge, philosophy, science, gifts, &c.—all vain, &c.

2. How necessary to possess it. Where obtained?— above. How?—by prayer—God's Spirit—the true fire.

3. How desirable to cultivate it. All its features richly, fully abound, &c.

4. How necessary to manifest it. Early Christians.

5. Its real blessedness. Essence of all enjoyment— of all bliss.

6. The essential qualification for glory. Heaven is love—its atmosphere, association, worship, song, service and glory.


## CXXXIII

## DIVINE FAVOUR ENTREATED

"I entreated thy favour with my whole heart."—PSALM cxix. 58.

How worthy is this prayer of our adoption. Of the adoption of all the Lord's people. Let us see,

I. What is entreated?

"Thy favour." God's gracious smile and blessing. For God's favour includes every possible good. But notice, it is favour in opposition to displeasure—in distinction from wages, for work done. It is favour or grace, for grace's sake. Not what we deserve, but what God freely bestows, and bestows according to the riches of His love and mercy.

1. It is *forgiving* favour, by which all sins are remitted and blotted out.

2. It is *adopting* favour. Making aliens and enemies, the friends and children of God.

3. It is *sanctifying* favour, by which we are made holy, and transformed into the Divine likeness.

4. It is *sustaining* and *preserving* favour, by which we are kept and secured from the evils by which we are surrounded.

5. It is *gladdening* favour,—so that our joy is made full, and abounds to the glory of God. How necessary, important, and precious is this favour of God! For it, there is no substitute. It is better than life, and the only antidote to the fear of death.

**II. How he entreated it.**

With his "whole heart."

1. It might be *expressed* in words. We have many such words of prayer in the Psalms, and through all the Scriptures.

2. It did *proceed* from the *heart*. All real prayer does so. With the Spirit, from the inner man—the understanding—the affections, and the will.

3. It was the *devotional* exercise of the *whole* heart. Not half-hearted. Not cold-hearted. Not nominal, or formal, but with all the moral force of the whole soul.

And now see,

**III. The grounds, or reasons, for the entreaty thus presented.**

We see a reason for this,

1. In God *Himself*. His grace is an ocean—full, overflowing, free, ready to be given.

2. In *ourselves*. We need it. Cannot dispense with it. Without it we are miserable, and shall be lost. We need it everywhere. At all times, and for all the purposes of this life, and meetness for the life to come.

3. We need it for *others*. To be lights to them—guides—friends—helpers—blessings. It is essential to our usefulness, &c. As we have this favour and abound in it, it will tell for the good of all around us. God's favour blesses us, and makes us blessings to others.

### APPLICATION

1. Do we enjoy this favour?
2. Are we seeking more of it,—to abound in it?
3. Do we seek it with the whole heart?
4. The Gospel offers this grace to all men.

## CXXXIV

### THE OBJECT OF OUR FAITH AND HOPE

" That your faith and hope might be in God."—1 Peter i. 21.

Faith trusts—hope expects. Faith accepts the testimony—hope expects the blessing. We first believe, and then hope. Faith and hope are welded links of the same chain, and the end of the chain holds on to Christ crucified, and Christ risen again. Now our faith and hope should not be,

**I. In ourselves.**

Our righteousness is as filthy rags. Our desert, death. Our estate, pollution. Our condition, utter moral insolvency. Our faith and hope,

**II. Should not be in our fellow creatures.**

Not in patriarchs—nor Moses—nor the prophets—nor

apostles—nor martys—nor priests—nor saints, living or dead—nor in the Virgin Mary.

**III. Should not be in angels.**

We may hail them as friends. Emulate their goodness. Rejoice in their ministrations—but they are not mediators, nor objects of faith and hope.

**IV. But our faith and hope should be in God.**

1. In the *Father*,—the source and fountain of all goodness and mercy.

2. In the *Son of God*,—the one mediator, sacrifice, and only Saviour.

3. In the *Holy Spirit of God*,—the fountain of grace the light—the truth and solace of our souls.

LEARN

1. To avoid *false trusts* and illusive confidences.

2. Learn that *God only* is the *living* fountain of waters. All else cisterns, broken cisterns.

3. Learn how *needful* is *self-examination.* Do we really, consciously believe and hope in God? Have we the evidence in our hearts, and the fruit thereof in our lives? Let us sing—

> " Now I have found the ground wherein
> Sure my soul's anchor may remain," &c.

CXXXV

## GOD'S UNWILLINGNESS THAT MEN SHOULD PERISH

" Not willing that any should perish, but that all should come to repentance."—2 PETER iii. 9.

THE sentiment of the text is expressed in every conceivable form in the Word of God. Ezek. xxiii. 11. It is so opposite to sentiments often published, that we do not

SKETCH CXXXV

wonder that men try to explain it away. But the
evidence in its support is absolutely irrefragable and
overwhelming.

**I. Let us look at the truth presented.**

"That God is not willing that any should perish."
That any wicked person should die in his sins. That
any transgressor should reject His infinite mercy. That
any of any class, or turpitude of heinous guilt, should
persistently by his indifference or unbelief, or procrastination, die out of Christ, without hope, and should
go down to the black dungeon of woe and destruction. Let us,

**II. Look at the evidences of the truth of this declaration.**

Here we have,

1. The *essential loving character* of God. God is love·
He cannot hate even the rebel, the traitor, &c., while
His holiness hates his sin, His love yearns for his
salvation.

2. The *provision* He has *made* for *men's* salvation.
Gave—sent—delivered up—did not spare His own Son.
Sent Him to seek—to restore, and bestow everlasting
life. All Christ's person—offices—mission and work,
confirm the text. John iii. 14-17. But by His Spirit
he takes the Gospel proclamation, and thus it becomes
all-powerful to save every believer.

3. His *declarations* and *promises*.

4. His *entreaties* and *expostulations*.

5. His *patient waiting* and *long-suffering*.

(1.) The subject is full of hope for mankind. He
wills not that any should perish.

(2.) The subject intimates how men only can escape
perishing—"By repentance." Change of mind—turning from sin to God, which is ever associated with
a believing acceptance of God's salvation.

(3.) The declaration of the text must be made known to every creature. Matt. xxviii. 18, 19; xvi. 15, &c.; Luke xxiv. 46, 47.

## CXXXVI
## THE NOBLE RESOLVE

"I will delight myself in thy statutes: I will not forget thy word." —PSALM cxix. 16.

THE statutes of the Lord are right, pure, good, necessary. Have ever been prized by God's people. This resolve includes,

**I. Delight in God's statutes.**

Involving a reception of them. Constant perusal. Divine meditation. And this as a joy and privilege, and not as a mere duty.

**II. Remembrance of God's Word.**

Retaining it in the heart. Using it when necessary. Joyous celebration of its preciousness.

**III. Why this resolve should be maintained.**

1. In honour of the Word. 2. In gratefulness to God. 3. For our general and special advantage. We must know God's statutes, to delight in them. Remembering God's Word will be our comfort and security. Meditation and prayer will give us a sanctified and profitable application.

## CXXXVII
## CHRISTIAN ABASEMENT

"How to be abased."—PHILIP. iv. 12.

THE text is the language of one of the greatest of the apostles—the great Paul.

**I. Look at his own self-abasement.**

"Less than the least of all saints." Chief of sinners. As nothing before God. See chap. iii. 7, 8 ; Gal. vi. 14.

**II. Look at his abasement.**

From false teachers. Galatians abounds in this.

**III. Look at his sufferings for his Master and the Church's sake.**

2. Cor. xi. 21-23, to end. What an inventory of sorrows and griefs ! and all this culminating in a martyr's death. Now let us see,

**IV. The principles of this abasement.**

1. Voluntary and cheerful. 2. Sustained by an invincible faith. 3. Constrained by the Saviour's love. 4. Maintained by the glorious crown in hopeful prospect. 2 Tim. iv. 5, &c. Learn, humility is the way to honour. The cross essential to the crown. "If we suffer," &c. Seek the spirit of lowliness. "Learn of Me," said Jesus, &c. So Philip. ii. 8. "Let this mind be in you," &c.


## CXXXVIII

## THE ILLUSTRIOUS SAINTS

" Of whom the world was not worthy."—HEB. xi. 38.

THE text refers to that glorious roll of God's servants, of the great and good, spoken of in this chapter. The text intimates their pre-eminent superiority to the world in which they lived. Let us see,

**I. This superiority.**

It might not always be in learning, philosophy, or art. It was moral, religious, spiritual.

(1.) They were the sons and daughters of Jehovah, and worshipped Him. (2.) They were the religious lights of their age and countries. (3.) They were models of living excellencies. Not perfect, but how superior to those around them! Enoch—Noah. (4.) They were the blessings of society. Job—Abraham—Joseph—Moses, &c. And let us now see,

**II. How the world treated them.**

Look how Noah was treated, and Lot and Samson and Jephtha and Daniel. The three Hebrews, Isaiah, Jeremiah. How Israel was carried into captivity. Many of the other prophets. Illustrious Baptist—holy Stephen —the wise and good—James, &c. See how,

**III. Their superiority was sustained.**

1. By *faith* in God and *trust* in His promises.

2. By the *grace* given in their suffering.

3. By the *presence* of their God and Saviour. In the lions' den. In the furnace.

4. By anticipating the *glorious* future *reward*. Abraham, Moses, David looked to the invisible God. Expected a heavenly residence—anticipated everlasting rest; and thus held on and held fast to the end, and died in the faith and hope of God's promised glory.

### LEARN

1. Christians ought to be better than the world in which they live.

2. Christ will confess His own, and reward them at His second coming.

3. Such worthy lives should inspire us with holy emulation.

## CXXXIX
## THE AVOIDANCE OF ERROR
" Do not err, my beloved brethren."—JAMES i. 16.

ALL fallible beings are liable to err. But it is alike the

duty and interest of all men to adopt the best means of avoiding it. Notice,

**I. The wide region of error.**

Error is possible on all subjects, which religion comprises—

1. On the nature and perfections of God.
2. On the person and offices of Christ.
3. On the work and operations of the Holy Spirit.
4. On the claims and prerogatives of the Scriptures.
5. On the nature of saving religion.
6. On the ordinances and duties of Christianity.
7. On the rewards and punishments of a future state.

**II. The best way of keeping out of this region.**

1. By cleaving to the clear teaching of holy Scripture.
2. Asking wisdom and understanding from God.
3. By avoiding a proud and self-sufficient spirit.
4. By humbly labouring to do God's will.
5. By testing all principles and doctrines with the holy, just and benevolent character of God.

APPLICATION.

We should hearken to the text—

1. From love of the truth.
2. From concern for our own spiritual well-being.
3. And for the honour of the religion we profess.

# CXL

## CHRISTIAN LOVE

" Love one another with a pure heart fervently."—1 PETER i. 22.

THE love of the brethren is the test of our Christianity, and the badge of our Christian profession. It is even the essential of the new man. Without it, all religious profession is mere glitter--an empty show—a noisy cymbal. But what is this love? Let us see,

**I. Its nature.**

It is admiration. Estimation, and complete complacency in the Lord's people. It recognizes them as brethren and sisters in Christ, and fellow-heirs of the grace of life. It will include attachment, fellowship, communion, and spiritual adhesion, and unselfish conduct and conversation.

**II. Its extent.**

All the Lord's people. It is not to be sectarian, denominational, local. It is not to be limited to persons of our order, creed, or mode of worship. Every saint of God—every disciple of Jesus—every saint walking in holiness.

**III. Its special traits.**

1. It is to be the *love* of the *heart*. All else is tinsel and make-believe.

2. It is to be the love of a *pure heart*. Not love of their person, with a fleshly attachment, but love pure as light, and sanctifying as flame.

3. It is to be *hot* and *intense*. "Fervently." Not coldly—not formally—not pretentiously—not confined to the tongue, but a holy flame, fervent. Not to be quenched—not to go out, but burn and shine in loving words and deeds—always to the glory of God.


# CXLI

## ON ENDURANCE

" Behold we count them happy which endure."—JAMES v. 11.

SUCH as—

**I. Endure in their work and toil.**

Labouring on till the Master calls.

**II. Enduring the trials and sufferings of life.**

As Job. Not rebelling—not mourning; but patiently bearing God's will.

**III. Enduring severe temptations.**

Not yielding, but resisting unto blood.

**IV. Enduring in the bitter warfare of faith.**

Standing fast—faithful—magnanimous—warring a good warfare.

**V. Enduring pains and persecutions for Christ.**

Bearing His cross. Imbibing His spirit. Treading in His steps.

**VI. Enduring the fatigues of the Christian pilgrimage.**

Faint, still pursuing. Going from strength to strength. Enduring to the end.

**VII. The blessedness of Christian endurance.**

Happy, or blessed are they,

1. In themselves. Having peace and a good conscience. 2. Blessed in their heavenward progress. 3. Blessed in their influence on others. 4. Happy in the hope of inconceivable and eternal glory, in the world to come.

Then the text may cheer, console, and invigorate the children of God. How wretched they who turn aside, who fail, and fall away.

# CXLII

## GOD OUR HELPER

"Behold, God is mine helper."—PSALM liv. 4.

MAN often stands in need of Divine help. It is good and pleasant to enjoy the help of our fellow-saints, but their help is limited, uncertain, and often valueless.

Not so God—He is possessed of every qualification, so there never can be failure with Him. Notice,

**I. When God is the helper of His people.**

1. In the *great crisis* of their *conversion.* He raiseth from the pit, delivers, saves, &c.

2. In the *troubles* and *afflictions* of *life.* These are many, varied, sometimes severe, &c. Job, the apostles; 2 Cor. i. 8-10.

3. In the *perils* and *conflicts* of their *warfare.* Psalm xxxvii. 5; cxlvi. 5; lx. 11.

4. In their *labours* and *toils* in His *kingdom.* Ps. cxxi. 1.

5. In *weakness, sickness* and *death.* Psalm xxiii; cxvi.

**II. What kind of a helper is God?**

1. Always near at hand. 2. Always efficient and sufficient. 3. Perpetual and everlasting.

**III. The conclusions to which the subject should lead us.**

1. Personal knowledge and reliance on God. 2. Unwavering faith and hope. 3. Constant prayer and supplication. He will be sought and enquired of. 4. Acknowledgment and praise. "Bless the Lord at all times," &c.


## CXLIII

### SAFE TRUST

" For I trust in thy word."—Psalm cxix. 42.

The whole of this long Psalm is about God's word. He tells us he delights in it—meditates in it—hides it in his heart—and in the text that it is his trust. God's word must be known, received and cherished, before it will be our trust. Observe,

**I. In what respects God's word is to be our trust.**

1. As the *directory* of our faith.

2. As the *charter* of our privileges.

3. As the *guide* of our feet.

4. As the *rule* of our life.

5. As the *inspirer* of our hopes.

**II. The reasons for this trust.**

1. It is God's *word.* And therefore Divine, true, pure, and essential.

2. It is *our word.*. God's gift to us.

3. It is necessary to *salvation.*

4. Full of *comfort.*

5. No *substitute* for it. Word of light, life, peace; profitable for instruction, &c. This trust must be personal, conscious, entire, always.


# CXLIV

## STRENGTHENED WITH ALL MIGHT

"Strengthened with all might."—COL. i. 11.

THE absolute weakness of man in things moral and good is ever presented to us in the Holy Scriptures. Our depravity has produced first indisposition to all good, and powerlessness to effect it—Christians, by the grace of God, feel this all through their experience. Theirs is the warfare—the flesh warring, &c. Now the perfection of the Christian character is not effected without the co-operation of the believer. "He works out," &c., while God "works in him," &c. Now the source of all the Christian's ability is presented in the text—"strengthened," &c. Now observe,

**I. The Christian's need of strength.**

Now this in many respects is evident.

1. He is to *stand fast* in the *Christian profession.*

The way slippery,—assailed, weak, &c. So he must be made able to stand.

2. He is to *advance* in the *Christian life*. A pilgrim, &c. Now he is to have journeying ability—strength for the pilgrimage. Besides, it is likened to a race—competition, speed.

3. He has to *work* for the Saviour. As Nehemiah and his co-patriots—as in the vineyard—and as a fisherman, &c. Now his hand and arm require strength.

4. He has to *suffer* for Christ. Trials, temptations, afflictions. Now he needs enduring power—strong in the passive virtues—so that he can do nothing in the Divine life without strength.

**II. Divine might is provided for the Christian.**

Observe, here is a reference,

1. To *might* or *power* for his use. It is evidently the might of God—the might of the Holy Spirit. Now it is thus explicitly stated; Isaiah xli. 10; so also Eph. iii. 15.

2. This might is *all-sufficient*. All might, all needed all degrees, at all times, for all purposes.

3. This might is *illimitable*. No measure, no bounds, no interruptions, no end. Now see,

**III. The process of strengthening the Christian by this all might.**

Here is the Christian's weakness—here is God's almightiness. Now this almightiness,

1. Must be *known*. There may be a well and a traveller dying of thirst close by, because he knows it not—a vessel in a storm, and a safe haven—a traveller in a tempest, and a refuge. Now God's moral might must be known. "They that know their God," &c.

2. It must be *supplied* from God to us. By faith we lay hold of God's might—even the touch of faith—faith to be healed—to stand, &c.—all things possible, &c.

3. It must be *realized*. Faith must ask, seek, and knock, "Lord, help me!" See Paul; 2 Cor. xii. 7. Until we feel it,

4. It must be *exercised*. God gives strength not to be latent but active—to be employed. So we are strengthened to expend it—lay it out. He who works can work, &c. Battles—runs. Now observe,

**IV. The evidences that we are thus strengthened with all might.**

1. Abiding *patience*. "All patience," in trials, through them, even to the end.

2. Evident *long-suffering*. Not only bearing without murmuring, but under extreme trials—not repelling our foes, but bearing with them.

3. In the spirit of *joyfulness*. Not sullenness, but cheerfulness—joyful in tribulation. This is the difficult thing; yet by the Divine might this can be done. They look joyfully on the spoiling of their goods—went to prison—sang praises at the rack and the stake, &c. Now these are the unmistakeable fruits of the strengthening power of God. Now observe,

1. The Christian's plea of weakness is unsatisfactory.

2. The Christian's resources ever sufficient.

3. Christian security absolute.


## CXLV

## GOD'S GLORIOUS POWER

"According to his glorious power," &c.—Col. i. 11.

POWER is a very comprehensive word. It varies in signification as you apply it to the material, scientific, mental, moral, spiritual, magisterial. There is the power or material force of a waterfall, stream, wind, avalanche,

&c. Scientific power is material power collected, directed, controlled—as in regulated air, in steam, electric forces. There is mental power, as in vigourous thoughts and ideas expressed in words. We see this in Shakspeare, Milton, Chalmers, &c. Moral power is seen in the influence of obedience and law, virtue, &c.; in the parent, master, citizen, &c. Spiritual power is that energy exerted on man's inner nature—regenerating and renewing the soul. Now let us look at some of the illustrations of God's glorious power.

Notice,

**I. It is the power of the glorious Deity.**

It is God's omnific energy. God's omnipotent might or almightiness. This power is essentially God's. " In thine hand is power and might." The voice of the Lord is powerful. " The thunder of His power," &c. " Right hand is glorious in power." " The Lord God omnipotent!" "Everlasting strength." So you will see how this power is the glory of God—it is linked to His eternity—infinity—unchangeableness—and all sufficiency.

Notice,

**II. It is the glorious power of Divine creatorship.**

Originating all materialism into existence. Commanding all things to be, &c. Look at the earth—the air— the seas! Look on high! Take the telescope, and visit the world beyond the ken of the naked eye. See Isa. xl. 12-26; Rom. i. 20, &c. Then the formation of what His power had created. Garnishing the heavens—fixing the ocean—settling the mountains.

Then there is,

**III. The glorious power of His dominion.**

The stability of the world. He commanded, and it stood fast. For the mighty arrangement. See Isa.

xl. 12 ; Deut. iv. 35; Nahum i. 3, &c. The sustaining
of the universe. The controlling of all creatures, and
all worlds. 2 Chron. xxix. 12. Now this dominion is infinite, irresistible, and everlasting.

Then notice,

**IV. This glorious power in Christ and in His word and gospel.**

Divine utterances are in creation and providence,
enough. He "speaks" and "wills," and it is done!
Now God's moral word, in Scripture, is mighty to lift
up nations. "To exalt," &c. His "gospel" is the
power of God, &c. But see it incarnated in Jesus.
Observe its operations on diseases, demons, death.
Satan and the elements of nature. See this power
going forth with salvation. Read Mark xvi. 17-20. All
the miracles of the apostles. All the inner working of
the spirit on the souls. "Our Gospel," &c. "I am not
ashamed," &c.

So we see,

**V. This glorious power in the building up of the Church and
preservation of His saints.**

"I build my church, and the gates of hell," &c.
"Who can harm?" &c. I give eternal life, and none
shall pluck, &c. See the early church of the Jews,
against it. Paganism against it. World against it.
Hell against. All that is mighty on the earth. Wealth,
rank, armies, &c. Yet the Church was built up. Millions converted. Saints saved, &c.; and so it shall be,

**VI. Till this glorious power shall triumph over all.**

Able to "subdue all things to Himself." Cast down
the prince of the power of the air, &c. "Bind that old
serpent, the devil." Blot out night and darkness—sin
and rebellion—misery and woe. "He must reign!"
Then death and hades shall be cast, &c. And then the
new heaven shall be seen. Rev. xxi. 1-6. Now such
are some illustrations of the glorious power of God.

The use of the subject is manifold—

1. Here we may wonder and adore.
2. Here we many exult and praise.    Then,
3. Here we may flee and trust.
4. Here we may rest and repose.
5. Here we are cheered in our resources—glorious power for the use of all God's saints.    Workers of all kinds, &c.    Here we look at the certain triumph of the future.


## CXLVI

## THE SAINTS' THANKS FOR MEETNESS FOR THEIR INHERITANCE

" Giving thanks unto the Father, which hath made us meet," &c·
—Col. i. 12.

Light and darkness are striking features.    Constantly used by nearly all the sacred writers.    They are expressive of good and evil—joy and misery—glory and woe. The light and darkness remind us, therefore, of our former and new spiritual condition; v. 13.    So "ye were darkness, but are now light," &c.    "Have no fellowship," &c.    " Ye are not of the night and of darkness," &c.    Now thus we shall see the signification of the text.    Notice,

**I. The inheritance.**

The inheritance of the text is two-fold.

1. An *inheritance* of grace.    A place in God's covenant —in God's family.    Into this family we are brought by God's adopting love, with all its privileges.    This is the spiritual kingdom of God in the soul.    The realized portion of the Divine redemption.

2. An *inheritance* of glory.    This is the inheritance on

the other side of Jordan. It is the completion of the saints' portion. "Lord will give both grace and glory," &c. Called to His eternal kingdom and glory. This is the saints future home. The Father's house— the mansion in Heaven. Now these two are really but one. Like the family on earth and in heaven. See Eph. iii. 15. Notice,

3. This *inheritance* is for the saints. The holy children of God. "Those translated." "Begotten again." Sons of God. The wicked reject it—despise it—neglect it, as Esau did his birthright. It is,

4. An *inheritance* of light. Light may refer to the spiritual condition of the saints, or to the inheritance, or both. But as applied to the inheritance, it signifies,

(1.) An inheritance of knowledge. Eyes opened. They have been taught to know Christ. Partial knowledge here. Full and perfect hereafter. 1 Cor. xii. 13. (2.) An inheritance of purity. Holiness is the characteristic of Christ's kingdom, here and hereafter. (3.) An inheritance of joy. Bliss. Light is sown, &c. This is now, therefore, the inheritance. It is their present portion, and future prospect. Isa. xxxv. 10; Rev. xxi. 3, &c. Then see,

**I. Their meetness for it.**

This is in the present tense—"hath made." A thing of present experience. Not at death or purgatory, but now. They have the title; but there must be fitness for the inheritance. And this is spiritual knowledge— "To know Thee," &c. Holy renewal of the soul. Born of and for the kingdom. Peace and joy in the Holy Ghost. Now these constitute the meetness, and include every thing. Observe, it is not wealth—rank —talents—learning. All these may belong to the children of darkness—but Divine knowledge, sanctifying and

blessed. Now this meetness is God's work or fitness
in us. "The Father." The great source. By the
grace of His Son. By the power of His Spirit. By His
sanctifying energy. By His work and ordinances, &c.
It is God's work, and, therefore, is not "self-made"
meetness. Nor priest-made meetness. Nor sacramental
meetness. But God—made meetness by regenerating
and adopting and sanctifying grace. Then see,

### III. The thanks due to God on account of it.

Thanks may be,

1. *Vocal.* "O Lord, I will praise!" &c. A new song
for the new creature. Or,

2. *Spiritual.* Making melody to the Lord in our
hearts. Inward gratitude. Or,

3. *Practical.* By a devoted service and life. One
holy psalm to the Lord. Glorifying God.

Now these thanks should be—1. Most earnest: not
formal. 2. Most constant and unceasing. And then, 3.
They will be eternal. For evermore. Songs of grace
will be followed by the praises of glory.

Now let the subject—

1. Shew the unity of the two kingdoms—grace and
glory.

2. The adaptation of the Christian to both.

3. The joyous, grateful character of the new life.

4. The absolute confidence of the true Christian.
The two linked. "I know whom, &c., and am persuaded He will keep;" 2 Tim. i. 12. "Fear not, &c., it is
your Father's good pleasure," &c.

## CXLVII

### LAW AND GRACE—MOSES AND CHRIST

"For the law was given by Moses, but grace and truth came by Jesus Christ."—JOHN i. 17.

THE evangelist directs our attention to the pre-eminency of the Lord Jesus over Moses, who was the glory of the Jewish economy ; and he does this by opening to us the differences in these economies of which they were respectively representatives. Moses was the head of the legal dispensation, and therefore stood essentially connected with it. Of the New Testament dispensation, Christ was the head, and though Moses had been favoured above all men in the communion he had with Jehovah, yet he never saw God, for God had said, "No man can see My face and live ; " but Christ, the only-begotten of the Father, had dwelt in His bosom, and came to declare Him to the world. Such then are the great truths presented in the text. Observe,

### I. We have Moses and the law.

This law might comprise the whole economy of the legal dispensation.

1. The *moral law* given on Sinai. That which is given at full length in the pages of Old Testament history; Exodus xx. Never were scenes so grand and sublime witnessed by mortals. The apostle referred to it; Heb. xii. 18; see also Deut. iv. 10, &c.

But it might mean,

2. The *ritual law*. Law of ordinances, sacrifices, ceremonials, &c., for obtaining purification, &c. Here was a grand pictorial system of religious rites, &c., which occupies the greater part of the book of Leviticus, and then,

3. There were the *statutes relative* to the *government* of the people, and by which they were all directed, from the rulers downwards. Well, the law in its threefold aspect, including the entire will of God concerning Israel, was given by Moses. He was appointed to be the voice of God to the people. Now the law thus given could not make the people holy, because it had to come in contact with depravity, which rendered perfect obedience impossible. But the law could shew God's just claims, and could produce a sense of guilt and condemnation, and could fill with fearful alarm as to the Divine penalty, and the law thus could be a school-master to teach men their need of a Saviour, and induce them to exercise faith in the promised Messiah.

Now see,

**II. What came by Jesus Christ.**

Now, while Moses was a deliverer, his especial vocation was lawgiver ; but Christ came expressly to reveal God's love, and to save, &c.

1. " *Grace came* by Jesus Christ." He brought grace, that is favour, to the undeserving and guilty. He did not bring a message of condemnation, but of salvation ; John iii. 17. Now by Christ came,

1. The *declaration* of *grace*. Jesus Christ taught expressly and fully the grace of God to man, thus He did what the law could not do. The law had no grace, but condemned the guilty, and handed them over to punishment. Jesus made gracious overtures to men, the worst, and to all.

2. He *exercised* and *dispensed* this *grace*. He did so to the extortionate publican—to the woman who was a sinner—to many beside, and last of all to the dying malefactor, and never rejected any.

3. He *set up* a *kingdom* of *grace*. His apostles and

disciples were to be prepared for it—hear Christ's declarations and orders; Luke xxiv. 46-49.

4. He came that *grace* might be *honourably imparted*. Not at the sacrifice of justice—not to the relinquishing of the law's demands—not to the giving license for sin and rebellion, but through Christ's perfect obedience, spotless purity, and sacrificial merits, that God might be the just God, and yet the justifier of the ungodly. So that grace came by Christ's lips in His teaching—in Christ's offices as the Christ and Saviour—by Christ's blood which He poured out as an atonement for sin— and now by Christ's Gospel and the working of the Holy Spirit. But by Christ came also,

2. *Truth.* The truth concerning God—the truth concerning His love and mercy—the truth of man's sin and peril and helplessness—the truth of promises now fulfilled—the truth of prophecies now accomplished— the truth of sacrifices and types now ended in the great sacrifice. Christ preached the truth—lived the truth— witnessed for the truth—and then sealed it with His blood—justified it by His resurrection—and confirmed it by the Holy Ghost sent down from Heaven. Christ Himself was both the grace and the truth. But now see,

### III. Christ's special qualifications for His work.

1. His Divine *Sonship*. "The only-begotten"—having the very nature of God—one with the Father—having His whole mind, and,

2. His eternal *fellowship* with the Father. "Who is in the bosom"—was so in the beginning—has ever been so—is so now. The delight of the Father, and by this communion Christ knew God—knew Him fully, perfectly. Moses had a few glimpses—Christ saw all His glory— Moses was in special communion a few times—Christ ever.

3. Christ had *revealed* God. God appeared in the cloud and with thunderings as lawgiver—but Christ declared His goodness, love, mercy. "As a father pitieth," &c. A forgiving God, &c. Then let us,

1. Hold Moses in reverence.

2. See the use of the law.

3. Adore and love the Lord Jesus Christ.

4. And receive into our hearts the grace and truth He has brought for our acceptance and salvation.


## CXLVIII

## MONEY, AND BIBLE TESTIMONY CONCERNING IT

" But they that will be rich fall into temptation and a snare," &c. —1 Tim. vi. 9, 10.

" But money answereth all things."—Eccles. x. 19.

NOTHING more paradoxical apparently than the testimony of the Bible concerning riches, or money. So the two texts. They are a good and a curse. A blessing and a snare. Answer all things, and are most uncertain, &c. Both books, Old and New Testament, give us counsel, &c.

I. Money in itself is a great good.

1. *Solomon* says—"Money answereth all things." Ecc. x. 19.

2. Hence *riches* are God's *gift*. See Deut. viii. 18; Job xxii. 24.

3. So there were *many eminently* pious, and yet rich. Abraham; Genesis xxiv. 35. Job; Job i. 3; xlii. 12. Solomon; 2 Chron. ix. 27. So in Christ's day. There were Nicodemus, Joseph of Arimathea, &c.; others. So in every age and nation. Observe,

4. Riches give great *facilities* for *usefulness* and *good* doing. What institutions it supports! What blessings conveyed! What influence exerted! What good of every kind diffused! Reynolds, Peabody, &c. Some of our living true noblemen and women. But notice,

**II. Money, however, is not to be enshrined in the heart.**

It is good in the purse. Good in the hand. Money is golden grain, seed corn. Not to be hoarded, but sown. For the hand, not the heart. For the wide liberal hand. Ruling hand to be governed, not to govern. Christ never craved it. The apostles disclaimed it. "Silver and gold," &c. How do I know whether I rightly value it, or love it? If I rightly value it, I shall be industrious in getting it. Wise in its expenditure. Cheerful in its distribution. Seed to be sown in the three acres,

1. Of the Lord's poor. 2. Of the Lord's Church. 3. Of the afflicted in the world.

If I love it—

1. There will be greed in getting it. Give me gold! Everything gives way to obtain it. 2. There will be clutching it—when possessed, anything but parting with it. 3. There will be hoarding it—adding to it. 4. Frequently talking about it. 5. Enshrining it in the heart. Money a good servant—good talent; but it is a curse in the heart. "The love," &c. It is gross idolatry —the veriest despotism—the cruelist tyrant.

1. It excludes God from the soul. Cannot love God and mammon. 2. Produces forgetfulness of God; Deut. viii. 13, 14. 3. It pollutes the conscience, and defiles the hands. 4. Is a rival to Christ. "The young man." 5. Renders salvation extremely difficult; Mark x. 21. 6. Is one of the chief causes of apostacy. "Demas," &c. So the text; v. 9. 7. Can never satisfy

the immortal mind. Material—gross. Eccl. v. 10, &c.
8. All the riches of the world cannot compensate for
the loss of the soul. "What shall it profit?" &c.
"Go to, ye rich," &c. The rich fool, &c. 9. Our text
summarises one bold declaration—the evil of the love of
money. The evils are legion. All sorts and all opposites. Pride and vanity—opposition and cruelty—
ambition and hardness of heart—blindness—deafness of
the soul—selfishness—sordidness—murders, &c.,—woman destroys her child—children kill their parents—
friends poison their confidents. By this, men league
with the world and the devil. "I will give thee all
these," &c. Now observe, there is,

### III. The remedy for this frightful evil.

1. A *conviction* of its *extreme folly*. It is madness—
moral insanity. When we see what it cannot do as to
body, or mind, or soul.

2. The *occupation* of the *soul* with the *chief* and *real*
good. The soul filled with God—the kingdom of God
—the fear of God—the supreme love of God—and
the constant realization of God.

3. The wise *estimate* of the *true* riches. The pearl of
great price. Wisdom—holiness—heirship to spiritual
treasures. Those of heaven and eternity. Hear Christ.
Matt. vi. 19, &c.

4. Daily *prayer* for *preserving* grace. Seek Divine
help. Seek Divine restraints. "Be anxious," &c.—but by
prayer.

5. A constant *remembrance* of our accountability for
its use. A talent that may bless or curse. The poor
may bless us, Christ commend, or God condemn. Ponder the subject. Seek the kingdom of God, &c.
Labour for the true riches, &c.

## CXLIX

## LOVE OF CHRIST, AND OUR LOVE TO HIM

" We love Him, because He first loved us."—1 JOHN iv. 19.

THE theme of John's epistle is love. The love of God to us. The love of Jesus as the Saviour. The love of saints to the Father and His Son. The love of believers to one another. The text leads us to the love of Christ and His people.

Observe,

### I. Christ is the fountain of love.

"He" first loved us. This is the universal and unvarying testimony of the Scriptures. Observe,

1. The *gradations* of Christ's *love* to us.

(1.) In His willingness to be our Mediator. Lo I "come." Not compelled. As Isaac, by faith, was ready, &c. He desired it—sought it.

(2.) In the assumption of our nature. Hence the Son of man. Made of a woman. Seed of Abraham—Tribe of Judah—lineage of David. But this step was wondrous. Not the nature of angels, but lower, &c. Not man — royalty—splendour—or sacerdotal—Priest. No! made Himself of no reputation. Bethlehem—manger—poor.

(3.) In taking the place of the substitute. Surety—Daysman — under law — suffering— soul sorrow — condemnation—death. "Bore our sorrows, griefs." Died the just for the unjust, &c. Sword, &c.

2. The *peculiarities* of His love.

(1.) Love to the base and the defiled—rebels, &c. (2.) Love unsought. Arising out of itself. For love's sake. (3) Unparalleled. Nothing like it. (4.) Infinite and inconceivable. Passeth knowledge.

Notice,

**II. In and from us love to Christ is asserted.**

" We love Him." This signifies, we esteem—admire
—delight, and are grateful to Jesus. Heart full of
Him. Now where this love is,

1. It is real and sincere. Not imaginative—not
rhapsody—impulse, &c. 2. It is conscious. " We love
Him." Know it—feel it. 3. It is evident. Its influence
is seen, for we love His word, sanctuary, ordinances,
day, people, commandments. 4. Supreme. Highest—
more than father or mother, &c. Look,

**III. At the connexion between the two.**

" We," " because," &c.

1. The love flowed from Him first.

2. Manifested to us.

3. Realized by us.

4. Then returned. As rivers to the ocean—light—
magnet.

5. Sustained.

### APPLICATION

First, who can utter the text. Second, let all seek to
feel it.

## CL

## THE EFFECTUAL FERVENT PRAYER

" The effectual fervent prayer of a righteous man availeth much."
—JAMES v. 16.

JAMES writes a great deal about prayer; chap: i. 5, 6.
It must be in faith, nothing wavering—a steady out-
stretched hand, looking, expecting, &c. He urges,
draw nigh, &c. He is speaking in the context of
prayer for others; v. 14, so in the text. Then he cites

Elias, and refers, in the concluding verse, to prayer in its converting agency; v. 19, 20. Now prayer for others is the subject of the text.

**I. The man who prays.**

"A righteous man." It does not mean an unfallen man, an innocent man, nor a perfect man—but a man,

1. In a *state* of *righteousness* or *justification*. Not in rebellion, not in enmity, but in a state of grace, accepted, justified.

2. A *renewed* man. One converted—born again.

3. An *obedient* man. One who serves God—who in heart and lip and life obeys God. Abel, Noah, Abraham, &c., were righteous, &c. So Zaccheus, so the Baptist, &c. Now an unrighteous man does not pray or feel his need, &c. But,

4. He is a *loving* man. He loves others, and feels for, prays for, &c. Love is the very atmosphere of evangelical and experimental righteousness. Now see,

**II. How he prays.**

In words, " effectual, fervent."

1. *Effectual* signifies inwrought. "Lord teach us!" Not mere outward—not saying or repeating, but put into the soul and inwrought, like veneering—like the works of a chronometer, like life in the body. Inwrought by " God's Holy Spirit;" Romans viii. 26; Jude xx.

2. *Fervent.* That is hot, earnest, vehement, &c., intense; see Heb. v. 7. It is said he prayed the " more earnestly." So of " Jacob," it is represented as " wrestling." Now these are the conditions or the features of the prayer spoken of in the text.

Observe,

**III. The obvious certain results.**

"Availeth much," that is in general succeeds, obtains the answer, &c. Now notice,

1. The *limitation*. "Availeth much." Not all—not always—as a rule it succeeds—failure is the exception. Christ prayed for His murderers, but we don't think they were all saved. Aaron, we should think, prayed for his sons, but they perished. So Eli for his sons—so no doubt David, &c., so many. It is "much"—not always.

2. See how Scripture *helps* us to notable *instances* when *prayer* did manifestly *avail*. Jacob was anxious for his family, &c., expected to meet an angry brother ; Gen. xxxii. 24, &c. Moses, the plague, the dying and dead, &c., the censer, &c.; Numb. xvi. 6; so the overthrow of Amalek; so Exodus xxxii. 10; xi. 14. Now the case of Elias in the text; v. 17, 18. Daniel's prayer closed the mouth of the lions, brought an archangel from Heaven; Daniel x. 10. The people prayed for Peter, and the gate of the prison opened; Acts xii. 5. Now in modern times prayer has been equally effectual. Instances numberless. Luther, Melancthon, Wesley Muller of Bristol, &c.

Now let us see in conclusion,—

1. The prerogative of prayer.
2. Its indispensable qualities ; and,
3. Be assured of its general victory.

## CLI

## GOD'S MERCY FILLING THE EARTH

"The earth, O Lord, is full of thy mercy."—PSALM cxix. 64.

MERCY signifies commiseration for the guilty and miserable. It includes the non-infliction of deserved wrath. Long-suffering and readiness to forgive the transgressor, on his acceptance of the Divine terms of reconciliation. In its widest sense it comprehends forbearance, compassion, grace and benevolent regard for the happiness of the wicked and utterly unworthy. Now of the Divine mercy, as well as of God's goodness, the earth is full, as stated in the text. Let us pursue this thought and see what it implies and involves,

**I. Mercy obviously governs the world.**

Not irrespective, much less in opposition to Divine holiness and justice and truth.

**II. Mercy has preserved our world from absolute woe and ruin.**

Since the entrance of moral evil, so repugnant to God's character and government, mercy has presided over the Divine councils, and has been manifested to all mankind, and from generation to generation.

**III. Mercy has assumed various forms and phases.**

(1.) Restrained deserved wrath. (2.) Foreborne punishment. (3.) Been long-suffering, patient,—been good and kind to the wicked—-to the just and the unjust—the evil and the good. (4.) Extended the probation of nations and individuals.

**IV. Divine mercy has been exercised to the vilest and most unworthy.**

**V. Mercy brought down an interposing Mediator and Saviour.**

Christ Jesus is mercy incarnate—mercy concentrated —mercy living, suffering, &c., for the ungodly. Dying for sinners, &c. Obtaining salvation. Opening the gates of the celestial paradise, &c.

**VI. Divine mercy sending forth the Gospel to all the world and to every creature.**

"Beseeching men to be reconciled to God."

**VII. The Divine mercy in the person and work of the Holy**

Spirit, for the convincement of sin and the regeneration of sinners.

VIII. Now this mercy may truly be said to fill the whole earth.

We notice this mercy,

(1.) It is free to all. Over all the Divine works. As the atmosphere of life to all. (2.) It is abundant. An ocean—yea infinite. Exod. xxiv. 6; Psalm lxxxvi. 15; ciii. 8. (3.) It is inexhaustible. Knows no diminution. (4.) It is eternal. "From everlasting to everlasting." Psalm ciii. 17. (5.) Yet it is sovereign in its exercise, and finds no reason for it but in the infinite depths of the loving will of God. See this stated, Exodus xxxiii. 9; Romans ix. 15.

The lessons from the subject are—

1. Men do not perish for any lack or limitation in God's mercy.

2. Divine mercy may be despised and rejected.

3. Of all sins, the refusal of God's mercy must be greatest.

4. Divine mercy is realized by faith in God's message of grace. Faith simply and unmeritoriously accepting it. Eye of misery, looking to the merciful Mediator —Saviour.

5. We have no intimation of overtures of mercy beyond the grave.

6. The minister's great message is mercy, and his great and onerous work to persuade men to receive it.


## CLII

## SALVATION BY GRACE

"For by grace ye are saved, through faith," &c.—Eph. ii. 8, 9.

THE subject is one of supreme importance—of individual concern and everlasting moment. The text is clear—full—unmistakeable. Let us,

**I. Define the terms of the text.**

1. *Saved.* Here it means our deliverance from the penalty of sin, by pardon, justification and acceptance with God.

(1.) The *renewal* of our *nature* by regeneration and sanctification. And of course it includes,

(2.) The *possession* of the *gift* of eternal life in Christ.

2. *Grace.* Favour not deserved—favour to the unworthy. Not wages for work, nor reward for goodness; but favour to the utterly unworthy.

3. *Faith* here signifies belief in Christ as our Saviour, and trusting in Him for its realization.

4. *Gift* of God may apply to faith. He gives the capacity and the power—as the eye and the ear—or it may apply to salvation, &c.

5. *Works* mean obedience to the Divine law—obeying the commandments, or observance of ceremonial institutions.

**II. The distinct signification of what is stated.**

1. *Negatively* our *salvation* is not of our own *good works.* We do not obtain it by obedience—no works are good till we are justified—we must be made good before we can perform good works. Man is a rebel, traitor, and unholy, so in that condition he has no good works to obtain salvation.

2. *Positively* it is of *grace.* Of God's rich free grace— the Sovereign pardoning, as an act of grace. Now salvation came from the infinite grace of the Father— flowed in the grace of the Lord Jesus Christ—is applied by the grace of the Holy Spirit—is carried on by the communication of the grace of God to the soul. Grace for us—grace to us—grace in us. Good works are the

evidence and fruit of salvation, and not the cause or source or means of salvation. See,

**III. The use we must make of these truths.**

1. *Accept* the *grace.*

2. *Renounce self* and imaginary *merit.*

3. Be *abased* and *humbled* before God; and then,

4. *Obey* the *commands* of *grace.* "Grace of God," &c., teaching us, &c. Not sinning, because grace abounds.


## CLIII

## THE CHURCH THE HOME OF THE FREE

"But Jerusalem which is above is free, which is the mother of us all. For it is written, Rejoice, thou barren, that bearest not; break forth and cry, thou that travailest not: for the desolate hath many more children than she who hath an husband," &c.—GALATIANS iv. 26-31.

THE apostle is presenting the allegorical contrast between Hagar and Ishmael and Sinai on the one hand, and Abraham, Sarai, Isaac and Jerusalem on the other. So the seed of Ishmael are the bondsmen, and the children of Abraham are the free—the line of the Messiah was by Isaac, not Ishmael—so Jerusalem is the symbol of the Christian Church; v. 26; Heavenly, royal, free and glorious. In one sense this is literally true. The first Christian Church was in Jerusalem, not Rome, so that is the mother Church of all Christian churches. But the spiritual holy Church of the Lord Jesus is,

**I. The heavenly Jerusalem.**

A city—Mount Zion; Heb. xii. 22. The city of God —royal, Divine, with walls, bulwarks, temple, palaces. Go round about her; Psalm xlvi. 4, 5; xlviii. 1, 3. Now the Christian Church is the heavenly Jerusalem— all in Christianity is heavenly—the Saviour from

Heaven—the kingdom of Heaven. Spiritual, celestial, from above—not carnal, ceremonial—but spiritual and heavenly. Notice,

**II. The heavenly Jerusalem is the mother of believers.**

See Psalm lxxxvii. 5; see Acts ii. 41, &c. Believers born in her—providing food for her children—instructing her children—disciplining her children—securing the best interests of her children—here all ordinances, exercises and blessings.

**III. All the children of the heavenly Jerusalem are free.**

Observe, the word is used in both verses, 26, 31.

1. *Free* from the *yoke* of ceremonial *bondage;* chap. v. 1-6.

2. *Free* from the *condemnation* of the *law.* "There is therefore no condemnation," &c.; Rom. viii. 1.

3. *Free* from the *bonds* of *sin.* Christ said, "Come unto me," &c.—being made free from sin, &c. Where the spirit of the Lord is, there is liberty.

4. *Free* from priestly *usurpation.* All sacerdotalism was swept away by Christ—all the ceremonials gone—Temple, altars, sacrifices, priests—no priest now but Christ—"He is a priest for ever," &c. No pope, cardinal, bishop, &c., can have authority over minds, consciences. As such,

5. *Free* from ritual *institutions.* Circumcision, offerings, visits to Jerusalem. Moreover,

6. *Free* in personal *choice* of the Master's *service.* "Thy people shall be willing," &c. All volunteers—none pressed into the Church against their will—must give themselves to Christ—to the Church—voluntary membership.

7. *Free* in the *exercise* of conscious *thought.* Amenable to Christ only, not to Paul or Cephas, except as they distinctly represented Christ. Individual, personal responsibility to God, and not to man.

8. *Free* from long complex *creeds*. This follows the others. How were saints received? what profession did they make? Take three instances—

1. The blind young man and Christ; John ix. 34, 35.

2. The first Church; Acts ii. 41. The word of Christ's death and resurrection preached—no creed, &c.

3. The Ethiopian eunuch seeking Christian baptism; Acts viii. 35-37. Such then is the liberty of the children of God—the freedom of the Christian Church, and this expressed in one passage as to what is necessary to salvation; Rom. x. 8, 9. The believers of the Gospel shall be saved.

### APPLICATION

1. The exactions of sects have no Divine authority. As to belief, worship, and as to sustaining the Church— all voluntary—no tithes, &c.

2. This freedom should be guarded—stand fast, &c.; chap. v. 1.

3. It may be abused. It is not free from God's authority, but man's, &c. Not looseness, licentiousness.

4. This freedom must be published.


## CLIV

## THE AFFLICTED AND BEAUTIFIED CHURCH

" O thou afflicted, tossed with tempest, and not comforted, behold, I will lay thy stones with fair colours, and lay thy foundations with sapphires," &c.—ISAIAH liv. 11, &c.

THE text is full of poetical beauty—it is a perfect picture of descriptions, illustrations, promises. It doubt- less related to the Old Testament Church—God's Israel —but it is equally applicable to the Church of the Lord in all ages. Observe then,

**I. The Church in its trials and perils.**

Observe here three things—

1. *Severity* of her *afflictions*. "Thou afflicted!"—various numerous, severe, floods, flames, bush on fire, &c.

2. *Imminent peril.* "Tossed," &c. Ship at · sea in storm—literally beaten about. See the instance of the vessel on the lake of Galilee—mariner, &c. Or like a castle' or lighthouse—sea coast—waves dashing over it, &c.

3. *Deprivation* of *comfort*. "Not comforted," &c. This is the climax, if afflicted—if there be comforts it may be borne. But here are none—no friendly presence, hand, voice, &c. Thus in bitter adversity—"sackcloth," "ashes," moaning, well-nigh desponding. See,

**II. The Church in her Divine encouragement.**

1. The *promiser*. "I," "Jehovah;" v. 10. The promiser able, present, true, faithful, loving, &c.

2. The *promises*.

(1.) A *substantial basis*. Foundations, literally, cement, stebium, adhesive, fast, firm, solid—bulwarks or battlements, agates, sapphires, &c. All kinds of gems—brilliant, costly, &c. Windows, agates, some pellucid gems—all the borders—"pleasant stones," wrought in, arranged, set so as to give magnificence and splendour. Now these are the externals of God's Church and palace. But then the promises,

(2.) Of the *internal*. Spiritual instruction—"taught" Divine truth, creation, providence, redemption, taught the deep and profound—the high and lofty—the grand and general—the holy and Divine—"all taught,"—all thy children—none ignorant—each a child of the light and of the day—all taught of the Lord, not of philosophers or priests, &c., but of the Lord Jesus—of the spirit of the Lord—of the word of the Lord, therefore perfectly taught, infallibly, savingly.

(3.) *Full* and *perfect* peace. Peace like a river, full, overflowing, perpetual—no "terror," no "alarm," &c.; v. 14. Peace from God—peace of God—peace in God, &c. Great, marvellous and everlasting. Such are the Divine encouragements of the Church. And,

1. These are explicit.
2. Sure—"Amen," &c.
3. Sufficient.
4. Abiding. Let the Church look up—look forward —rejoice.


## CLV

## THE BLESSINGS OF THE LORD'S DAY

"This is the day which the Lord hath made ; we will rejoice and be glad in it."—Psalm cxviii. 24.

A division of time is essential to us. God eternal has the ever present now surrounding Him. No past—no future. "I am that I am!" Seasons distinguish the times of the year. Months form twelve milestones on the yearly road to futurity. But the earliest division was that of the day: Gen. i. 5. Observe, it was the evening and the morning were the first day. Evening first: darkness—night and repose. Then the morning of light—vigour and activity. But the end of the sixth day, and there came the Sabbath, or the rest; and this ushers in a septennial division, which is to last for thousands of years. The seventh, or Sabbath, belonged to man in paradise—to the antediluvians—was then incorporated into the Jewish ecclesiastical code, and remained to the coming of Christ. Now there is a new creation—the kingdom of Christ. The Gospel era and the seventh day hangs heavily on the moving dispensa-

tion: till at length it passes away, and the first day of
the week takes the first rank in the religious observances
of the Christian Church; and now the text is as true of
the Lord's Day, as of the Jewish Sabbath, and much
more expressive.

Now observe,

## I. This day was specially made by the Lord.

1. There was the *dim dawn* of Judaism preceding it.
The darkest part of the night. How dreary the condition of the Jews! How ignorant! How superstitious!
What mixtures of good and evil! How perverted the law!
How symbols and shadows obscured the heavens! But
at last came the day of God—the day of truth, and
the day of salvation.

2. There was the *dark night* of Christ's death and
burial. The crucified Teacher, the murdered Messiah. Slain on the tree—buried—all dark. What a
night, from Friday at three, till the early morning of the
first day of the week! And now clouds depart—morning
star shines—the sun arises—angels proclaim the glad
day, and the glad tidings. Now comes the "day of
Christ and the Gospel," to last to the end of the world.

But, notice,

3. This *special day* of the Lord becomes a permanent institution of the Christian Church. Has been
so in all ages—all countries and peoples is so still.
Millions hail it—rejoice in it—and exclaim with highest
delight—"This is the day!" &c. Now let us,

## II. Enquire for what purposes the Lord hath made this day.

It is in every sense "the Lord's day." Best title—
better than Sabbath—better than Sunday. This, and
the first day of the week, were attached to it from the
beginning.

1. It was *made* for the *manifestation* of the Sun of

Righteousness. The sun seen by day. Moon and stars by night. Now the risen glorious Son of God is to rise, shine, to diffuse Divine beams of Gospel light. Christ must have a day in the week for Himself. Thus revealing Himself—the Father—salvation—immortality. It is that we may see the Son, &c.

2. It was *made* for the *diffusion* of saving light. "Let there be light," &c. During the six days there is to be toil—secular enterprise—work, &c. Now the Gospel is to be pre-eminent—now the Word is to run—now the soul is to be illumined—now day is to cheer the soul. "Arise, shine."

3. It was *made* for *special work*. God's work—soul work—putting forth energy, &c. Preaching—teaching— praying work—all good may be wrought. The Church's market day. The day for hiring into the vineyard. Spiritual work is for the Lord. The idea of the day.

4. Made for *special privileges*. Lord hath made it to be, our weekly festival. So in connection with the Lord's Supper for ages. Fellowship of the Lamb—communion with God—holy exercises—joyous delights. It comes with ten thousand blessings. It begun with the cry, "The Lord is risen!" It ends in the upper chamber where Christ comes and meets His disciples. Such are some of the grand purposes. Observe,

**III. How we should treat this day of the Lord, when it comes to us.**

If possible we should,

1. *Prepare* and *look* out for it. The people do so, for the sun, in the northern countries, where there is no day for six months. How desirable it is. Many cannot,— the masses now can.

2. *Hail it* with *holy* thanksgiving. Welcome day! Welcome to body, to mind, to spirit! With all our hearts —welcome! Let us rejoice and be glad.

3. *Treat it* as it *deserves.* Not secularize it—not stupify it by indolence—not darken it with gloom; but use it, 1. For the Lord; then, 2. For ourselves; 3. Then for the Church; 4. For the world's good; 5. Make it as long as possible. Early rising—all the day employed—not abridged, &c. So that it shall ever leave its blessing behind it. 5. Link it to eternity. It is of heaven—from heaven—ends in heaven. Soon this will end, and what is to follow? The eternal rest—the eternal day—the eternal worship, and the eternal blessing.

### APPLICATION

1. This day we all absolutely need.

2. This day God has in love and mercy given.

3. This day must be accounted for.

4. This day may be a blessing or a curse.—Now, which? O! say, "This is the day," &c.

## CLVI

## THE WAY OF SALVATION

" The same followed Paul and us, and cried, saying, These men are the servants of the most high God, which show unto us the way of salvation."—ACTS xvi. 17.

OUR text is the declaration of a soothsayer; yet it was true and most important. It contained a summary of Divine knowledge, and the words are ever pre-eminently momentous. A ruined humanity is distinctly implied. If men are good and holy and secure, we need no word about salvation. If any class of men are so, then to them there is no evil—no guilt—no peril. Salvation means nothing. Some assert that they are good when under the laws and restraints of civilization. Others, when men are educated. But all history attests the wickedness of man under all the highest condition of civilization and learning. Take Rome or Greece in their greatest glory. Now the testimony of impartial history is, that men are corrupt and sinful; and if there be any great moral governor, they must be in peril. But the Scriptures only reveal the way of salvation.

Observe,

### I. The way itself.

Now, the true way of salvation is the Lord Jesus Christ. This is no mere hypothesis. He said " I am the way," &c.; John xiv. 6. Not only the way maker, the way revealer—but the way itself. Now salvation is restoration to God. He is the mediator—the uniter—the reconciler. Forgiveness of sin—remission of sin in His name, and precious blood. Justification. Freely by His grace. By Him justified from all things, &c. Sanctification — washed in His precious blood. By His truth and spirit. Victory over evil. "More than conquerors through Him," &c. By His cross we overcome. Eternal life in Him—with Him—by Him. How clear that "Christ is the way." The symbol was the ladder, uniting earth and heaven. The two sides—the Godhead and the humanity, we hold them both. Its association with angels. God above it. Resting firmly on the earth. Now, observe, how all that relates to Christ is this way. His incarnation—His spotless life—His Divine inauguration—His perfect obedience—His complete example—His glorious miracles—His sufferings and death—His cross and desertion—His resurrection —His ascension—intercession—Divine power and glory.

Notice,

### II. The revelation concerning it.

1. It is the *way Divinely appointed*. Elected of God—sent—designed. God's seal on Him.

2. The *way scripturally attested*. To Him all scripture

refers.  The earliest promises.  The ancient types.  The
numberless sacrifices.  The fulness of prophecy "all"
point, &c.  Abraham saw—Jacob, Moses, David, &c.
The Baptist.  Then the apostles, evangelists, &c.  John
in the vision, &c.

3. The *way so graciously adapted*.  Near to us.  Down to
our deepest guilt.  Helplessness—worthlessness.  For
the vile, undeserving.  Not money, nor rank, nor merit.

4. The *way universally revealed*.  Christ's commission
meets the whole case—"all the world"—"every creature."
No one can go beyond.  We need not fear going out
of the line.  Each—all—everyone—no exception—
exemption.

5. The *way* to the *exclusion* of *all others*.  One God—
one Mediator—one Spirit—one system—one Gospel—
one name—one fountain—one cross.  Two passages of
Scripture on this vital part of the subject.  Act iv. 12 ;
Gal. i. 7-9.  So the passage, "No man cometh to the
Father, but by Me."  Such then, briefly, is the revelation
concerning this way.  Observe, then,

### III. Our duty and interest concerning it.

To see,

1. Our *personal interest* in it.  We surely desire to be
saved.  We, therefore, should make it a personal matter.
It is a subject not only of theology, but religion, for personal concern—" What must I do ? " &c.  " How shall I
escape ? " &c.

2. Our *distinct apprehension* of it.  To see it clearly,
distinctly.  Not Christ and something else.  " Christ
the way."  Not Christ and ceremonies—Christ and
Moses—Christ and churches—Christ and creeds, &c.
" Christ alone."

3. Our *hearty acceptance* of it.  Make it ours by a living
faith, and entire trust, and cheerful obedience.  A way

to be chosen—adopted—walked in—come to God by Him—to eternal life by Him.

4. A *way* to be *distinctly published.* "We preach Christ," &c. Not ourselves—Christ. "Know nothing else." "God forbid!" "Count all," &c.

"'Tis all our business here below," &c.

It should be distinctly published. No haziness—no mists — no obscurity — no metaphysical subtleties. Plainly, openly, clearly to say, "Christ is the way of salvation."

Now here we come, in application, to the necessity of securing places for the proclamation of this grand subject—

1. They preached Christ in the synagogues. They preached Christ in the Temple—in the market places, &c.; from house to house: so we. But it is essential,

2. That there should be adapted places at hand. Commodious. Standard places for the banner of mercy. Places of assembly—places for the express subject and object, to proclaim the way of salvation.

3. Such is this place. Everything here subordinate to Christ. Nonconformity—baptism—doctrinal theology.

CLVII

A REVIVAL DESIRED

"Wilt thou not revive us again, that thy people may rejoice in thee?"—Psalm lxxxv. 6.

Let us see,

I. What is implied in a revival of religion.

Religious deadness and formalism. Religious indifference and supineness. Religious apathy and slothfulness.

Religious compromise and worldliness.  Religious covet-
ousness and mammonism.   Now see,

**II. What a revival involves.**

1. Look at the dull dead fire in the grate.

2. At the arid scorched field.

3. At the fruitless garden.  Here are emblems to help
us to understand, &c.   It involves,

1. The *excitement* of the people to *greater interest* in
Divine *things*.

2. The more *earnest attention* to Divine *ordinances*.

3. The more *fervent spirit* of believing *prayer*.

4. More *cheerful* and *active* labour to *win* souls.

5. A more *entire* personal *consecration* to God's *glory*.

**III. God is the great and only source of religious revivals.**

" Wilt thou not revive us ?" &c.

1. God *only can*.  His spirit in its grace and power—
not by might, &c.

2. God *desires* to *revive*, &c.   Hence His promise—" I
will pour out," &c.   Rain, dew, streams.   But,

3. God *wills* that we should *seek* it by prayer.  Prayer
is felt need—inward desire.  So Moses, Ezra, Nehemiah,
so the apostles, so in all ages, &c.

The text indicates,

**IV. The result of such a religious revival.**

That thy "people may rejoice."

1. It is *joyfulness*.  Not dreariness, not enviousness,
not murmuring, not fault-finding, but "joy," "rejoicing."

2. It is *joyfulness* in God.  "Rejoice in thee."  God
glorified, praised.

3. *Holy joyfulness*.  More light—more life—power.

4. *Devotional joyfulness;* v. 7.  More prayer.


APPLICATION

1. See the deep need of such a revival in us, in our
Churches, schools, &c.

2. The appeal we should make to God.
3. The believing experience we should cherish.

## CLVIII

## THEISM AND CHRISTISM

" Ye believe in God, believe also in Me."—JOHN xiv. 1.

THE sorrow of the disciples was, indeed, heart sorrow. Christ not only sympathized, but gave them the remedy. Faith in Himself. We select the text independently of the context; and we do so to emphasise the importance of faith in the Lord Jesus Christ. Two things are before us,

**I. A recognition of Theism.**

"Ye believe in God." That is Theism. There are two kinds of Theism.

1. *Philosophical.* A belief in a personal Deity, from a consideration of the works of nature. See Rom. i. 20; Psalm xix. 1. From the government of the world. Acts xiv. 17. Now the evidences of design are so various and numberless. A sceptical rejection of a personal God is the greatest credulity, &c. So thought Socrates and Plato and others among the Greeks; and Cicero and Seneca among the Latins. Now this is philosophical Theism. But there is,

2. *Revealed* Theism. And this the Gentiles had not; but the Jews had it. Patriarchs, prophets, &c. " What advantage hath the Jew ?" &c. The Old Testament Scripture was a revelation of a personal God—a Divine Supreme Being. Gave His portrait, attributes, &c. : government and will are revealed, and the disciples were Theists of this order. " Ye believe." Now many

suppose this belief is enough. But hear the Divine
word: "He that cometh," &c. Heb. xi. A rewarder.
He must know God clearly, fully, personally, and the
way to Him. The Jews had only the twilight. They
had types, sacrifices, services; but they were in the
condition of Philip, enquiring, "Shew us the Father,"
&c. Now Christ came,

3. To *give* a *full* and *mature view* of Theism. So
Christ's answer; v. 9, 10. The Trinity. In our complex material and spiritual state we require Theism
to be made palpable. Christ embodied, or incarnated
God. He, Emmanuel, &c., God in Christ. Pourtrayed
to be seen, heard. Now perfected Theism was one
part of Christ's work. But even this was not enough.
We must rise from Theism,

**II. To direct Christism.**

"Believe also in Me." Two things,

1. The *faith itself*. It means more than "credence."
It signifies "knowledge," "trust," "acceptance." The
belief of God in Christ, and in Christ as messenger,
as mediator, as sacrifice, as Saviour. The one and only
one, &c. "Look!" &c. "Behold!"

2. The *great purposes* of *such* a *faith*.

(1.) As our infallible teacher. Hear ye Him! Last
days, hath spoken, &c. (2.) As our perfect example.
(3.) As our righteousness and atonement. Only way
to God. By Him only. Pardon, peace, holiness, eternal
life. This belief also,

1. Is what the sinner needs.

2. Is what the believer in God needs. A merciful
High Priest.

3. Is what the world needs. Theism failed to lift
up the world. Christ is the light to the Gentiles. He is
to destroy the kingdom of Satan. He is to claim the

world He had made and redeemed. All things were made by Christ, and for Him. Now this faith in Christ must be personal. Dost *thou* believe? &c. Conscious. "I know whom," &c. "I do believe," &c. Saving. Passing from death unto life. "He that believeth shall be saved." As Noah and his family in the ark—as the Israelites in the wilderness, by the serpent of brass. John iii. 14.

In conclusion—

1. Christ is the great object of faith; yet it includes the Father and the Divine Spirit.

2. Nothing else meets our case.

3. Nothing short will be effectual. Not faith in nature—in providence. Not faith even in the Bible—not faith in ordinances—not faith in obedience; but personal faith in a Divine personal Saviour. Examine and test. Realize this, for this is life—eternal life, &c. Unbelief is death, &c.

## CLIX
## TRANSGRESSIONS BLOTTED OUT

"I, *even* I, *am* he that blotteth out thy transgressions for my own sake, and will not remember thy sins."—ISA. xliii. 25.

MANY questions may arise as to our moral condition, guilt, peril, &c.; also as to whether there is forgiveness, and if so, who can forgive? and in what way, and how do we obtain it? The text solves most of these problems. Let us see,

### I. Our need of forgiveness.

This is evident on account of our transgressions. If innocent or holy, pardon would not be applicable to our state. But we are all guilty before God. All have sinned—all gone astray—none righteous—no not one. The text refers to one species of moral evil—"Transgression"—violations of the Divine law. Now our transgressions,

1. Are of a *diversified character*. Against various laws and statutes of God. Against both tables. Against Divine providences, mercies, privileges, &c.

2. They are *numberless*. None but God can know them. Think of those perpetrated every day, week, month! Those of the year—of many years—past lives! More than the hairs of our head, &c.

3. They are our own *individual* transgressions. In some sins there may be many partakers, &c.; but still as a rule, our transgressions are such as we have knowingly and wilfully committed. So they are distinctly ours.

4. They are *aggravatedly heinous*. As committed against a good and gracious God—heavenly Father—kind Saviour—infinite love and longsuffering. As they have been committed in the midst of many privileges, blessings, &c. Hence, they are as scarlet, as crimson, foul, black and enormous.

5. These transgressions are *recorded*. This is the symbol of the text, as though God had a book in which they are written down. See Revelations xx. 11, &c.

6. These transgressions are *connected* with Divine *penalties*. Punishment—including shame, degradation, misery, woe, remorse, death!

7. No created being can *deliver us* from the *results* of our transgressions. No priest, or prophet, or apostle, or saint, or angel, or Virgin Mary. Christ the Son of God has power, that is, might, to forgive sin. God's prerogative to blot out transgression. Then observe,

**II. The Divine declaration as to blotting out transgressions.**
" 'I, even I,' am He that blotteth," &c.   The form of
this declaration is striking.   " I,' I," the word *even* is in
italics.   I the Creator; v. 15:  the Jehovah; v, 3:  the
Holy One of Israel; v. 3: your Redeemer; v. 14.

1. He has *sovereign right* to do so.   He is the supreme
monarch—the God against whom all sin is committed.
He, therefore, as supreme, and having all authority, can
blot out, &c.

2. His infinite *love* and *mercy disposes* Him to blot out
transgression.   This is the Divine nature and the Divine
name.   This is clearly stated, Exodus xxxiii. 18, &c.

3. This Divine *nature* and *name* Christ the Saviour
*possessed* as the Son of God.   " In Him dwells all the fulness," &c.   Full of grace and truth.   He was appointed
the Mediator, and by and through His person, merit and
work, we obtain forgiveness of sin.   It is important to
observe, there is salvation in none other.

4. By faith in the *Gospel* of Christ we realize the
*removal* of *our sins*.   We behold the Lamb that beareth
them away.   Hear His gracious free words of pardon,
&c.,—" Justified, &c., from all things," &c.


### APPLICATION

1. God thus blots out all sins and transgressions.

2. He blots them out utterly and for ever.   There
shall be no more remembrance.   As a stone cast into
the sea.   The erasure is complete.

3. How solicitous we should be to hear God speaking
thus to our hearts, by His Holy Spirit—" I, even I."

4. There  is  no  excuse  for  the  unforgiven.   " He
that believeth not," &c.

## CLX

## THE TEMPLE AND THE DIVINE PRESENCE

"But the Lord is in his holy temple: let all the earth keep silence before him."—HAB. ii. 20.

**I. God is present in three temples.**

These are exclusive of the Temple in Jerusalem.

1. In the temple of the consecrated heart.
2. In the temple of his true Church.
3. In the temple of celestial glory.

**II. All God's temples are holy.**

1. The heart made so by cleansing blood.
2. The Church by His sanctifying Spirit.
3. Heaven by its unsullied purity.

**III. Terrestri̇ ̇eings should be silent before God.**

"All the eai  ."

1. All *dwellers* on earth. High and low—monarchs and subjects. "Worship Him all ye gods," &c.

2. All *worshippers* on earth may pause with the sublimity of silence. No words can fully glorify God, or adequately express our veneration, awe, wonder, and adoration, or express our perfect praise.

3. Such *silence* may be most acceptable to God. As expressive of our humility and reverence and self-abnegation; and as indicating our profound views and emotions of God's greatness and majesty.

The subject condemns—

1. All trifling and thoughtless worship.
2. All mere noisy, declamatory worship.
3. All rash and heedless worship.
4. The Holy Spirit alone can make us true and acceptable worshippers. Psa. xcvi. 1-10; John iv. 24; Philip. iii. 3.

## CLXI

## GOD, AND WHAT HE IS TO HIS PEOPLE

" For the Lord is good, a strong hold in the day of trouble ; and he knoweth them that trust in him."—NAHUM i. 7.

THIS is a true portrait of Jehovah. He is drawn and thus presented in all the photograph galleries of the Bible.

He is,

**I. Essentially good.**

His name, God, signifies the good. His nature is good; so His perfections; so His works and ways, His laws and ordinances. His goodness fills heaven and earth. It is infinite, unchanging, everlasting.

**II. He is the shelter and defence of His people.**

A "stronghold in the day of trouble." His people have their troubles—Israel. The prophets and saints in all ages. So the Baptist, disciples, apostles, all saints. Now God is a stronghold, where they are *secretly* preserved—strongly protected, and absolutely secured. His name, His love, His fidelity, unchangeableness, make Him a sure defence, an impregnable fortress and strong tower. He is so to all His people, and in all their troubles.

**III. He recognizes all who trust in Him.**

He knows them—observes them—approves of them—distinguishes them—and saves them.

Learn from the subject—

1. The connection between God and His people. It is mutual, constant, unending.

2. The Divine claims of God on our trust and confidence.

3. The safety of the Lord's people at all times and places.

## CLXII

## THE ELEVENTH COMMANDMENT

" A new commandment I give unto you, That ye love one another as I have loved you, that ye also love one another."—JOHN xiii. 34.

THESE words of Jesus have been fitly styled the eleventh commandment. Christ himself calls it a new commandment. Yet not essentially, for the second great commandment was in this direction—" And thou shalt love thy neighbour as thyself," &c. But the whole text strikingly illustrates the idea of "new," when it is added, "As I have loved you." Now in this wide and deep sense, it is indeed new: But look,

**I. At the commandment itself.**

" Love one another." Now "love" includes commiseration, compassion, goodness, sympathy, benevolence, beneficence, &c. Good feeling towards others—good doing, &c. See, it is unlike,

(1.) Isolation, or separateness. (2.) Selfishness and indifference. (3.) Hate and evil - disposedness. (4.) Envy and uncharitableness. As in the text, it includes approbation, complacency, oneness, and kind feeling, &c. Now Paul describes it in 1 Cor. xiii. Read its items, and see its counterfeits—alms-giving, self-emulation, extraordinary gifts, &c.

Observe,

**II. The model on which it is to be constructed.**

" As I have," &c. Notice,

1. Like Christ's, it *must* be *first*. Before they love us, or at least before they manifest it. Also it,

2. May be *undeserved*. Christ loved before they were worthy, yea, in one sense, they never had a worthiness He had not given.

3. It must be *most free*. Like Christ's. Not extorted. Like the stream or the air, light, &c.

4. It must be *self-sacrificing*. Like Christ's. How Christ's love brought Him to the earth. Incarnate—abased—suffering—died, &c.

5. It must, like Christ's, be *practical* in its *results*. Bearing blessings—conveying mercies—bestowing gifts.

6. It must, like Christ's, be *lowly*. Not pompous—vain-glorious—ostentatious.

7. To all Christ's *disciples*. Each and every one.

8. It must be *abiding*, like Christ's. Having loved his own, He loved them to the end. Now see,

**III. The appropriateness of the designation.**

"A new commandment," &c.

1. It is the commandment of the *new dispensation*.

2. Invested with *new authority*. "I" give unto you. He is our Lord, our Divine Head and Master.

3. It is *identified* with *new illustrations*. Moses and the prophets loved God and the Church, but not as Jesus. In Him it lived supreme. His breath, words, deeds, life, death.

4. It is *supplied* with *new resources*. How are we to exemplify it? By Christ's grace—by the Spirit's work in the soul.

5. It is to be the *distinguishing feature* of the *new* kingdom. The sign — the motto — the badge — the glory! Not a kingdom of ceremonials, sacrifices, but of love. Love is the essence, substance, and ground of Christianity.

APPLICATION

1. Christ's disciples are bound by this commandment.

2. For it there is no substitute.

3. In it is the perfection of blessedness. Thus we are one with God, and the Lord Jesus Christ, by His Holy Spirit dwelling in us.

## CLXIII

## BLESSINGS FOR THE STRANGER

" The Lord recompense thy work, and a full reward be given thee of the Lord God of Israel, under whose wings thou art come to trust."
—RUTH ii. 12.

THE words of the text are addressed by Boaz to Ruth. The narrative of Ruth's character and conduct are given in the first chapter. And now she begins to realize the blessedness of her decision and choice.

Notice,

**I. Ruth's work.**

" Thy work." (1.) It was a work of deep and generous sympathy: chap. i. 16. (2.) Of strong faith. (3.) Of great self-denial. (4.) Of remarkable love. (5.) Of pious perseverance. Notice,

**II. Ruth's reward.**

She obtained the favour of Boaz, &c. But her reward was, (1.) The Divine acceptance. (2.) Temporal and spiritual blessings. (3.) Messianic honour; Matt. i. 5. (4.) And union and fellowship with God's Israel.

Notice,

**III. Ruth's security.**

Her security was, (1.) Divine. "The Lord God of Israel!" and his sheltering wings. (2.) It was most consolatory. The figure is most indicative of union, repose and comfort. (3.) It was inviolable. No one could disturb or harm, or destroy. (4.) It was in harmony with her believing confidence. "Under whose wings *thou art* come to trust." Observe,

How beautiful this picture of Boaz and Ruth!

How good is God's providence!

How all work and sacrifices for God shall be abundantly recompensed!

## CLXIV
## MATERNAL PIETY

" For this child I prayed : and the Lord hath given me my petition which I asked of Him," &c.—1 Sam. i. 27-8.

The text is the pious declaration of Hannah's conduct and experience, and the noble resolve she makes on account thereof.  She refers,

**I. To her devotional solicitude.**

(1.) Her condition was one of motherly sorrow and vexation.  (2.) Her recourse was to God by prayer. (3.) She sought of the Lord a special favour.  (4.) For this special favour she evidently prayed most confidently.  See,

**II. The Divine favour she experienced.**

(1.) God heard her supplication.  (2.) God was favourable to her plea.  (3.) God granted her the desire of her heart.

**III. The spirit Hannah manifested.**

(1.) Profound reverence for God.  She gave Him all the glory.  (2.) A personal testimony as to the value of prayer.  (3.) An unselfish recognition of God's claim to her child.  (4.) A full consecration of Samuel to God's service.  Herein she exhibited the power of personal religion.  A noteworthy example of maternal self-denial, and a supreme concern for God's glory and her child's highest happiness.  Her prayers and tears and self-denial gave to Israel one of her holiest men and most faithful prophets.


## CLXV
## JEWISH PREROGATIVES

"The Jews had light and gladness and joy and honour."—Esther viii. 16.

The Book of Esther is a beautiful exhibition of the

marvels of providence in relation to God's people. We
have their imminent peril and their extraordinary deliverance. The result is described in the text. "The
Jews had light," &c. Observe,

**I. They had light.**

Darkness gone—mists dissipated—clouds dispersed.
God gave them light, and turned their night into day.
This light is the privilege of all God's people. They are
the children of light—walk in the light; and light is
sown for them, &c. This light is knowledge, holiness,
and spiritual transformation into God's likeness. 2
Cor. iii. 18.

**II. They had gladness.**

Of dispelled fears. Rescue from perils. Of God's
loving-kindness. This was spiritual gladness—grateful
gladness—sustaining gladness. They had,

**III. Joy.**

Not merely the emotion of grateful feeling, but of
settled happiness. Not tears, nor fears, nor doubts, nor
griefs, but joy—joy of the Lord, their strength. Joy of
assured mercy, inward confidence, and blessed hope.
"We joy in God," &c. "God is our exceeding joy."
Their joy was personal, national (the Jews, &c.), universal. Kingdom of God is righteouness, peace, and
joy in the Holy Ghost.

**IV. They had honour.**

From the Queen, King, people; but especially from
God. By prayer and fasting and faith they honoured
God, and now God honoured them. Such is the portion
of all saints. They are honoured by angels. They are
honoured often by the great of the earth, as was Joseph,
Moses, David, Daniel, &c. The prerogatives of these
Jews are ours spiritually. Divine honours are abiding,
substantial and everlasting.

## CLXVI

## WORKING IN GOD'S HOUSE

"And they came and did work in the house of the Lord of hosts, their God."—HAGGAI i. 14.

THE text states a most important fact in relation to God's house, the second temple. God's spirit stirred up sundry persons to work therein. Two of these were exalted, distinguished persons — "Zerubbabel" and "Joshua," the High Priest, and then is added, "All the remnant of the people." Notice,

**I. God's House is for work as well as worship.**

So the Tabernacle, Temples —so the Christian sanctuary—so the Church of God. Worship is momentous, essential, God-glorifying, and blesses the spiritual worshipper. But there must be work as well as worship.

1. *Teaching* work. Building up the Church in knowledge, truth and holiness. So God has given some "teachers," and apostles, or evangelists may do this.

2. *Pastoral* work. Shepherding the sheep. Caring for and watching and feeding the flock.

3. *Disciplinary* work. The duty of the whole Church: 1 Cor. v. 4.

4. *Edifying* work. See 1 Cor. xiv. 8-26, to end; Rom. xii. 3-8.

5. *Benevolent* work. Caring for widows and the poor. James lays great stress on this: James i. 27; 1 John iii. 14-17; so 2 Cor. ix. 1, &c.

6. *Praying* work. See instances: Acts i. 14; xii. 5-12.

7. *Restoring* work. Seeking wanderers from the fold: Gal. vi. 1; James v. 19, 20.

**II. God's work must not be neglected.**

Or it would be disobedience, soul-guiltiness, and cruelty to our fellow-men.

**III. The obligations and spirit in which it should be done.**

(1.) With cheerful alacrity. (2.) With earnest sincerity. (3.) With constant fidelity. (4.) With prayerful dependence; and with (5.) Faith and hope in God's promised help. It is obligatory on every Christian personally—on the whole Church generally.

### APPLICATION

1. God our Lord and Master knows the workers.
2. And will help and bless them in it.
3. And reward them in the last day.

## CLXVII

## A FEARFUL INDICTMENT

" She obeyed not his voice ; she received not correction ; she trusted not in the Lord ; she drew not near to her God."—ZEPH. iii. 2.

THE charges in this indictment, against Jerusalem, are numerous and striking. But let us see if they are not true extensively of mere nominal religionists, in all ages, and so true now.

Let us see,

**I. What is implied.**

(1.) That God had spoken. His voice had uttered His will. (2.) To the Divine word had been added *correction*. Discipline had been adopted. The rod of chastening employed. (3.) God has demanded confidence, reliance on His word and covenants and promises. (4.) The Lord supplied the means of devotion. Prayer appointed by God. Throne of mercy approachable.

But see,

**II. What is declared.**

(1.) She obeyed not the voice. Lived in witting and

wilful and continued rebellion to God's holy and just command. (2.) She received not correction—did not listen to the rod—did not bow before corrections—did not learn, nor be abased, nor return to God. The correction in vain. (4.) Did not trust in God. Either self-trust, or human confidence, or resting on ceremonies and outward forms, and not in Jehovah. (4.) And continued in a prayerless state. Did not call, "or draw near to her God." There was the outward compact—the general profession and appearance of religious harmony, but prayer was neglected, or was restrained altogether.

We notice,

(1.) These changes, how true every one of them of many professors in our day.

(2.) These changes, where true, exhibit great moral declension.

(3.) And must expose to the Divine displeasure.

(4.) Immediate consideration, self-abasement, penitence and supplication, can alone raise the soul to a condition of spiritual health, happiness and security.


## CLXVIII

## PIOUS RESOLVES AND EXHORTATIONS

"Therefore I will look unto the Lord; I will wait for the God of my salvation; my God will hear me."—MICAH vii. 7.

How desirable to turn from men to God—from earth to Heaven! So thought the prophet: see v. 1 to 6, for some of the reasons. Notice,

### I. The relationship claimed.

Jehovah is recognized as the God of his salvation, and as his portion, "my God." Mine by covenant—mine by

promise—mine by personal realization—mine to love,
worship, obey and honour.

**II. His holy resolutions.**

He would,

1. Recognize God *habitually.* "I will look unto the
Lord." By faith, with solicitude to know His will.
With dependence and trust, in every time of need.
Acknowledge Him always, &c. Set God before him.
Seeing Him, the invisible, &c.

2. He *would wait* for God. Not only look to Him and
wait on Him, but also wait *for* Him in trouble, affliction, persecution, and in personal, relative, or religious
trials. Psalm xl. 1. This waiting is the work of faith,
patience and submission.

**III. His confident anticipations.**

"My God will hear me." Now, God can hear. God
has heard his people's cry. Israel in Egypt—Jonah, &c.
God has promised to hear. God has delight in hearing.
He will not turn away His ear. And God so hears as to
give answers of peace. He ever sustains, comforts,
or delivers His people. 2 Cor. i. 4 to 11.

### LEARN

1. The text is adapted to promote prayer, faith
and patience.

2. To cheer, and fill with hope and joy in God
our Saviour.

3. Our Divine Advocate, the Lord Jesus, ensures us
the Father's favour, and the Holy Spirit's aid in all our
supplications.

## CLXIX

## PURITY OF RELIGIOUS SPEECH

" For I will turn to the people a pure language, that they may call upon the name of the Lord, with one consent."—ZEPH. iii. 9.

THE prediction of the text is not yet fulfilled. A great many differences among God's people arise from using dubious, or mysterious terms, and taking language out of its obvious signification. Hence, nearly all sects, have their peculiar phraseology, denominational terms, which gives a sort of free-masonry recognition. The text expresses God's purpose to give His Church a language that shall be pure and, obviously, one language that shall be spoken by all His people.

Observe,

**I. The pure language predicted.**

Even, at present, Scripture language differs with various versions—different translations. In some of these, words have been perverted, obscured, or changed. God's Word shall be purified. By devout, unsectarian learning and labour, we shall have the Bible as near to original exactness as possible. Then the language of Scripture will be, (1.) Lucid. (2.) Exact; and, (3.) In close harmony with the original word, as spoken by prophets, the Saviour, apostles, &c.

**II. The influence of this pure language.**

It will be great—(1.) In reference to Denominations. (2.) Churches. (3.) Creeds; and, (4.) Religious conversation. It may materially alter, (1.) The tests of orthodoxy. (2.) The terms of fellowship. (3.) The fulminations of anathemas; and (4.) Bring God's people into happier and more united union and love with each other; then Bible authority will be more reverenced, and

Church catholicity be more manifest; and the Lord Jesus more honoured. Notice,

**III. The certainty of this prediction's accomplishment.**

1. God declares He will effect it. He can do so, and His word is inviolable.

2. The demands of His Church require it.

3. The glory of the latter days renders it essential.

### APPLICATION.

1. Let us ignore sectarian terms and forms of speech.

2. Let us seek to speak that all the Church may understand and be edified.

3. Let us live and look for the realization of the text.

## CLXX

## THE TWO ESSENTIAL LINKS

"In truth and love."—2 JOHN 3.

IN the first verse, the Apostle speaks of the elect lady and her children, and adds, "whom I love in the truth." Now let us look,

**I. At the link named first.**

That is, "Truth." It may signify, (1.) A knowledge of Divine truth, as given to us in Holy Scripture; or (2.) A reception of evangelical truth, in its saving efficacy; or (3.) The power of truth, in delivering the mind from error and superstition and sin. Giving liberty, &c. "Ye shall know the truth," &c.; or (4.) Fidelity to truth—by speaking it, and professing it, and being under its practical influence; or (5.) Rejoicing in the truth of the Divine faithfulness, and being witnesses for it.

**II. The second link is love.**

1. True love to the Divine Tri-unity—Father, Son, and Holy Spirit.

2. Unfeigned love of the brethren in Christ.

3. The sympathy of compassionate love for all mankind; or,

4. Love of Divine truth, as exhibited in the Gospel system—doctrines, ordinances, profession of Christ. Having loving communion and companionship with the disciples of truth.

(1.) Now both of these are links of the same heavenly chain. (2.) Truth must be received, before Divine love is experienced. (3.) We believe the truth, and then love. Faith worketh by love. (4.) They are ever to be found connected with each other. Truth can only thrive in the atmosphere of love. And love is mere natural emotion, unless living in the vital air of truth. (5.) Both indispensable in the realization of true religion. (6.) The union of the two will flourish in eternal harmony and oneness. (7.) Sin is falsehood and enmity; Religion, truth and love. As two flowers, they grow side by side in the garden of Holy Scripture. They constitute the essentials of the Gospel, and dwell in the hearts of all the children of God.


## CLXXI

## THE JOYFUL PASTOR

" I have no greater joy than to hear that my children walk in the truth."—3 JOHN 4.

THE truth is most probably the true Gospel of the Lord Jesus Christ—or the true words of Bible revelation—or the true experience of a renewed servant of God.

**I. The unconverted walk in error, darkness and sin.**

II. The converted are brought to the knowledge and into the way of truth.

III. Believers must advance in the truth.

"Walk," progress, clearly, constantly and persistently in the way of truth. Go from elementary to the higher truths.

IV. It is a source of joy to the pastor when his flock thus walk in the truth.

For, (1.) It is the way of salvation. (2.) The way of peace. (3.) The way of usefulness. Thus also (4.) God is glorified. (5.) The Church edified and confirmed. So on every account the good pastor rejoices when her children walketh in truth. Truth is the foundation of God's government. The glory of the Gospel. The girdle of the Christian soldier; and the power by which Satan shall be bruised under the feet of the disciples of Christ. Let us seek the truth—buy it—sell it not— hold it fast, and so abide in it for ever and ever. To secure our children's walking in the truth, the pastor must exhibit it fully, clearly, in its purity, power and sublimity. He must exemplify it in his lips and life and profession; and live and labour under the aid and guidance of the spirit of truth.

## CLXXII

## THE VETERAN APOSTLE

"Such an one as Paul the aged."—PHILEMON, 9.

THE design of this short letter was to plead for a runaway slave, who had become converted by the Apostle's ministry, and in urging sundry pleas, he refers touchingly to his own advanced life, as "Paul the aged."

Notice,

## I. The early period of his life.

A Pharisee in faith—a blasphemer of Christ, and a bitter hater and persecutor of the Church of the Lord Jesus. Then he was a young man, learned, gifted, and zealous for the Jewish faith. Observe,

## II. The transition period of his life.

He was now rising into full manhood. Was probably about twenty-nine or thirty years old. He was rising into fame, and was on the highway to distinction, honour and wealth. But he was arrested in his career—convicted of his extreme error and sin—brought to the feet of Christ a suppliant for mercy. Truly converted. United with the Christian disciples. Became a preacher and an apostle of Jesus. Then we come,

## III. To his long, active, Christian and apostolic life.

Damascus, Jerusalem, Judea; but chiefly among the Gentiles; Rom. xv. 19. Corinth, Athens, Philippi, Antioch, Ephesus, Rome, &c.: in all the regions round about he went forth in the fulness of the Gospel of Christ. And now,

## IV. He is a prisoner and worn out servant of Jesus.

About thirty years of toil, persecution, suffering, &c., for the Gospel's sake. Now bowed down with years, but more with a long career of trials and distresses, &c. Read 2 Cor. xi. 21. Aged in years—in knowledge—in grace—in holiness—in usefulness. A shock of corn ripe for the garner. A steward waiting for his Lord. A soldier looking for the reward. A racer on full stretch for the goal. An ambassador returning to his sovereign. 2 Tim. iv. 6-8.

### LEARN

1. How lovely is aged piety. Glorious setting sun—autumn tints—harvest fruits, &c.

2. What reverence it should command!
3. What hopes inspire!
4. What gratitude display!

## CLXXIII
## THE SEEN INFLUENCE OF FELLOWSHIP WITH CHRIST

" They took knowledge of them that they had been with Jesus."
—ACTS iv. 13.

SEE context, and occasion of these words being spoken. All intercourse is beneficial or detrimental.

**I. It was a true declaration.**

(1.) Peter and John had been with Jesus from the beginning to His ascension. (2.) They had been most intimate with Jesus. (3.) Had been favoured with special tokens of His grace. (4.) And placed in circumstances of high trust and responsibility.

**II. The truth of this declaration was most manifest.**

They took "knowledge of it"—saw it clearly—they beheld it. (1.) In their high Christian intelligence. (2.) In their dignified self-possession. (3.) In their fearless fidelity to Christ and His Gospel. (4.) In their undaunted intrepidity, and disregard of human consequences.

### LEARN

1. How they honoured the Saviour.
2. Exalted their office.
3. Cheered the Church.
4. And led the people to glorify God.

## CLXXIV

## PAUL'S THANKSGIVING FOR HIS CORINTHIAN CONVERTS

" I thank my God always on your behalf, for the grace of God which is given you by Jesus Christ."—1 Cor. i. 4.

PAUL'S deep interest in all that concerned the best interests of our common humanity, especially in the true welfare of the saints in Christ Jesus, and more so in the spiritual happiness and progress of his own converts to the faith of Christ, how strikingly is this seen in the text.   Observe,

**I. The occasion of his thanksgiving.**

"For the grace of God given," &c.   Now this grace, or favour, would include—

1. The Divine *purpose* of grace, manifested by God in the fulness of the times. Titus ii. 11.

2. The grace that was *embodied* in Christ, and revealed in the Gospel.

3. The grace *displayed* towards them, by the proclamation of the word of life.

4. The grace *wrought* in them, by the saving operations of the Holy Spirit.   Now every phase of grace or favour, had God for its source, Jesus Christ as its medium, and the blessed Spirit as the agency of bestowment.

Notice,

**II. The nature of the apostle's thanksgiving.**

1. It was thanksgiving to *God*, to the Father, Son, and Holy Ghost.   To the apostle's God.   "My God."

2. It was thanksgiving *most ardent*.   The very terms he uses denote warmth and ardour.

3. It was thanksgiving he *constantly* celebrated. " Always."   Did not forget—did not wax cold, or become formal.

4. It was most *affectionate* thanksgiving. The sacred offering of unfeigned love, true genuine affection.

5. It was *comprehensive* thanksgiving. See v. 5, 6.

**III. The lessons the subject suggests.**

1. The spiritual connection between minister and people.

2. The best evidence of a true-hearted Christian teacher. To remember pupils when absent—to take note of their spiritual condition—to advise them by Christian counsel, and to thank God for all their privileges and blessings.

3. Ever to perceive the source of all good. " I thank my God." He that giveth, let him glory in the Lord; and he that giveth thanks, let him give thanks to God.


# CLXXV

## JEREMIAH'S MISSION

" Then said I, ah Lord God, behold I cannot speak; for I am a child. But the Lord said unto me, say not, I am a child," &c.— JER. i. 6, 7.

SOME saints have been consecrated from the womb. The Baptist was—Jeremiah was; v. 5. The remarks very striking. Now here is predestination and election to office. Then came the time of the calling of Jeremiah out to his work; v. 4, &c. Now Jeremiah's exact age we don't know, but he was evidently in the morning of life. Now God's call was clear, precise, peremptory. Let us look,

**I. At his objection, as given in the text.**

Now the objection was not unreasonable. His early age,

1. Would indicate *inexperience*. He could not have much experience, &c.

2. Insufficient *knowledge*. To teach—to counsel others especially in Divine things.

3. Modest *diffidence*. He could not be expected to be like a bold hero, &c. Youth is none the worse for this.

4. His *age* and its *defect* time would remedy. Let me wait and learn and know and get qualifications.

5. Now *such* might be *involved* in his objections. He evidently felt what he said. He speaks feelingly, &c.

Now see,

**II. How God overrules his objections.**

1. God refers to His *pre-ordination*. "Knew thee;" v. 5. "Sanctified." Took out of his nature the unfitting. "Ordained," &c. All these before his birth. Then God refers,

2. To his divine *commission*. "Go to all that I shall," &c.; v. 7. He had prepared Jeremiah, and he now gives him his high commission. Did not leave him to seek his sphere and work. "Go to all that I shall send thee."

3. He was to *speak* God's *words;* v. 7. Not his own. Did not require his own knowledge, but the Lord's.

4. He *pledged* His Divine *presence;* v. 8. "I am with thee," &c. Shield—help—deliverer.

5. Then there was the *supernatural communication;* v. 9. God put His words into the prophet's mouth. Now the Divine answer met all that could be objected.

The subject itself,

**III. Is full of important lessons.**

1. God, and not man, *arranges* the affairs of His *moral* kingdom. He is the proposer—architect. He plans, &c. as to the work, and the agency, &c.

2. God *qualifies* the instruments He *employs*. He has

His own college, &c. He knows what they require, and He fully equips them for their work. No other qualification will do.

3. God often *selects* His agents, not as men would do. Men would select the mature—He the young. Men the learned—God the illiterate. Farmers, ploughmen, fishermen. Men, the respectable and the *élite*—God, the poor, &c. 1 Cor. i. 26.

4. God gives His *own message* to the messengers. He sends (text,) "My words!" They are to speak His words—deliver His commands. The preaching He commanded—"Thus and thus saith the Lord."

5. The *ministry* of God's servants is *mighty* for good or evil; v. 10. How great the results! how portentious! solemn! &c. Jonah — the Baptist — Jesus — the apostles, &c.

Finally—

Let us listen when God speaks.

Obey when He commands.

Trust when He promises.

## CLXXVI

## GRAND VISION OF UNIVERSAL PEACE

" But in the last days it shall come to pass, that the mountain of the house of the Lord shall be established in the top of the mountains, and it shall be exalted above the hills; and people shall flow unto it And many nations shall come, and say, Come, and let us go up to the mountain of the Lord, and to the house of the God of Jacob; and he will teach us of his ways, and we will walk in his paths: for the law shall go forth of Zion, and the word of the Lord from Jerusalem. And he shall judge among many people, and rebuke strong nations afar off; and they shall beat their swords into plough-shares, and their spears into pruning-hooks: nation shall not lift up a sword against nation, neither shall they learn war any more."—MICAH iv. 1-3.

MICAH prophesied seven hundred years before Christ. The prediction has not been accomplished. It is yet future—not alone—universal knowledge—holiness—stands in the same category. Isaiah ii. 1, identical. Zech. ix. 10; Psalm lxxii. 7. Let us look,

I. At the period stated.

"The last days," v. 1. Gospel times. From first coming of the Saviour to the second. Daniel ii. 28; Heb. i. 2. First, three hundred years incessant wars up to our days. The last fearful collision. Cannot be far off, &c. Notice,

II. The subject of the prediction.

"Mountain of the House of the Lord." Symbol of the Church and kingdom of the Lord Jesus Christ.

1. *Elevation.* Mountain rises up—seen afar off—Church raised.

2. *Stability.* Mountain stands—all are as of old.

3. *Pre-eminence.* "Top of the mountains, above the hill." See the various ranges. So the various dispensations. Patriarchial—Mosaic—Prophetical—higher and yet higher.

4. *Religious association.* "House of the Lord." Not the Altar—the Tabernacle, nor Temple, but the assembly—the Church of the Lord Jesus, so often called—Christ the Head and Lord—which house believers are.

III. The prediction itself.

1. The *establishment* of the Christian system; v. 1, —shall be established. It has been assailed, persecuted, &c., by every combination of earth and hell; yet it grows, advances, and is now established.

2. Its *universal* visibility. "On the top of the mountains"—shall be seen by the wide world. "Arise and shine," &c.

3. Its *attractive force;* v. 1. "People flow," &c. "Many nations," &c. Drawn—raised—united by truth —flow up —water finds its level—from heaven to heaven —by love.

4. Its *sanctifying power;* v. 2. To be taught God's ways. To be obedient to God's ordinances and commands. "Law." "Word." From Jerusalem. There Christ gave the command and commission.

5. Its *pacific influence;* v. 3. Rebuke of the war spirit. Deliverance of God's judgment, as to the folly, iniquity, cruelty of war. The intellectual growth of Peace principles. The transference of hostile weapons; v. 3. Agriculture and arts—peace. Then, observe, the utter abolition of war—not learn war any more. Then there are,

6. The *blessed results;* v. 4.

7. Its *absolute certainty.* "The mouth of the Lord!"

### APPLICATION

1. How grand the vision!

2. How cheering!

3. How it is linked with the triumphs of knowledge— the success of the Gospel—the glory of Christ—the salvation of the world.

4. Our duty in reference to it. To teach it—preach it—exercise it—pray for it—believe, &c.

# CLXXVII

## SMALL THINGS

"For who hath despised the day of small things?"—Zech iv. 10.

OUR text is a question, and refers to small beginnings.

The day of small things. The child's birthday is such.
The commencement of things in general. The new
birthday. The digging of the foundation for a building.
The first day at school. The first day at business. The
first day in Christian life. But I use the words merely
as a topic—"small things"—and the use we should
make of them. How regard them, &c.

Observe,

**I. The different nature and magnitude of things.**

There are in nature the variety of the great and
small. Mountains, rivers, trees, &c. Cedar and hyssop
—different seas. Above there are planets—large and
small. Stars of first and second, or fourth magnitude.
Men great and small. Everywhere we see the great
and small. Then notice,

**II. The connection between the great and small.**

The great mountain made of small grains. Rivers—
small drops. The day of small moments. The thousand
years of small days, &c. Great men have risen from
small experiences. Sir I. Isaac at one time did not
know his letters. Demosthenes stammered, and could
not utter five sentences, &c. Moses floated a helpless
babe on the Nile. Christ had to be carried away from
the fury of Herod. So there is the link uniting the
great and the small. Look at the Church and kingdom
of Christ. Grain of mustard seed. An upper room held
it in Jerusalem. A ship contained the Puritan Fathers,
the real founders of American independence.

**III. Small things may be connected with great results.**

Pharoah's daughter's visit to the Nile. The little
maid's talk with her mistress. The small stone slung in
the hand of the son of Jesse. The small cloud in the
time of Elijah. The small spark ignites and destroys.
The small leak, and the ship founders.

**IV. Small things may be connected with much of our happiness.**

Temper is often spoken of as a small thing—tongue—the spirit—regard to small duties make the material of a good and useful life. Most people depend on small things, not great ones.

**V. God shews His special regard to small things.**

Bruised reed—smoking flax—small faith—a small prayer—publican—woman—dying thief—small gifts—a cup of water—the widow's mite, &c.

**VI. True Christian philosophy therefore teaches the regard we should pay to small things.**

A small deviation from the right, and it may end in gross error—apostacy—ruin. Punctual regard to our word and engagements. Daily adding to Christian virtue. Constantly doing some small good. Exercising small talents—sowing small seeds; so that we may learn not to despise small things—not to be discouraged by small things; yet not to be satisfied with small things. Aim upwards—onwards—great-wards. "Be strong in the Lord." Seek great things from the Lord, &c.


## CLXXVIII
### AGREEMENT AND FELLOWSHIP

" Can two walk together, except they be agreed? "—Amos iii. 3.

THE text contains an important principle. If there be mutual walking, there must be general agreement. The agreement, we say, must be general—it need not be minute and particular—but it must include oneness in most, especially in important things.

**I. We must be reconciled to God, if we are to have holy com munion with Him.**

The Divine Majesty can have no fellowship with treason, rebellion and wickedness. God, who is light, and the Father of lights, can have no communion with darkness, or His purity with our corruption and depravity. So that man must be converted, renewed, sanctified, before he can walk like Enoch, or Noah, or Abraham, walked with God. So we see the same truth illustrated,

**II. In reference to Christian agreement, in order to mutual harmony and peace.**

Infidelity and faith cannot walk together, nor sceptical doubts, with full assurance of God's love. There must be agreement as to,

1. The *way* in which *they* are to *walk*. If they choose opposite ways, they cannot walk together, or ways that diverge from each other. In this there must be positive agreement, and they must have mutually decided for the same paths.

2. They must be *agreed* as to the *end* of the *way* in which *they walk*. Journey to the same land, or city of habitation. So that they both must be sure that the way leads to the object of their desires and hopes. Like fellow-pilgrims, journeying to the place the Lord has promised them.

3. They *must* be *agreed* as to the *walk* itself. Walking is advancement—going onwards,—and how? and in what? and in what way is this walk to be conducted? What application of time and means are to be devoted to it! What speed and persistency to be employed! What means of solace and quietude, as well as what processes of diligence and care and toil! In all these things they must be agreed, if they are to walk together.

4. They *must* be *agreed* as to the *spirit* they must *cherish*.

How can the dull and morose and murmuring, walk with the joyous, contented and happy ? How can love and uncharitableness, or meekness and wrath, or humbleness and pride, walk together ? How can generousness and avarice, fervour and formalism, or decision and vacillation, walk together ?

5. They *must* be *agreed* as to the *sympathy* they shall *cherish*. Sympathy knits hearts together. It magnatizes and attracts and cements and binds in one, kindred souls. The sensitive and tender and feeling cannot walk with the selfish, the frigid, and the unfeeling. By sympathy the twain are made one and bound together in the indissoluble bonds of heaven-born charity. Now this fellow-feeling should be manifested with regard to general beliefs, modes of worship, principles of faith, and the conduct of life. The closer the accord and concord, and the sweeter the luxury of the fellowship flowing out of them.

**III. The subject bears on the conjugal state, and the agreement of family life.**

1. How *common* is the *absence* of this *agreement*. No mutual ties—no fellow-feeling—no evidences of self-sacrifice. The currents of daily life and conversation running in opposite directions. Each seeking his own things.

2. How *disastrous this is*. To the heads of the family. To the children. To the domestics. To all who come into this atmosphere of discord and contradiction. What a blight upon the house ! What a curse to the family ! What a haunt for evil spirits ! What a place for Satan ! What a sea of storms and tempest and perils !

3. How *desirable* to *avoid* this life of *disagreement* and *sorrow*. Surely young persons should be circumspect in forming attachments and unions. Those who are to

live within the constant wear and tear and friction of life, should be well assured of heart agreement, and of the existence of a well-spring of pure affection.

4. How *important* to seek this *spirit* of *agreement* where it does *not exist*. Natural means—such as, self-controul, —cherishing good temper—avoiding occasions of vexations and disputes, may do much. But God's grace can, with these, do much more. Prayer to God for the new heart and right spirit, and for growth in the milder graces, and more heavenly virtues of saving piety. Prayer for and with each other, and asking that the spirit of unity and mutual love may be shed down upon them.

## CLXXIX

## WALKING WISELY

" See then that ye walk circumspectly, not as fools, but as wise."— EPH. v. 15.

THERE are many important and precious things in the world, but none superior in intrinsic value to time. Every thoughtful mind admits this, confesses this, and yet how few use it wisely, and apply it to its most important ends. The Apostle felt this, and hence the exhortation—" See then that ye walk," &c. Observe,

I. The text exhibits a beacon.

The walk of fools. The folly of the text is not mental, but moral—not of the head, but of the heart. How do fools walk?

1. *Thoughtlessly.* Do not think, reflect—act on impulse, excitement.

2. *Rashly.* Essence of folly is to be rash, precipitate. Wisdom examines calmly, and decides slowly.

3. *Without rule.* All wise people act by rule. Students, men of science, mechanics, labourers, the farmer, God does so. The fool has no settled principles of action.

4. Without *regard* to *results.* Certain actions tend to certain ends. Improvidence, extravagance, bad company, habits, &c.

5. Without *regard* to *God.* " The fool hath said," &c. Or he is like unto us, &c.

6. Without *regard* to *contingencies.*

1. The fool who had laid up, &c. 2. The foolish virgins. 3. The foolish one who says, I will go and buy and sell. As the foolish mariner, who is not prepared for the storm. Here is the beacon,

II. **The text exhibits the safety-light.**

To walk circumspectly. The word signifies, the eye looking all round—taking all into account. All contingencies—all perils—all duties. Here is the " wise,"

1. As the *wise* Abel, renouncing *self,* and looking to the *sacrifice appointed.* See the contrast. Cain and evil. Not trusting to ourselves. Pharisaism is folly.

2. As *wise* Noah, preparing for the future. The deluge, &c. Heb. xi. 7.

3. As *wise* Moses, who preferred the honours and wealth of Heaven, to the treasures of Egypt. Heb. xi. 24.

4. As *wise* Daniel, who choose a self-denying and temperance life to the luxuries of the royal table. Daniel i. 3-8.

5. As the *wise* Virgins, who had lamps, oil, and were waiting.

6. As the *wise* Merchant, who sold all to obtain the peerless pearl of great price.

III. **How this walk is to be maintained.**

1. By making the *Holy Scriptures* the rule—" Able," &c. Psalm cxix. 99, &c., 105.

2. By seeking the *spirit* of *wisdom*, to direct and keep us in the way. "If any man lack wisdom," &c. Spirit of wisdom and counsel.

3. By *walking* with the wise and good; Prov. xiii. 20. So David—"I am a companion," &c.

4. By seeking the *grace*, to give us the power of *walking circumspectly*. Power within—God helping—all fails without this.

5. By *using* the means of Divine *appointment*. "Not forsaking the assembling," &c.

### APPLICATION

Notice the beacon light. Beware, &c. Follow the safety light.

## CLXXX

## TIME'S REDEMPTION

" Redeeming the time, because the days are evil."—EPH. v. 16.

TIME is measured duration — eternity unmeasured. Simile: ocean fathomed—ocean fathomless. Time is measured, and exhibited by the revolving of the earth round the sun,—that is the year. By the revolving motion of the moon,—that is the month. By the rotatory motion of the earth on its own axis,—that is the day. Then we have artificial, yet scientific, measurement of the hour and the minute and seconds.

Now let us look,

### I. At time generally.

1. The *measurement* of the *progress* of *life*. A time to be born—to die. Time begins with the first breath of inspiration, and ends with the last of respiration. Observe,

2. The *uninterrupted progress* of *time*. Never stays—

never rests, sleeps, or varies. Will not, till the angel, &c.

3. Its *silent career*. No noise—no indication between its periods, years. None ever heard its wheels, or the rippling of its waves. A deep, ever flowing stream.

4. Its *inevitable tendency*. Like the rivers, it runs into the eternal ocean. Bears all towards that destiny.

Observe,

**II. Time in its special relation to us.**

It is "our" time the text refers to.

1. Men have their *special allotment* of time. All ages —countries—all individuals.

2. This is of *very diverse quantity* and *amount*. The antediluvians, and ours. Some only a moment, hour, day, year, seventy, eighty, &c.

3. *Time* is the *tenure* of our *probation*. The lease of our accountable life. The exception—infants and imbeciles, all others. It is the day of labour, stewardship, &c.

4. *Time* is ever associated with *privileges* and *blessings, lessons, mercies*. Daily good, &c. Ours is the acceptable time, and day of salvation—Gospel light.

But observe,

**III. This special time of ours is fearfully abused.**

1. Often applied directly to evil. 2. Often wasted on trifles. 3. Often absurdly and wickedly mis-appropriated. Much time to folly—little to wisdom. Much to the body—little to the soul. Much to this world—little to eternity. 4. Time past is gone for ever. No return of a year, week, day, or moment. Gone for ever! Yet observe,

**IV. Time may and should be redeemed.**

"Redeeming the time," &c.

1. By a *wise* and *orderly arrangement* of it. Seeing how it should be set out. Sleep, rest, recreation, business, religion.

2. By *crowding* into it *all* we *can*. Diligence, industry. Having no blank pages. Ever active. Soul formed for this.

3. By a *constant reckoning* with our own *consciences*.

4. By *doing* all the *good* we can in it. Deeds—measure life—not years. There may be an aged child —a man of eighty, and no ends of life obtained. A child of hoary hairs of young life—crowded with good. Now the text gives,

**V. An important reason for redeeming time.**

"The days are evil."

1. The *days* have the *evil* of *vanity*. Swift, rapid, soon gone—man's especially. Look at the trees—the mountains—not so the men, &c.

2. The *days* are *full* of the *evil* of *peril*. To trifle, to waste, to kill it—so easily done.

3. Moral *evils environ* us. Atmosphere, influences, &c.

4. We may *lose* our *ability* to be *useful*. Infirmity, sickness, &c.

Now we appeal,

1. To the young. Now is the time to begin.

2. To parents. Have fixed arrangements. Train up a child, &c.

3. To the old. Be up, &c.

4. To all Christ's disciples. Work to be done, &c.

5. Before us the grave.


## CLXXXI

## THE UNITY OF THE SPIRIT

"Endeavouring to keep the unity of the spirit in the bond of peace."—EPH. iv. 3.

THE address of the apostle is most tender and affecting.

He was a prisoner in Rome for the Gospel's sake; he therefore reminds the Ephesians of this—"I therefore, the prisoner of the Lord," &c.; v. 1. He urges a walk of Christian holiness, &c., worthy of their profession. He then presents the spirit they are to cherish towards each other; v. 2. Four things, and all to be cherished in "love." Then he presses on them the necessity of "endeavouring to keep the unity of the spirit," &c.

Notice,

I. The unity, existing.

You cannot keep what you don't possess; this unity. therefore, was a reality, a fact.

But observe,

1. It was not *uniformity* of which he *speaks*. This did not, nor ever can exist. It is seen nowhere. Diversity, variety every where. Trees, plants, flowers, creatures. So in the human species, colour, size, craniological development, &c. So of angels. But it was,

2. *Unity*. Now varied plants belong to one order. All men have this unity physically. "God has made," &c. Human oneness, erectness, brain, heart, general system the same. So in God's children. One spiritual nature, one body in Christ, members one of another. One vine, one Temple, &c. This exists as a Divine result—we cannot make it nor hinder it

3. This *unity* is *spiritual*. By the Spirit, of the Spirit, having the Spirit. "The Spirit beareth witness," &c. "Because we are sons of God," &c. "If any man have not the Spirit," &c. The same Spirit calls, convinces. renews, witnesses, sanctifies, comforts, guides, &c.

4. This *unity* is *universal*. Over the world—in all ages, countries, colours, tongues, sects, &c. But the apostle obviously assumes,

**II. That this existing unity may be broken.**

It may be broken,

1. *Outwardly.* So Paul distinctly states; 1 Cor. iii. 1-3. Sectarianism breaks it—tears the Saviour's robe—partitions off the Church, &c. It may be broken,

2. *Inwardly.* By envying, strifes, evil surmisings. Selfishness breaks it, spiritual pride breaks it, vain glorying breaks it, anger and bitterness break it, unforgiveness breaks it. Now both the inward and outward unity may be broken, and hence exclusiveness and hatred are the result. But the apostle,

**III. Impresses upon us the course we should adopt.**

"Endeavouring to keep the unity," &c. Now there is to be put forth,

1. *Real effort.* "Endeavouring." Seek it, live for it. labour for it, pray for it, cherish it.

2. It must be *meek* and *humble effort.* Not boisterous, loud, dogmatic; but calm, quiet, &c.

3. It must be *forbearing effort.* Others may differ, but it may be the result of ignorance, prejudice, education, divers influences, &c. Now bearance with their infirmities, and forbearance must be cultivated.

4. It must be *constant effort.* Perils and difficulties constant—a part of our creed, profession, experience and practice, and that daily.

5. It must be Divine *relying effort.* Looking to the grace of God—trusting in the Divine aid. Not in our own spirit or strength, but in the Lord's.

Now the application of the subject may supply us with motives—

1. Our own well-being. This unity is our adorning, our comfort, and our growth.

2. This unity honours the Divine Spirit. He seeks to work this in us. He is glorified by it.

3. It answers the great prayer of the Saviour—His last, &c.; John xvii.

4. It is the power of the Church of Christ.

5. It will be the grand attraction of those without.

## CLXXXII

## THE JOYFULNESS OF GOD'S HOUSE

"Joyful in my house of prayer."—ISAIAH lvi. 7.

THE text is only the fragment of a sentence, yet complete, &c., and it is of universal application, independent of dispensation, age, or circumstances, and admirably adapted to our gathering to-day.

**I. The persons to whom the text refers.**

It obviously relates to Gentiles, v. 3; but to religious Gentiles.

1. *Public professors* of God's name; v. 3.

2. *Obedient* to the Divine *will*, pleasing God; v. 4.

3. Who are in *covenant relationship* with God. "Take hold," &c.; v. 4.

4. *Love* the *name* and *service* of the Lord; v. 6.

5. *Delight* in His *Sabbaths*; v. 2, 4, 6.

Notice,

**II. The declaration made.**

"I will make them joyful."

1. In *taking away sadness* and its *causes*. Sin, condemnation, slavish dread, horrible pit, &c.

2. By *giving* the *spirit* of *adoption*, the evidence of their sonship, the source of their blessedness.

3. By *inspiring* hopes of the *future*—"rejoicing in hope." Christ in you the hope, &c. Seeing the distant land, &c.

4. By the *sanctification* of their *providential experiences*.

All things working. &c.    God guiding, protecting, blessing, return to Zion singing.    But observe,

**III. The special place of this promise of God.**

"My House of prayer." The Tabernacle was God's House—the Temple—every holy Synagogue. Now, wherever two or three are gathered. &c.

1. Our *places* of *worship belong* to God. They are for God, to God, and God dwells in them, meets, communes, sanctifies, and owns.

2. They are *pre-eminently houses* of *prayer*. Here God is known as the hearer of prayer, answerer of prayer. Here is the true prayer-book to guide our prayers, promises to prayer, the spirit of prayer. Not exclusively hearing, meditating, &c., but prayer pre-eminently.

Now notice,

**IV. The character and connection of this joy with God's House of prayer.**

1. See the *connection* with the *exercises* of this *house*. Joy and prayer. Joy and the Word. Joy and the ordinances. Joy and the praises. Joy and the blessings. How clear all this. But look at it,

2. In *connection* with the *persons* as well as the *exercises*. God's people there—God's ministering servants there—God Himself there, Father, Son, and Holy Spirit. "Wherever," &c. "Lo, I am with you," &c.

3. See it in *connection* with the *experiences* of this *house*. Most persons have been enlightened there, convicted there, converted there, sanctified there, comforted there, fed there, &c.

4. See it in *connection* with *this house* and the *house above*. House of God, the gate of Heaven. Ladder here, angels here, foretaste here. As Mount of Olives to Christ. Now the subject,

1. *Exhibits* the *blessedness* of *true religion*. Not dark-

ness, not gloom, despondency—but "joy," abundant, Divine, heavenly, everlasting. Subject exhibits,

2. The *preciousness* of God's *House*. "Lord, I have loved," &c. "Blessed are they," &c.

3. The corresponding *duties* and *privileges*. "I have been there," "Not forsaking," sustaining, &c., helping. We should bring others with us to share the blessedness. All men desire joyousness of soul, here it is supplied. Then "Come with us and we will do you good."


## CLXXXIII

## THE BLESSED SERVANT

"Blessed is that servant whom his lord when he cometh shall find so doing."—MATT. xxiv. 46.

VIGILANCE, fidelity, and readiness for His coming inculcated by the Lord Jesus, to watch, work, and be ready. It is obvious how essential they are to the sentinel, to the seamen, to the pilgrim, and, as in the text, to the servant or steward. Now let us see the truths the text involves.

### I. The Lord's people are His servants.

This is true of all and each, every class and age and condition. The Christian life is servitude, but not slavery or serfdom. All the angels serve God, do His will, hearken, &c.

1. Now the *entrance* on Christian *service* begins by taking His *yoke*, &c., thus we become the servants of Christ.

2. The *progress* of the Christian *life* is *active* service. Doing the Lord's will, obeying Him, keeping His commandments.

3. In this *service* there is *variety* of *office.* There are

the lowest and the highest and the intermediate. Apostles were the highest, &c. The private Christian is a household servant of the Lord. No character without a sphere. Work and place for all.

4. This *service* is *life-long*, fidelity to the end. Serving God is the golden thread of spiritual being woven into the web of our probationary life. Much work for the new convert, the mature Christian, the aged saint; death even does not end it, for observe,

5. This *service* is of *perpetual duration*, for ever; see Rev. xxii. 3. But it is to the present service that ends with this life to which the text refers. Observe,

**II. The coming of the Lord and Master—His second coming.**

1. Is *matter* of *certainty*. Predicted, promised, necessary. He must come to complete His purposes and consummate His kingdom.

2. At His *coming* His *servants* will be *rewarded*, Matt. xxv., &c., rewarded according to their work and to the riches of His grace. To secure this reward,

3. His servants should be found *watching* and *waiting* for His *coming*. This is the central idea of the text. Now let us see what this includes—1. To be at work. 2. To have conscious sense of faithfulness. 3. Not to be occupied with other things. 4. Not to be indifferent, &c. 5. But looking and longing for His appearance. But observe,

**III. The blessedness such a state will secure.**

See Rev. xvi. 15.

1. There will be the *blessedness* of the *Divine recognition:* Christ will observe and distinguish: He will note, &c.

2. The *blessedness* of *public acknowledgment*. His "well done" will be uttered in the ears of the assembled throng.

3. He will *bestow* the *reward*, "enter thou," &c. He

will admit into glory, give the crown.  Paul expected
this.  Now this blessedness—1. Is certain, it is in the
service and with it inseparable.  Truth, fidelity, &c., all
secure it.  2. Universal to all the servants; none too
great or obscure; each and all.  3. Immortal.  Every
gem in the crown shines for ever: all the honours un-
fading: the glory everlasting.  Now the subject,

 1. Suggests *personal enquiry*.  Are we Christ's servants?

 2. Careful *supervision*.  Are our *accounts* right, state,
talents? &c.

 3. Do we *expect* the Lord, and are we *waiting* for
Him? &c.

 4. How *devoted* we should be, so as not to fail of the
final blessedness.


# CLXXXIV

## SOWING AND REAPING

"But this I say, He which soweth sparingly shall reap also sparingly ; and he which soweth bountifully shall reap also bountifully."
—2 Cor. ix. 6.

THE Bible is a book of similes.  Figures and parables
abound.  One of the very frequent, that of the figure, is
of "sowing."  Hence in Job we read of sowing wickedness.  In the Psalms sowing "in tears"—" going forth,"
&c.  So Christ's rich parables : so the devil sowing tares :
so Paul speaks of sowing to the flesh : so in the text—
sowing and reaping.  Now there is the idea of seed—
ground, and putting seed into the ground.  Now no one
expects to reap without sowing, and of the same kind.
But the text refers to the abundance, that is the one
idea.  Bad seed sown abundantly, and there will be an
abundant result : so good, as in the text.  Now there
are several analogies I want to bring before you.

## I. The self-cultivator.

The mind, the heart, the soul like soil, to be cultivated. And corresponding, there is the seed of knowledge. There is the seed of wisdom. There is the seed of Divine truth. In each case, as is the sowing, will be the reaping, reading, reflection, study, persistence; and there will be a good religion of knowledge. So of wisdom. So of religious moral truth in the soul.

## II. Look at the sowers of knowledge and truth in others.

Look at your children, families. See how true of your vicinities, town, schools. Scanty sowing, &c. Liberal sowing, &c.

## III. Look at the religious teachers.

Apostles, bishops, evangelists. All sowers of best seed. And so results. So now he who sows largely, freely, constantly, will reap in proportion. So the Apostle said, "Freely ye have received, freely give."

## IV. Look at the beneficent sower to which the text refers.

Acts of goodness—deeds of kindness—seed of loving works. Now bountiful sowing,

1. Is sowing *up* to our *means;* chapter viii. 2, 3. So the widow and her mite.

2. It is *embracing* all sowing *seasons.* In the morning, evening: beside all waters. Having an eye to all opportunities. As ye have opportunity, &c.

3. It is *continuing* to sow. Not ceasing. Life work to the end. Till the evening.

4. It is *abounding* and *increasing* in sowing. The skill increasing. The power increasing; age, &c.; love to it increases. Now see,

## V. The declaration of the bounteous sower.

1. He shall *reap.* This is the Divine law in nature, in mind, &c. So in religion the good seed does not die: but it lives: deep in the earth it lives. So good deeds live, &c.

2. He shall *reap more* than he sows. Without this sowing would be useless, if it were grain for grain. But the one seed yields thirty, sixty, or a hundred fold.

3. He shall *reap abundantly.* Proportion for proportion —much seed—much return. But this abundant reaping,

4. Is of God's *blessing.* He blesses the springing— Fountain of life. Increase is of the Lord. The seed is His. The rain, the dew, the sun, the electrical currents. God gives the increase.

Observe—

1. All Christians should be sowers. 2. All should aim at bountiful sowing. 3. All may cherish the hope of corresponding reaping. 4. God will not fail to give the return. 5. So the sparing sower, cannot expect other than sparing results—it must be so. 6. The reaping is of both worlds. Now we reap as well as sow. Joy, happiness, satisfaction. But the grand reaping time is beyond and above. Just examine, prove, seek God's grace for right views, feelings, dispositions, toils, &c.


## CLXXXV

### THE PRAYER GOD WILL NOT DESPISE

" He will regard the prayer of the destitute, and not despise their prayer."—PSALM cii. 17.

No religion without prayer. All Pagan religions have it. Mahomedanism abounds in it. Scenes I have witnessed of it. The sound from the minarets, calling the believers to prayer several times a day. Jews under the law were distinguished for prayer—Christianity is saturated with the spirit of prayer. Directions, cautions and promises we have in every conceivable form. Now the text contains two distinct declarations in reference to prayer. Now let us look at these two declarations in their various bearings.

**I. God will not despise their prayer.**

To despise is to scorn, to contemn. Now the declaration obviously involves the truth that there are prayers God will despise. Our subject therefore, will be best discussed by looking at such prayers as God despises, that is, treats with His Divine scorn; and,

1. He will *despise* prayers that *seek* to do *evil*. Malicious prayers, vengeful prayers. Prayer must be without wrath. Such prayers are in reality seeking curses and maledictions.

2. He will *despise* the prayers of mere *terror*. Wicked profane persons, when in danger only, pray. Often sailors in storms—soldiers in battle—persons in sudden peril; see Proverbs i. 23.

3. He will *despise* all *ostentatious* prayers. Mere parade of piety, learning, or display of gifts, or shew of goodness; Matt. vi. 5; Matt. xxiii. 5, &c.

4. He will *despise* merely *long* prayers; Matt. xxiii. 14. So Christ's Divine model is in a few sentences.

5. He will *despise* all mere *talkative* prayers. Just prattling to God—prayers with a bushel of words to a few ideas—vague, diffuse, wordy.

6. He will *despise* all *assumptious* prayers. Teaching God, or preaching to God, explaining to God as if He did not understand, or in prayer preaching to those who hear us, or dictating and telling God what He ought to do.

7. He will *despise* all *uncharitable* prayers. Prayer can only rise on the wings of love. Hear Christ; Matt. v. 23.

8. He will *despise* all *unbelieving* prayers. "He that cometh to God must believe," &c. Faith essential—

without it prayer is mockery, contradiction, absurdity. It may be weak faith, but faith is essential.

9. He will *despise* all *ungrateful* prayers. Prayer and thanksgiving must be the two links of acceptable devotion. Make your request with thanksgiving; 1 Thess. v. 17.

10. He will *despise* all *self-meritorious* prayers. Resting on our supposed excellency or merit—leaving out the Mediator and His work, &c.

11. He will *despise* all *presumptuous* prayers. Where we ask God to do for us what we can do ourselves, or ask what involves a miracle, or for personal convenience, without regard to others, or God's general providence and His government of the world. To pray for removal of epidemics and dwelling in dirt.

12. He will *despise* the *insincere* prayer. Mere lip devotion—nominal dead form. Now these must be our beacon lights when we pray. But the text refers to,

II. The prayer He will not despise.

" The prayers of the destitute."

1. Who feel their need. 2. Who realize their dependence on Him. 3. Who acknowledge their sins and unworthiness. Publican, &c. 4. Who press their suit. Woman of Canaan, &c. 5. Who honour His word by confidence and persistency. Will not let thee go, &c. 6. Who ignore themselves. Deep in the valley. 7. Who pray in Christ's name, &c.


APPLICATION

1. How condescending God is. To the poorest, most wretched, forlorn, widow, orphan, beggar, &c.

2. How good God is to all.

3. How all-sufficient God is to His people.

4. How we should learn to pray and seek His grace.

## CLXXXVI

## GOD'S GOODNESS AND WONDROUS DEALINGS WITH HIS PEOPLE

" And ye shall eat in plenty, and be satisfied, and praise the name of the Lord your God, that hath dealt wondrously with you ; and my people shall never be ashamed."—JOEL ii. 26.

THE original signification of the text will be seen by a careful perusal of the chapter, where God's judgments are exhibited; v. 1-12; where repentance is enjoined; v. 12 ; and the Divine mercy is predicted; v. 14. Then the scene is brightened by Divine mercies and gracious assurances, of which the text is a part. But let us look at it in reference to spiritual experiences and blessings.

Notice,

**I. A striking statement.**

That God has "dealt wondrously" with His people. This is universally true of all God's people, and sometimes the evidences are more than usually extraordinary. See it,

1. In God's *words*, as *sympathy* and *compassion*. As with Israel in Egypt, &c. For it is not usual to take deep interest in the vile and worthless, and utterly undeserving. But such were many of those, called and saved by the grace of God. Woman sinner—dying thief—Jerusalem sinners—defiled Ephesians—persecuting Saul, &c. How wondrous,

2. In the Divine *appliances* for *their salvation*. Providential means—extraordinary visitations—remarkable incidents, &c. Take the case of John Bunyan. Remarkable men raised up and sent forth as the sceptical John Newton—the Boanerges, John Nelson—converted prizefighters, &c.

3. In the *free* and *abundant bestowment* of Divine

*mercy.* See it on the day of Pentecost. God's mercy plenteous—pardons abounding—grace as a river—showers of blessing—multitudes saved.

4. In the *transforming power* of the Holy Spirit. How wondrous the changes wrought! The translations from gross darkness into the Divine and saving noon-day light. How all moral maladies and leprous defilement are removed, and all holy graces and virtues imparted. The palaces of Satan, now the temples of the Holy Ghost—slaves enfranchised—demons expelled—rebels forgiven—heirs of wrath and hell, now heirs of God and joint heirs with Christ Jesus.

5. In the *glorious* and *exalted privileges* conferred.

Sonship and its dignities—covenant mercies pledged—Divine fellowship bestowed—immortal joys and hopes imparted. "Beloved, now are we the sons of God," &c.

6. In the *special providences afforded.* As with the Patriarchs, Israel, David, Daniel; so the apostles, &c. See 2 Cor. i. 4-11. All things working for good, &c. Rom. viii. 28-39. Observe,

II. The plentiful provision.

"Shall eat in plenty and be satisfied." This table of Divine bounties is spread in the wilderness, and it is covered with good things. This cup of mercy runneth over. This manna fell fast and thick and daily. This meal and oil do not fail. Now this abundant provision,

1. Is *royal* provision. A king's banquet. A royal store-room. The provision of the infinite source of all blessings.

2. It is, therefore, of every *rich variety.* All kinds of good things from the folds and pastures and clouds and heavens and the depths of the sea. Every conceivable spiritual good.

3. It is more *than sufficient.* Enough and to spare—boundless, and increasing—flowing superabundance.

4. It is *perpetual.* Every day—every moment—an enduring feast—a perennial spring; and, therefore, no marvel,

5. That it should be *satisfying.* "And be satisfied." The mercy, the love, the kindness, the blessing, are all adapted to man's necessities and miseries, and yield full and lasting satisfaction. But, notice,

### III. The magnanimous spirit displayed.

"And my people shall never be ashamed." Not ashamed,

1. Of the *author* of *their blessings.* God, in Christ, by the Spirit. They shall exult and glory in the God of their salvation.

2. Of the *gracious experience* they *have realized.* "Come all ye that fear God, and I will tell what," &c. The restored blind young man; John ix. The demoniac—the leper—woman of Samaria.

3. Of the *noble* profession *they* have *made.* Of the army into which they have enlisted—of their captain—of their brethren—of their principles and exercises and prospects. So Paul, "I am not ashamed," &c. So Christ's demand, "If any man be ashamed," &c. But they shall be the bold, undaunted confessors of the Lord Jesus. Such is this rich text in its spiritual aspects. And now let us—

1. By faithful self-examination prove ourselves, and see if we are the subjects of the wondrous changes and privileges and blessings, the text presents.

2. Seek grace to honour God by holy devotedness to His service.

3. To invite the weary way-worn souls around us to be partakers of like blessings. "Come with us," &c.

4. To cherish humbleness, gratefulness of spirit, and glorify God in all things, by His grace given unto us.

## CLXXXVII

## MOUNT ZION AND ITS BLESSINGS

"But upon mount Zion shall be deliverance, and there shall be holiness.—OBADIAH 17.

THE true mount Zion is the Christian Church, unto which it is said "we are come," and not to the mount that might be touched, and that burned with fire, &c.; Heb. xii. 18-22. And this New Testament Zion was typified by the original Mount in Jerusalem, and there are many striking analogies between the two. But we look at the text in its two distinct statements as to deliverance and holiness. Notice then,

I. **The New Testament Mount Zion and its deliverance.**

It is here that we have deliverance from,

1. *Sinai* and the *law*. Here there is condemnation and curses, blackness and wrath, terror and destruction, but in mount Zion is the new covenant, the one efficient Mediator, &c. Here appears the Saviour and the blessings of the Gospel, pardon, peace, adoption, &c., eternal life. Notice,

2. Here is *deliverance* from Jewish *ceremonials*. No longer are we allied with Aaron, Levites, sacrifices, Tabernacle services, or ancient festivals, cloud and all have disappeared, and now in Christ and the Gospel we have all in their spiritual significancy and saving influence; see Heb. ix. 10.

3. Here is *deliverance* from *national* and *local religion*. No longer are the tribes required to go up to Jerusalem. The Temple is gone—the glory departed—Jerusalem in heaps—the division wall is no more—Jew and Gentile stand on equal terms before God. All believers are priests. All of every nation who work righteousness

are accepted of God. The Kingdom of Christ is for the whole earth. The Gospel for the world and every creature. Now this deliverance had been typified in some measure by Israel's redemption from Egypt. It is liberty in and by Christ Jesus. Liberty of soul and spirit, and deliverance from the twilight and imperfect knowledge of the legal economy, into the full daylight and glory of Christianity. Here Christ wrought our deliverance, and here the delivering grace of God was first exerted; Luke xxiv. 46. But there is not only deliverance upon mount Zion, but,

## II. There is holiness.

We have,

1. An *immaculate Saviour.* Not like Aaron or Moses, frail, &c., but the holy Child Jesus—the holy Youth Jesus—the holy Man Jesus—the holy Prophet, Priest, King. Essentially holy in His ministry, in His life, in His work; the channel of holiness,—the model of holiness—the teacher of holiness. The Divine purifier. The cleanser and healer and transformer, &c.

2. A *holy sacrifice.* Not spotless beasts, but a spotless Christ! Hence the value of His blood, and the efficacy of His mediation. It was not only the holy blood of a holy man, but the holy blood of the Son of God, and therefore partook of the efficacy of His divinity.

3. Here was to come down the *spirit* of *holiness.* In Jerusalem they were to wait for the great promised gift of the Holy Ghost, and as He came down in cloven tongues of holy flame, so, too, holy influences like a river were to flow out from Jerusalem or Zion.

4. Here would be holy *influences* and *privileges*— ordinances of the Gospel. A holy Church with its immunities and fellowship and holy services and blessings. Now holiness is the one great end of the grace

of God, the work of Christ, and the operations of the Spirit. In holiness we are restored to God, regain the Divine likeness, and have the meetness for glory, immortality, and eternal life. Now see in the text,

III. The permanent results of this deliverance and holiness.

"They shall possess their possessions." Not Judea or the Promised Land, but the possessions it fore-shadowed.

1. A *possession* of *grace here*. In a state of favour or grace we come into the possession of every conceivable needed good. We enter the Divine kingdom, and are endowed with all its privileges and favours. Cove-nanted mercies, and precious promises, and realised spiritual enjoyments; partakers of the unsearchable riches of infinite grace.

2. Then the *possession* of *glory* hereafter. "He will give grace and glory." "Called to His eternal king-dom and glory." Heirs of a glorious inheritance. Heirs of God and joint heirs with Christ. So Christ shall appoint unto you a kingdom, &c. "Fear not, little flock," &c. And the Spirit of grace is the earnest of this their future inheritance. Such, then, is the deliver-ance, and the holiness, and the possession. Now let us enquire,

1. If we feel our interest in these privileges and blessings? Are we delivered, sanctified, and have entered into the possession of the Divine favour, and the hope of eternal life?

2. The satisfaction such an experience should produce. "Let the children of Zion be joyful."

3. The devout and holy walk, becoming a state so exalted and blessings so Divine.

4. We appeal to such in bondage to come in faith and obtain the deliverance revealed and offered in the Gospel of Christ.

## CLXXXVIII
## SONG OF THE STRONG CITY

"In that day shall this song be sung in the land of Judah; We have a strong city: salvation will God appoint for walls and bulwarks."—Isa. xxvi. 1.

THE text refers to the Church of God. The Church is one in all ages and countries. The Church is ever the butt of attack from men and devils. Ever hated, persecuted, scorned, &c. The Church, notwithstanding, still exists. Bush—covenants, promises. Now let us first look at the cheering statement of the text. See next the harmony of the text with other Scriptures; Psalm xlviii. 12; cxxv. 1, &c.; Zech. ii. 5.

Now let us see,

**I. The description of the Church of God.**

It is a city—Zion—the type—city of God—glorious city. Its King, Jehovah; attendants, angels; inhabitants, the godly. It is a strong city—foundations, rock, protection, the Divine presence—wall of fire. Invincibility, cannot be destroyed—oldest in the world. Its magnificence shall increase—be the glory of the whole earth. Observe,

**II. Its impregnable walls and bulwarks.**

"Salvation."

1. The Divine Saviour *dwells* in it.

2. Salvation is *secured* to it.

3. Salvation has ever been the *issue*. Israel in Egypt —in Babylon. New Testament Church. It must be so,

1. Unless God is overcome. 2. Or truth fails. 3. Or Satan triumphs. 4. Or the ungodly are victors. 5. Or the promise and covenant fail. Then see,

**III. The appropriateness of the song.**

1. For it is true. 2. It is cheering. 3. It is comforting. 4. It shall be enduring. Notice the singers—

prophets and priests, apostles and ministers, pastors and people, teachers and children—the whole Church of Christ.

APPLICATION

1. Let us learn this song.

2. Often practise it.

3. Anticipate its increasing importance. See Revelations.

4. Remember, it will be sung for ever.

CLXXXIX

## COMING TOGETHER FOR THE WORSE

"Now in this that I declare unto you I praise you not, that ye come together not for the better, but for the worse.—1. Cor. xi. 17.

GREAT disorder existed in the Church at Corinth. Divisions, confusions, &c. Abuse of sacred things—neglect of order, &c. Made a common meal of the Lord's Supper; and so the Apostle writes, instructs, counsels, &c., and shewing not only that thus convening they were not the better, but really worse.

Let us then notice,

**I. The assembly for public services of the Church of Christ.**

This was from the beginning—to this they are exhorted—not forsaking, &c. Three special objects,

1. To *worship* God. This is an essential duty and privilege. So the Psalms are as applicable to us as to the Old Testament saints; Psa. xcv. 6; xcvi. 9.

2. To *commune* with God's *people*. Go up in company —religious sociality—" as iron "—they came together—" at once they sing," &c.—parents and children—brethren and sisters—neighbours and friends.

3. To obtain *blessings* for *ourselves*. To get know-

ledge, counsel, blessings, adapted, &c. Comfort, joy, strength, hope, submission, &c. So we might add to these, to exhibit the banner of religious truth before the world. Observe,

**II. We may come together in the House of God and not be the better for it.**

So says the text, "not the better," &c. In many things we may see this,

1. In *hurriedly* coming together. Calm composure is requisite in approaching God. Hurry confuses, unsettles, ruffles and prevents meditation, and distracts the soul; a few minutes calm would enable us to draw near acceptably, &c.

2. When we come *carelessly*, without object. We go, of course, it is the order, the rule; others do it, we must, but the why and wherefore overlooked, no immediate design or express reason.

3. When we *treat* the assembly as an *ordinary gathering*. It is not merely intellectual or merely social, but it is spiritual, Divine, to meet God, the most momentous, &c., to do with the soul and eternity.

4. When we come in the spirit of ceremonial *self-righteousness*. To do so much in the way of duty, merit, work for pay, &c., to be better than others.

5. When *faith* is not in exercise. Hearing, singing, praying, and no faith—is it not a mockery and a snare, without faith?

6. When we come in a *bad, uncharitable spirit*. Towards the minister, towards some of the brethren, or towards any of the Lord's people. Some make it the place of their bickerings, bad tempers, spirit looking with bitterness, &c. Our Lord meets this case; see Matt. v. 23.

7. When we go away and forget the *end* of assembling. Benediction and immediate forgetfulness—the world

and every-day affairs, &c.—not look, or wait, or expect the blessing—not harrow the Word in by prayer.

**III. The text assumes if we are not the better for assembling, we are certainly the worse.**

"But for the worse." How obvious is this. See it in, 1. The worship spoiled. 2. Duty perverted. 3. God displeased. 4. Soul disappointed. 5. Satan gratified. Now let us see in application how we should—

1. Immensely prize our social privileges. How dear! How sacred! How precious!

2. Resolve to make the best of them. Give them the first place; keep them there.

3. Sanctify them by prayer—before—in—after.

4. And follow them by reflection and watchfulness.

## CXC

### THE BLACK PASSION

"Who is able to stand before envy?"—Prov. xxvii. 4.
"Envy is the rottenness of the bones."—Prov. xiv. 30.

Envy is a sense of pain, and often of hatred at beholding the excellency, prosperity, or happiness of others. In itself it is the very rottenness of the bones, and is most malignant in its influence on others.

**I. See it in families.**

The first family—Cain and Abel. Jacob's family, the brothers towards Joseph.

**II. See it in kingdoms.**

Saul and David; 1 Sam. xviii. 6. Haman and Mordecai; Esther v. 13. The Princes and Daniel; Dan. vi. 3, 4. Herod and the infant Jesus; Matt. i. 15, 16.

**III. See it in relation to religion and ecclesiastical institutions.**

Some of the Israelites and Moses; Exo. ii. 14; so also

Aaron and Miriam; Numb. xii. 2. Paul and the Judaizing teachers; Philip. i. 15, 16. The Jews and the Lord Jesus Christ; Matt. xxvii. 18.

In regard to this black passion—(1.) How it abounds. (2.) How it defiles; hardens the heart and curses the soul. (3.) How it spreads ruin and woe among families and homes. (4.) How it leads to awful sins and fearful crimes. (5.) How it is incurable by human appliances. (6.) How the grace of God alone can cure it, and save us from it. (7.) How we should earnestly pray and strive to get the entire victory over it. (8.) How Divine love in the soul extirpates it, and effectually delivers us from it.


## CXCI

## THE MONARCH OF THE GLORIOUS FUTURE

"And the Lord shall be King over all the earth."—ZECH. xiv. 9.

THIS prediction is not yet accomplished, but it is in harmony with many prophecies. It stands in connection with God's purposes, covenants, and promises. Look,

**I. At the glorious Monarch.**

"The Lord." The Lord Jesus. He is the supreme King—King of kings—Prince of Life—Lord of Glory— the King Immortal. He shall wear the many crowns; Rev. xix. 11-16; Heb. i. 8; 1 Tim. vi. 14-16. Notice,

**II. His specified domains.**

He is King of Glory—Lord of Angels—supreme over the universe. But the text refers to our world, "He shall be King over all the earth."

1. The earth was *made* by Him; John i. 1-4.

2. As such the earth *belongs* to Him. "Lord of all," King of the whole earth.

3. He *governs* the whole earth.

4. He has *redeemed* the earth.

5. He will *restore* the earth to purity and bliss.

6. He will *triumph* over all His foes. "Subdue all things to Himself;" Philip. ii. 10-11.

7. He will *graciously* and *gloriously* be adored and loved and obeyed by all the earth; Rev. xi. 15-17.

Observe,

1. The clearness of the prediction.

2. The power of Christ to effect it; and therefore,

3. The absolute certainty of its accomplishment; see Psalm lxxii. 17-19; Isaiah liii. 10-12. He bore the cross for all, and He shall wear the crown over all.

4. How we should live and labour for this glorious consummation. "Come, Lord Jesus, come quickly!"

## CXCII

### WEARYING GOD WITH OUR WORDS

" Ye have wearied the Lord with your words."—MALACHI ii. 17.

As true now as in the days of the prophet. As true of the ungodly and the merely formal, as of the ancient Jews. We need scarcely to state, that we might expect God to be wearied with blasphemous words—profane words—false words—proud words—flattering and vain words. But we often weary God,

**I. By mere ceremonious words.**

Words good and suitable and reverent, but being uttered without sincerity or truth. We use them in worship—in profession; but they have no real significancy in our hearts and lives. How true this is frequently of praying words, and praising words! Words merely.

**II. By forgotten words.**

Uttered and not remembered—vows—resolves—purposes, &c.

**III. By insincere words.**

Strong expressions—feeble feelings and influences. Extravagant and exaggerated modes of speech in religion and religious conversation; worship, &c.

**IV. God is thus wearied.**

By our oft-repeated and unmeaning words. He knows the heart—tries the spirit. Demands truth in the inward parts. Abhors hypocrisy and all vain dissemblings.

Let the subject lead us—

1. To seek the gracious, purifying influences of the Holy Spirit. "Create in me," &c. 2. To be watchful of our lips. Life and death are in the power of the tongue. Words will finally condemn or justify us. 3. To imitate the Lord Jesus, in whose mouth was no guile. 4. Ever to seek so to speak and walk as to please God. A sanctified mouth glorifies God.


## CXCIII

### SINFUL INFATUATION

" But they refused to hearken, and pulled away the shoulder, and stopped their ears," &c.—ZECH. vii. 11.

THE counsel of the Lord given to His people was most just and reasonable. It was alike in harmony with humanity and religion; see v. 8-11. But their conduct was base, rebellious, and god-defiant. How often sin presents these aspects of vileness. Observe,

**I. They refused to listen to the Divine message.**

An act of greatest daring and culpability—as children of God—as subjects of God—as almoners on His bounty —as the objects of His forbearance and mercy.

**II. They withdrew their acknowledged obedience and submission to God.**

"Pulled away the shoulder," that is, rejected God's yoke, and cast off their allegiance.

**III. They closed the means of communication.**

"Stopped their ears," &c. So shut out God's message, and all intercourse with Him. How daring and reckless and presumptuous!

**IV. They hardened their hearts against God.**

Made their hearts as an adamant stone. How impious! and resolved to set God at defiance. What moral suicide; v. 12. Therefore we need not marvel,

**V. At the ruin in which they were involved.**

"Therefore came a great wrath," &c. A punishment most just. Their great folly—great daring—and great defiance of God, brought upon them "great wrath." Sin and penalty in accord—sowing and reaping—rebellion and ruin—impiety and distrust.

How men still set God at defiance! And how certainly they involve themselves in utter ruin. How needful to warn, reprove, and exhort men to flee from sin, and thus from the wrath to come.


## CXCIV

### INFINITE FULNESS

"The fulness of Christ."—EPHESIANS iv. 13.

THE four words of the text have an infinity of meaning. We detach them from the context and look at them alone, and in their express signification. And thus we shall be led to a higher estimate, and a more entire appreciation of the Saviour. In Christ all is perfect, complete, no deficiency. Let us see in reference to the text,

**I. What it comprises.**

1. *Divine fulness.* "Fulness of the Godhead," &c. Equality with the Father.

2. *Human fulness.* Man, Son of Man. Made in all things, &c. All the essentialities of our humanity.

3. *Mediatorial fulness.* Filling the great void with His mediatorial presence. United inseparably to God, and graciously to man.

4. *Gracious fulness.* Full of grace. A combination of mercy, compassion, tenderness, love, &c.

5. *Efficient fulness.* As to wisdom—as to power—as to adaptation. He could do all He undertook. Confound Satan—redeem man—glorify God.

6. *Unchanging fulness.* "Jesus Christ the same yesterday, to-day, and for ever." No exhaustion. Like the sun, or ocean, or air, &c., and therefore,

7. An *eternal fulness.* A fulness for the past ages, and the present dispensation—and all the ages to come, and for eternity itself. He is the Eternal Life. Such is, in brief, the fulness of Christ. Now let us consider Christ's fulness,

**II. As to what it demands.**

1. Our *personal knowledge* of it. To know or understand it. To know the fulness of Christ which passeth knowledge. Look at it,

(1.) By comparison—fulness of the first Adam, Noah, of Abraham, Melchisedeck, Moses, David, &c. Yea, of the holy angels. All these shadows—Christ the substance. (2.) See it from its communications—He has imparted of His fulness in all ages, &c., to billions of recipients; John i. 16. "Of His fulness," &c.

2. Our *personal realization* of it. To know and then to experience it. To hear His voice and feel His power.

3. Our *personal confidence* in it. We need to be ever supplied with every grace. Well, it is in Christ for us. Grace upon grace—grace to help us, &c.

4. Our *joyous gratefulness* for it. Thanks be unto God, &c. Praises to Him. Exulting—rejoicing in the Lord always.

5. The *publishing* of *this to others*. Ministers—parents —teachers—Christians in all spheres. To tell of this fulness of Christ to the blind—the diseased and wretched —the poor and the perishing, &c. A full salvation for every grade of sinners. Such then is the fulness of Christ, and our duty in reference to it.

### APPLICATION

1. We cannot exalt Christ too highly.
2. We cannot trust too implicitly.
3. Or ask too much. Hitherto ye have asked nothing, &c.

## CXCV

## THE GLORIOUS MANIFESTATION OF THE SAINTS

" For the earnest expectation of the creature waiteth for the manifestation of the sons of God."—ROMANS viii. 19.

THIS is one of the grandest chapters in all the epistles of the New Testament. The Christian character is here depicted in its origin,—process—spiritual advancement —dignity, privileges and future glory. And then by a bold figure, creation is represented as waiting earnestly for the glorious consummation of the text.

Let us consider then,

### I. Creation in its expectant attitude.

Creature here most be read in connection with verses 21, 22. Now the creature, or creation, represents the world in which we dwell. The home of man. The earth that God has given to the children of men. Psa. cxv. 16. Now let us just look,

1. At creation in *connection* with *man.* I mean the creature, the earth. The Mosaic record ends; Gen. i. 25, 26. Then let us look,

2. At creation, under the *spell* of *evil.* It was a garden of delight. Temple for God and man. But sin entered, and the curse came down. Gen. iii. 17. Now see,

3. The *harvest* of *woes* that creation reaps. Sterility —pain—decay. It becomes one grave-yard. One inferno of evil. The first man a murderer. After 2000 years, hear Jehovah's description; Gen. vi. 5-7. Now remember,

4. The *woes* of the post-deluvian world. Idols— slavery — suffering — plagues— famines—pestilences — war and gory battle-fields—storms—tornados—earthquakes—sea wrecks—home scenes of bitter pain. The hospital, infirmaries. The crowds of the sick, blind, deaf and dying. On the earthly creation, written vanity, &c.; verse 22.

5. The earth's grand *future renovation* by fire. Purified by flame; 2 Peter iii. 10-13. With this read John's description as beheld in vision (Rev. xxi. 1-4), and it is for this,

6. The creature, or creation, is *waiting.* As the mariner waits the break of day. As the prisoner waits for liberty. For all this creation travaileth, groaneth, waiteth earnestly, and with joyful expectation. Then see,

**II. The emancipated creation in connection with God's people.**

"For the manifestation of the sons of God." As the chaotic earth waited for the Mosaic creation, and the first of the human race; so the creation now waits for the manifestation, &c. Now notice,

1. The *title* of God's people. "The sons of God."

(1.) By restoration; (2.) Adoption; (3.) Regeneration.

2. The *present state* of God's people. Obscurity. As the sun eclipsed—world knoweth us not—hidden ones —hid with Christ. But this obscurity is only for awhile.

3. For there *shall be* a *manifestation* of the sons of God. They shall appear with Christ. They shall be seen and known—"Come forth"—"Shine," &c.

1. Will relate to their *distinct visibility.* Seen of God —angels—men.

2. To their *aggregation together.* They have been separated by time. The first sons of God—succeeding generations — different dispensations — never met together—the great family gathering.

3. To the *exhibition* of their Christian *excellencies.* The marvels of their experience, goodness, piety, graces, virtues, &c. Religion in all their diversified individualisms.

4. To the *recognition* of their *labours* and *deeds* of worth. Christ gives a slight sketch; Matt. xxv. All the heroism, self-denial, sufferings, deaths. All the confessors, martyrs, &c.

5. A *revelation* or *manifestation* of their *future* glory. "Now are we the sons of God, but it doth not yet appear," &c.

6. It will be an *eternal manifestaion.* No night; Rev. xxi. 10; v. 22 to 26.

**III. We may unite in this expectancy of creation, for this glorious manifestation of the sons of God.**

Observe—1. We are specially concerned. 2. We have the promises of it. 3. We are believers in it. 4. We are hoping for it. 5. We are suffering with the creation—we groan within, &c. And, therefore, if we suffer, &c.; v. 17.

APPLICATION.

1. The restricted manifestation. It will be of God's children. "Sons of God."

2. The basis of our character and hopes. In Christ —on Christ—with Christ.

3. The grand attraction this should be to Christian sufferers in our world.


## CXCVI

## THE SAVIOUR'S ONE OBJECT

" For the Son of Man is come to seek and to save that which is lost."—LUKE xix. 10.

No declaration of greater importance than this. It is the life blood of the Gospel. It is the best news, &c. Now look,

### I. At the condition of mankind.

1. "Lost" by the *apostacy* of our first parents. In the first Adam—glorious, holy, blessed. All lost in Him. Honour, inheritance, life.

2. Lost by *actual transgression*. "All we like sheep." All sinned—all rebelled. Not one righteous, &c.

3. The *universality* of this lost condition. All the world—every man—all ages, nations, conditions.

4. The utter *helplessness* of this state—no power of self-deliverance—none can deliver, &c. Observe some similitudes that exhibit it as a lost sheep, lost traveller, lost criminal, lost ship, lost slave, as a maniac.

### II. The great Restorer.

1. His *title*. "Son of Man." One of our race. His humanity real, evident; yet,

2. He was the *Divine* Son of man. His humanity was so. Conceived of the Holy Ghost. God dwelt in Him. The Son of God. The Lord Jesus Christ.

3. His *mission*. "He came" from heaven—from the Father. He came into the world.

Observe—(1.) He came to seek. His ministry was itinerant—seeking the lost sheep. (2.) He came to save. From ignorance, by teaching. From error, by His life. From misery, from demons, &c., by His compassion. From sin, by pardon. From the power of darkness, &c. To save—by renewal—by restoration —by adoption—by the gift of eternal life. (3.) He came to save all the lost. "God so loved," &c. We know and testify, &c. (4.) He came to die. To rise from the dead—to save the lost. Gave Himself. "The Lamb of God." Propitiation. "Behoved Christ to suffer and to rise," &c. (5.) He came to ascend. To save the lost. Ascended on high, to send the Holy Ghost. (6.) He came to set up the Divine agency. Preaching, &c. "Go ye," &c.

Observe—

1. All men are in a salvable condition—need not perish, &c.

2. By faith men receive Christ and His salvation.

3. The finally lost reject Christ, and thus perish.

4. Ministers' duty to proclaim the text.

# CXCVII

## THE CHARACTERISTICS OF PAUL'S PREACHING

" And I, brethren, when I came to you, came not with excellency of speech, or of wisdom, declaring unto you the testimony of God: for I determined not to know anything among you, save Jesus Christ, and Him crucified," &c.—1 COR. ii. 1—5.

Now look at the text and see,

I. The line of ministry the Apostle did not adopt.

1. He did not appear among them as an eloquent orator; v. 1.

2. Nor as a philosophical casuist; v. 1.

3. Nor as a a plausible proselyter; v. 4.

**II. Look at the spirit under which he had been present with them.**

1. Under *conscious inability*; v. 3, "weakness."

2. With great *doubtful solicitude,* v. 3; fear of himself, adversaries, results, &c.

3. With great *mental trepidation,* v. 3, "much trembling," anxiety for souls, as those rescuing the ship wrecked, saving from flames, raising from the disease and miseries of sin. Observe,

**III. The great and one theme of his preaching.**

"Determined not to know anything," &c. The words are most intensified, therefore they are not to be taken,

1. In their *absolute literalness.* He dwelt on other themes, on the whole system of Christian theology, on all Christian duties, virtues, and graces.

2. But Christ crucified was the *chief* idea. This was the Gospel, the sum and substance of it; no Gospel without it.

3. This was the *central* idea, the sun of the Gospel system, the heart, the life, the basis of the whole.

4. This was the *constant* idea; every day, every sermon more or less, every subject, every epistle.

5. This was the *universal* idea, Christ crucified for all; Gospel for all, cross for all. "The Lamb of God taking away the sin of the world," &c.

6. To *this* idea the Apostle consecrated *all* his *being,* head, heart, tongue and life. He determined piously, devoutly, not to know anything, &c., and he maintained it to the end. Now Paul had three reasons for this:— (1.) This was his mission. (2.) This glorified Christ. (3.) This only could save souls.

APPLICATION

1. What a spirit to be cherished! Deep humility, self-abasement, &c.

2. What a work to be prosecuted!

3. What sympathy and aid to be secured! "Brethren, pray for us," &c.


## CXCVIII

## THE CHURCH, THE MYSTICAL BODY OF CHRIST

"From whom the whole body fitly joined together and compacted by that which every joint supplieth, according to the effectual working in the measure of every part, maketh increase of the body, unto the edifying of itself in love.—EPHESIANS iv. 16.

THE symbolism of the Church rich and diversified. It is a house and family; a building and temple; a garden and vineyard; a mother and virgin; a city; a nation; an army; a sheepfold. But the most striking is that of the body, the mystical body of Christ. Now look at,

**I. The Church itself—" body," " whole body."**

1. Its *visibility*—can be seen; Christ's body could, they saw Him, beheld Him. The Church. The incarnation of the Spirit of Christ. A city of light.

2. *Substantial*—not a *shadow*, but real; we read of joints, &c.

3. *Vitality*—not a *corpse* or *effigy* ; not dry bones and dead, but breath and life in it.

4. *Unity.* Body, not bodies; one, v. 4; one body.

**II. Its Divine Head.**

" Who is the Head, the Head of the body, the Church." Christ is so,

1. *Essentially.* It would be a trunk without the head. Joints may be removed or be wanting, the head essential.

2. *Divinely*.  God's Son.  The Divine Christ.  Christ in His true Godhead.

3. *Humanly*.  The Son of Man, same nature as the body.

4. *Mediatorially*.  The Head for a Divine purpose.  To sanctify the body—unite the body to God, no other.

**III. Its manifold members.**

As in the human body; see 1 Cor. xii. 12, 14.  All believers all over the world are the members of Christ. Faith unites to Christ, nothing else does; John i. 12, &c. Here numerically many, it has a sort of ubiquity, of all ages and dispensations.

**IV. Its symmetrical union.**

1. The many members united together.

2. United to Christ the Head.

3. United in order by Divine wisdom, "fitly" and "compacted," in their right place, and for their several objects and uses.

**V. Its vital activities.**

1. *Working*.  Designed for this—the hand, &c.  This one great end of the body and its members—not ornament only, but work.

2. In every *working* part.  Without this paralysis—death.

3. *Working* in the *measure* and way designed—not all visibly working.  Look at the body—much unseen working.

4. *Effectual working*—accomplishing the end—lungs effectual—heart also—nerves—veins—arteries effectual. Then,

**VI. Its vital efficient resources.**

"Edifying."  "In love," &c.  By the love of God the Father, and the Son, and the Holy Spirit.  By mutual love of the members.  By the universal love to each and all the members.  Edifying—building up—in growth, strength, efficiency.

APPLICATION

1. How beautiful this picture of loveliness, &c.
2. Our place and privileges and responsibilities.
3. Our "spirit" love. "By love serve one another."
4. The end to be kept in view "edifying."

## CXCIX

## PAUL'S GLORYING

"But God forbid that I should glory save in the Cross of our Lord Jesus Christ, by whom the world is crucified unto me, and I unto the world."—GAL. vi. 14.

LET us look—

### I. At the Cross itself.

It was not the literal Cross—the beam and transverse piece to which Christ was nailed. Of this the crucifix is the sign. It was the death of Jesus on the Cross. Christ crucified—the culminating point of Christ's sufferings—altar of the world—the sacrifice for all sin and all sinners. It was the priest and victim occupying the gap, to stay the plague of wrath. Observe,

### II. Those aspects of the Cross which produced the averment of the apostle.

1. There was the *Illustrious Sufferer*, "our Lord Jesus Christ."

2. He *gloried* in the *amazing efficacy* of the Cross. See the brazen serpent. So the Cross healed—pardoned.

Now this efficacy—(1.) Is in the Cross, as explained really not typically—or symbolically. (2.) Abidingly —never is exhausted. (3.) Universally, extends to the whole world, &c.—and every man. (4.) Stupendous victories of the Cross. In Jerusalem 3000—Samaria, &c. — over himself — over paganism — idolatry — and Grecian philosophy—Athens, &c.—over every kind of sin; Eph. ii. 1. By this everywhere the apostles and evangelists overcame.

3. He *gloried* in the *special doctrines* of the Cross.

(1.) Man's ruin and need of it. (2.) Man's salvation through the intervention of another—Christ died for us —suffered, &c. (3.) This intervention being an act of inconceivable love. (4.) This act of Christ's suffering and mediation followed by the gracious operations of the Holy Spirit. (5.) The belief of this atoning death of Jesus bringing salvation into the soul. (6.) Our acceptance and eternal life as the result of Christ's death, and faith resting on it.

4. He *gloried* in the *restoring* and *exalting power* of the Cross.

(1.) To restore from barbarism to civilization. (2.) From idolatry to pure worship. (2.) In restoring men from degradation to a Divine humanity. (3.) In restoring the lowest of our species to glorious dignities and privileges—slaves—the masses—the poor.

5. He *gloried* in the *destined universal triumphs* of the Cross. We have spoken of the past victories. Hear Christ—"And I, if I be lifted up," &c. It struggled for 300 years with the paganism of the Roman empire and shivered it. It encountered the grossest idolatry, &c. in Britain and exploded it. South Sea Islands—New Zealand—Fiji, &c. Hear the apostle; Philip ii. 7-11.

Now Paul believed it, and thus gloried in the Cross, &c.

### APPLICATION

1. There is no substitute for the Cross. Not the crucifix! Not the wafer! Not the sign! Not the Cross on a church, &c. These are all fictions and make-believes.

2. We ask about our personal connection with it. "I" should glory. All in New Testament religion is

personal. Do you, &c., know—believe—glory.

3. We should have the apostle's spirit in all places and times.

## CC

### GOD REALIZED BY HIS PEOPLE

" Our own God shall bless us."—PSALM lxvii. 6.

THE Heathen nations had their numerous gods,—gods for every phase of nature, for all seasons, and for all events. But these gods were senseless idols, puerile, contemptible, and valueless; so also were all those who trusted in them. See Psalm cxv. But Jehovah was the God of Israel, and as such the object of their faith and hope. In Him they trusted—to Him gave homage, and in Him exulted, as in the text. See also the same spirit exhibited, Psalms xcv., xcvi., xcvii., xcviii., &c.

Observe,

**I. The Divine Being in the text—" God."**

This Being was unknown to the Heathen, but He revealed Himself to the holy patriarchs, and especially to Abraham and Moses. Our God,

1. Is a *spirit.* Not material. Angels are in a secondary sense spirits; but it is obvious that they have ethereal vestments, and can manifest themselves, and be seen by men; but not so God. John iv. 24; 2 Cor. iii. 17; Col. i. 15; Heb. xi. 27.

2. *Self-existent,* He, the Creator, has no maker, from Himself and in Himself absolutely, underived—before all things. Deut. iv. 35; Isaiah xliv. 6.

3. *Eternal.* From eternity to eternity, God. No beginning nor capable of any end of His existence. Isaiah lvii. 15; Rom. i. 20.

4. *Unchangeable.* Or He would not be absolutely perfect. " The same yesterday, to-day, and for ever." So

in His essence, attributes and purposes, of one eternal, unalterable mind. Without variableness or shadow of turning. Malch. iii. 6; James i. 17.

5. *Omnipotent*, or Almighty, of unlimited energy. Able to do all things worthy of His effectuating. Gen. xvii. 1; Jer. ii. 18; Rev. xix. 6.

6. *Omniscient.* Knowing all things, accurately, distinctly, infallibly, and with these His essential natural attributes; possessing every moral perfection of wisdom, holiness, goodness, truth, mercy, and tender compassion, the glorious central of overspreading unmixed love, at once the basis of his character and glory of His name. Job xxi. 22; Heb. iv. 13. Such is the Divine Being exhibited in the text "God." Observe,

**II. His relationship to us.**

Our "God," not merely the God of the universe, the only God, the God of the seraphim and the holy angels, but our God. The God—

1. Of *our being.* Our Maker, Father, Source of existence. Gen. ii. 7; Isa. lvii. 16; Job. xxxiii. 4; Psalm cxxxix. 14.

2. Our *good Benefactor.* Fountain of all goodness, the giver of every good and perfect gift. In whom we live and move, and have all things richly to enjoy. Exod. xxxiv. 6; 1 Chron. xvi. 34; Psalms xxxiv. 8; xxxiii. 5.

3. Our *Divine Lord* and *Ruler.* To whom we are subject and owe all loyal obedience and worship and love and gratitude. 2 Kings xix. 15; 2 Chron. xx. 6; Psa. xcv. 3.

4. Our *covenant God.* Who remembered us in our lost estate, and in infinite condescension and mercy entered into gracious covenant relationship with His Son for our redemption and restoration to holiness and eternal life. 2 Sam. xxiii. 5; Jer. xxxi. 31; Heb. viii. 8.

5. Our *gracious* God, who has called us, and adopted us into His Divine and heavenly family.

6. The God of our *open profession* and worship. Ours by obedience to His call, and faith in His name, and avowal of delight in His service.

7. Our *God* for *ever* and *ever*. In close unbroken fellowship, and eternal oneness and joy. We are His people for ever and ever. God is ours consciously by the indwelling of His spirit, and by our union with our Divine Lord, His only Begotten Son Jesus Christ. Observe,

**III. The blessed assurance of this relationship—" Shall bless us,"**

1. With all the *good we need*.

2. With the *evident tokens* of His *favour*. His smile—His spirit—His presence—communion, &c.

3. With the *rich treasures* of *His grace*, unsearchable, unspeakable, unchanging and everlasting.

4. With *eternal life* and *glory*, " not see death," have abiding life, fulness of life, and joyous life in glory everlasting. Such are the chief, and including all other blessings which our God will bestow on us.

A few words in conclusion—

1. These blessings are of His sovereign *bestowment*.

2. Are *laid up* for us in His Son, our Lord Jesus Christ, in whom all fulness dwells.

3. Are *realised* by us as we ask and believe.

4. Are *absolutely certain*, as based on His immutable word, ratified by His solemn oath, and sealed with the precious blood of the Lord Jesus.

5. And are *experienced* by *all* His saints in the dispensation of His grace and love. Yes, " God, our own God will bless us." Grateful acknowledgment and entire consecration are His right and due. To our God be glory evermore !

# INDEX